P9-ELW-456

WrestleCrap and Figure Four Weekly Present

THE DEATH OF WCW

WrestleCrap and **Figure Four Weekly** Present

THE DEATH OF WCW

R.D. REYNOLDS and BRYAN ALVAREZ

ECW PRESS
ecwpress.com

Copyright © ECW PRESS Ltd., 2004

Published by ECW PRESS
2120 Queen St. East, Suite 200, Toronto, Ontario, Canada M4E 1E2

All rights reserved. No part of this publication may be reproduced, stored in a retrieval system, or transmitted in any form by any process — electronic, mechanical, photocopying, recording, or otherwise — without the prior written permission of the copyright owners and ECW PRESS.

NATIONAL LIBRARY OF CANADA CATALOGUING IN PUBLICATION DATA

Reynolds, R. D., 1969–
The death of WCW: wrestlecrap and figure four weekly present —
    /R.D. Reynolds and Bryan Alvarez.
ISBN 1–55022–661–4
1. World Championship Wrestling, Inc. — History. I. Alvarez, Bryan II. Title.
GV1195.R48 2004   796.812'0973   C2004-902617-8

Editing & production: Emma McKay
Design & typesetting: Guylaine Regimbald — Solo Design
Cover design: Crystal Baer
Cover photos: Mike Lano
Interior photos: Mike Lano, Jeff Cohen, John Lawson
Printing: Transcontinental

This book is set in Cronos MM
Fourth printing

DISTRIBUTION

CANADA: Jaguar Book Group, 100 Armstrong Avenue, Georgetown,
    Ontario L7G 5S4

UNITED STATES: Independent Publishers Group, 814 North Franklin Street,
    Chicago, Illinois 60610

PRINTED AND BOUND IN CANADA

To Hunter and Steph

Bryan Alvarez's Thank-Yous:

Gladys "Granny" Gibson, Carlos and Valerie Alvarez, Tony and Nikki Leder, Cliff and Carlos, Autumn Swankosky, Alex Marvez, Ed Dwyer, Karl Stern, Brent Kremen, Galatea, Craig Proper Jr., Vincent Verhei, Keith Lipinski, Kyle Wolf, Mike Lano, Buddy Wayne, Tim Flowers, Frank Culbertson, Ritchie and Tami Magnett, Lynne and Don, Ryan Sagmeister, Whitney Neugebauer, all the readers of *Figure Four Weekly*, all my friends and family, and all the wrestlers with whom I worked over the years who didn't manage to kill me.

R.D. Reynolds Would Like to Thank:

My wife Crystal for believing in me; my family: Mom, Jeff, Sue, Aaron, Steph, Mike, Maggie, Aubrey, Morgan, Josh, Teresa, and especially my Dad, whom I miss dearly; my friends: Eric Kuehling, "Diamond" Dan Garza, Casey Stephon, Dan Harcourt, Fred Roehner, Troy Ferguson, Jeff Cohen, John Lawson, Larry Tipton, Mark Manford, and Jon Heilman; Terry and Sally Corman, as well as everyone at Firehouse Image Center; Matt at X-Entertainment.com; Greg Ogorek at GlobalInternet.net; my fellow WrestleCrappers: Blade Braxton, Madison Carter, Alfonzo Tyson, Bill Brown, and all my loyal readers, who made the first book a success, and therefore, gave me the opportunity to write this one. Extra special thanks to John Tenta and Bobby Heenan, who have both been nothing short of amazing to meet and talk with; both men are a credit not just to wrestling, but to mankind in general

Both authors would like to especially thank Emma McKay, Guylaine Régimbald, and everyone else at ECW Press for green-lighting this project, then taking a very fact-heavy manuscript and actually making it readable.

Finally, a huge thank you to Dave Meltzer, without whom there would be no book. Well, there would be a book, just one filled with countless errors.

TABLE OF CONTENTS

PART I
The Birth

PART II
The Rise

PART III
The Fall

PART IV
The Death

FOREWORD

When the ultimate history of American pro wrestling is written, there is probably no story more important, with the exception of the history of Vince McMahon Jr. and the World Wrestling Federation, than that of World Championship Wrestling.

It's a story about what should have been. WCW was, at its zenith, the single hottest company the wrestling world had ever seen, a title it should have held for years. The idea of a pro wrestling company being part of the Turner family was a panacea. Wrestling had, in most parts of the country, been a hand-to-mouth business. In many parts of the country, it was a huge TV ratings success, and many cities had traditions of drawing good crowds on a regular basis. But every place had its ups and downs. Many formerly flourishing cities over the years, from Detroit to San Francisco to Los Angeles to Atlanta to Toronto to Montreal to St. Louis, had great long-term traditions. In all cases, however, they went down the tubes in very quick order. That was the nature of the beast.

But being under the Turner umbrella could have, and arguably should have, changed everything. The backing of a billion-dollar company should not only have opened the doors to better marketing, but should also in theory have created a promotional synergy that would put the company on the entertainment map that its rival, McMahon's WWF, had been on since 1984. But to those in charge of the wrestling end of things, it was questionable whether anyone in the Turner regime had a single clue what promoting professional wrestling was all about. Indeed, by the time Ted Turner suggested putting *Nitro* head-to-head with the WWF's flagship program *Raw* on Monday nights, pro wrestling in North America was in a terrible depression. The thought of splintering the audience between the two promotions was seen by many in the wrestling business as suicide.

Instead, something amazing happened. *Raw* and *Nitro* didn't split a finite group of wrestling fans, but instead spent the next several years creating millions and millions of new viewers. The Monday-night wrestling audience grew from about 4 million in 1995 to more than 12 million at its peak in 1998, when both companies were on a roll.

And make no mistake about it—WCW was on one hell of a roll. It went from being a company that no one had much interest in to being the most powerful company in the history of wrestling, one capable of drawing 30,000 people to major stadiums without even having to advertise one match.

The man behind WCW's rise to fame was Eric Bischoff, who raised the stakes by paying top dollar and getting the most marketable talent in the world. He brought fans big-name stars and filled the undercards with the best wrestling anywhere. He brought in big-name celebrities, many of whom actually drew money for the company. But Bischoff's biggest contribution was probably the fact that, under him, WCW modernized the in-ring style of American pro wrestling, a style that had languished behind those of both Mexico and Japan for years. Other promotions, such as Paul Heyman's Extreme Championship Wrestling, tried to do the same, but they never had the money to keep the talent they were developing, and they were doomed when WCW started copying their style. Even the mighty WWF didn't have the star power, or the talent depth, and its "big man" style suddenly looked slow and outdated compared to the far more athletic product WCW featured at the time.

The irony of Bischoff being the man who did all this is nothing short of amazing. Prior to his rise up the ranks, Bischoff was little more than a backup announcer, hired largely because he wasn't very good, and thus would never be a threat to lead announcer Jim Ross. He grew frustrated at how badly the company was run, and he somehow leapfrogged over everyone to gain control over a business of which he had limited knowledge. His battle plan was really not all that different from McMahon's years earlier: that is, he would spend huge money for the top talent and raid the opposition. McMahon did this in 1984, and his rival promoters laughed at him for overspending. But it was McMahon who had the last laugh, as those promoters quickly went bankrupt while he became the most successful wrestling promoter who ever lived.

In the mid-1990s, Bischoff gave McMahon a taste of the medicine he'd given the rest of the wrestling world. The end result should have been the same, except, in the end, Bischoff didn't understand his fan base. Perhaps even more crippling was the fact he was so close with pro wrestling's ultimate charmer, Hulk Hogan, that he thought he'd never have to worry. Bischoff really believed that Hogan *was* pro wrestling, because for so many years, he was. In addition to Hogan, Bischoff also had every other huge star under contract: Roddy Piper, Randy Savage, Ric Flair, and countless others. Hogan's initial matches with all these men were huge hits, and cast the die for years to come.

The problem was that, after years of seeing the same men in the main events, fans yearned for something new. What Bischoff and WCW were presenting became very stale. This wasn't the same as the Rolling Stones doing a tour every few years; this was the wrestling legends of the '80s dominating television shows in 1999.

It wasn't only Bischoff's lack of foresight that led to the company's downfall. The wrestlers themselves took advantage of and ruined the greatest system they could have possibly ever worked under. Bischoff would often allow these men to have total control of their careers, although he'd learn (only not soon enough) that putting old wrestlers in charge of a business that had changed rapidly, but one they still thought was the same as it was in 1991, was a recipe for disaster. WCW had squandered its future because the hungry younger wrestlers were not allowed into the main events. The guys in those spots jealously guarded them, ran them down to management, and soon all the fresh young stars began to hate their jobs and sought employment elsewhere. Before long, every advantage WCW had was gone, and its future was mortgaged at the feet of the older wrestlers. It would never get that bright future back.

In the end, WCW was a victim of its own success. Bischoff had created a successful formula, one that he held onto for far too long, and one that ultimately started the downfall of the company. Once the snowball started to roll, those in charge had no idea how to stop it.

This book explains, sometimes on a week-to-week basis, how the company was built into the most successful pro wrestling promotion in history, only to squander it all away. It's a story of how a bright future was basically destroyed in one horrible calendar year, and why, just over one year after that, it was gone. Sadly, pro wrestling may never be the same for it.

There are so many lessons to be learned from WCW's downfall that you would need a book to detail them all. Thankfully, the book has finally been written. It's a book that everyone in wrestling—even though most lived through it—really needs to read in order to remember the mistakes and avoid repeating them.

Because, sadly, since the death of WCW, we've seen far more examples of copying what killed it than of copying what made it successful.

Dave Meltzer
August 2004

INTRODUCTION

Here Lies World Championship Wrestling 1988-2003

World Championship Wrestling was not supposed to die.

Anyone with even a basic understanding of its inner workings knew this to be true. As the company began to hit its peak around 1997, all signs indicated that WCW was destined to thrive and prosper. The promotion had so many unfair advantages, it seemed that not only would it continue to expand its profits, but it would also eventually turn every other wrestling promotion in the country into dust.

And why wouldn't it?

More importantly, *how* couldn't it?

The promotion had the single greatest array of talent the wrestling world had ever known. The two men who defined professional wrestling in the 1980s, Hulk Hogan and Ric Flair, both made their home in WCW. The most popular wrestlers of the 1990s, including Sting and Bret Hart, competed in WCW rings, as did Scott Hall and Kevin Nash, who revolutionized the business as the Outsiders, and shortly thereafter formed the nucleus of the infamous New World Order. The company had the most talented in-ring workers: men like Chris Benoit, Eddy Guerrero, and Dean Malenko, as well as the greatest high-flyers from around the world—Rey Mysterio Jr., Juventud Guerrera, and countless others. And, perhaps above all, WCW also employed the man who would lead the industry into the next millennium, the man fans flocked to arenas to see: Bill Goldberg. Such a roster of talent had never been seen in a single pro-wrestling promotion before.

When their flagship show *WCW Monday Nitro* was created, many older fans returned to watch the stars they'd grown up on, creating the largest wrestling audience the cable industry had ever seen. WCW was in a place no company had been since Vince McMahon took the World Wrestling Federation national in the mid-1980s: that is, poised to kill the WWF once and for all. Many wrestlers were eager to jump ship to WCW, some looking to increase their paydays, others out of fear that the WWF wasn't long for this world. Essentially, they were looking to survive.

WCW was looking beyond that. *Nitro* had surpassed not only *Raw* in the ratings, but every other program on cable television. They weren't just the number-one wrestling show; they were the number-one cable show, period. Every week, *Nitro* presented three hours of live action, featuring cutting-edge story lines, amazing matches, and production values the likes of which the wrestling world had never seen before. In addition to the sky-rocketing ratings, WCW was one of the biggest and most profitable touring groups in the country, as fans swarmed to arenas for live *Nitro*s and for the monthly megashows. Fans who couldn't attend the matches live ordered in record numbers via the miracle of pay-per-view, spending upwards of $30 a month just to watch the special events. And let's not forget the insane amounts of merchandise sold, from T-shirts to posters to magazines to bandanas to wrestling teddy bears to key chains to beanie babies to sipper cups to every stupid tchotchke piece of crap imaginable—all with the WCW logo slapped right on it.

Everything was making the company money, to the tune of more than a $55 million profit in a single year.

So let's restate once more, for the record, that WCW was not supposed to die.

In fact, not only was WCW never supposed to vanish from the face of the Earth, but the mere thought that the company could ever perish was laughable.

How could this company go the way of the dodo? WCW zealots would tell you—inaccurately, but that's beside the point—that it had been around for over 100 years. *One hundred years!* Not only had it been around longer than any other wrestling company, they'd insist, but also longer than almost any other viable form of entertainment. It had been around longer than movies or television. It had been around longer than the National Football League. By God, WCW wasn't just a wrestling company, it was an American institution!

As impressive as it was that the company could trace its roots back "nearly to the days of Abraham Lincoln," more impressive was the fact that it was owned by the biggest media mogul in the entire universe, Ted Turner—the real reason why the company could not, would not, die. There was simply too damn much money behind it. Turner had purchased the company in the late 1980s almost as a toy, a hobby, and, if truth be told, he wasn't greatly concerned if the thing ever made a dime. Anything it lost was just pocket change, and anything it made likely was as well. But since wrestling had been a cornerstone of the Turner networks since the launch of the Superstation, he pledged to keep it around, no matter what.

So he had their shows airing on his networks, TBS and TNT, and in prime viewing hours: Monday nights, Wednesday nights, Saturday nights, and Sunday nights. Think about that: in any given week, more often than not, WCW was being featured on the Turner networks during prime time. If another timeslot was needed for a new show, or perhaps a bimonthly special, Uncle Ted was just a phone call away. Backed with the power of the Turner networks, promotion of the pay-per-view events was nothing short of grandiose.

How on Earth could anyone imagine that World Championship Wrestling might die?

After all, if the company was going to die, it would have done so years before it ever hit it big. WCW would have died in 1993, when it lost $6 million filming expensive promotional movies featuring exploding boats and one-eyed midgets. It would have died when an allegedly racist "Cowboy" took the reigns and attempted to create a slave tag team comprised of two black men, pissing off Hall of Famer and Turner higher-up Hank Aaron in the process. It would have died when it lost its number-one draw, Ric Flair, to the competition.

It would have, and perhaps it should have, but it didn't.

World Championship Wrestling didn't die; in fact, it laughed in the face of death and came out smiling, making more money in 1997—over $50 million—than it had lost in all its previous years put together. WCW wasn't dying; it was growing and expanding, becoming the wrestling company against which all other wrestling companies would ever be measured. WCW was the benchmark of success in the wrestling industry. The fans knew it, the wrestlers knew it—even the WWF and Vince McMahon knew it. WCW was so successful, in fact, that it didn't matter what stupid mistakes were made because the revenue would always keep coming in. The ratings that came in on Tuesday mornings would justify whatever they did, as would the incredible buy rates and live attendance figures.

Yes, WCW was on top, and it knew just how to stay there: by never changing anything.

After all, why shuffle the card around in order to give new talent a chance on top? The stars it had been using for years—the Hogans and

Nashes and the rest—well, they'd been stars for years, and they'd certainly be on top for many more to come. Sure, there were younger and arguably more talented guys on the roster, but they weren't proven commodities. The fans couldn't buy these guys as main-eventers; after all, these wrestlers had never been put in such an important position before, and who knew if they could handle the pressure? Besides, Hogan and Nash were the big stars in the eyes of the fans. If anyone tried to convince the WCW brass otherwise, these two wrestlers would be more than happy to explain their role in bringing WCW out of the dark ages and into its rightful position as the number-one wrestling company on the planet.

Question: Why fix what wasn't broke?

Answer: Because if it wasn't broken, it certainly was worn out.

Almost as quickly as they had grown, the ratings tanked. As the WCW fan base began to depart in record numbers, the ratings spoke volumes. Audiences were tired of seeing the same old, same old, and they voted with their remote controls. Not only did the ratings collapse, but the all-important pay-per-view buy rates also tumbled, eventually falling right off the cliff. The wrestlers who'd supposedly brought the company to its zenith began to quarrel backstage, some choosing to vanish like thieves in the night rather than shoulder any blame that this was somehow partially their own doing.

Countless millions were spent on quick fixes that did nothing but drive fans away. Regimes changed backstage. New script writers were brought in. New sets were built. New pay-per-view events were created. Rock and roll bands were brought in to do mini concerts.

None of it made a damn bit of difference. All these short-term fixes amounted to little more than putting a bandage on a cancerous tumor.

World Championship Wrestling wasn't supposed to die?

Right.

PART I The Birth

*"Ted called me up and said, 'Hey, Vince, guess what?
I'm in the rasslin' business now!'"*

—*Vince McMahon, Owner, World Wrestling Federation*

CHAPTER 1

1988-1996: Mr. Turner's Baby Boy

While many believed World Championship Wrestling could never die and were stunned in 2001 when it actually did, an even larger group believed the company probably should have died countless times before then, since it had consistently lost so much money. The misconception that WCW was a huge money-loser in its formative years should be dispelled right off the bat. In truth, WCW lost around $6 million per year in the first five years of its existence—not a horrible figure at all, considering what they were giving Turner: four hours of excellent ratings every single week of the year. Some within the Turner organization squawked at the losses, but Ted Turner himself didn't. In fact, Turner was such a cheerleader for the company that when a board of directors suggested shutting WCW down in 1992, he told them that wrestling built the Superstation, and as long as he was in charge, it would always have a home there. He also told them never to bring the idea up again. They didn't.

Since Turner was so strongly behind WCW, it seemed that regardless of what happened or how much money the company lost, it would always be around. No matter what, no matter how bad things could get, many within the company were unafraid. This sense of security often led those in charge to bad decisions. They could throw away money, alienate their employees, and even their fans—Ted Turner would always be there to bail them out of a jam.

For all the reasons why the company could have and arguably should have died, it did have history on its side. After all, this was a company that had been around almost 100 years . . . or at least that's one of the myths rabid WCW supporters would have you believe. The truth is a bit different.

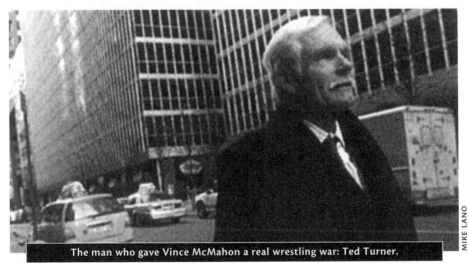

The man who gave Vince McMahon a real wrestling war: Ted Turner.

MIKE LANO

When promoter "Big" Jim Crockett died in 1973, he passed his assets—including Jim Crockett Promotions, which ran pro-wrestling shows—on to his son, Jim Jr. For decades, the Crocketts, like other National Wrestling Alliance (NWA) promoters nationwide, tried to bring prestige to their organization by claiming that their main title, the World Heavyweight Championship, dated back to 1905. Their champ, they claimed, wore a belt with a lineage that could be traced to such turn-of-the-century legends as George Hackenschmidt and Frank A. Gotch.

Truth be told, the NWA that helped form WCW has roots in 1905 about as much as the rap group NWA does. The confusion stems from the fact that there were two different NWAs: the turn-of-the-century National Wrestling *Association*, and the modern-day National Wrestling *Alliance*. Today's NWA was formed in 1948 by six promoters at a meeting in Waterloo, Iowa. They named Des Moines promoter Pinky George the first president and Kansas City promoter Orville Brown the first champion. Lou Thesz won the title in 1949, then won the National Wrestling Association title in 1950. Because the group controlled all the major titles, the NWA Championship became the most prominent belt in the world for almost forty years. In April of 1984, it was one of three "big" titles in the U.S., along with the world titles of the AWA, promoted by Verne Gagne, and the WWF, promoted by another junior, Vincent Kennedy McMahon.

The original Vince McMahon—Vincent James McMahon, to be precise—was the son of boxing and wrestling promoter Jess McMahon. Vince Sr. had promoted the World Wide Wrestling Federation (they dropped a "W" in 1979) since 1963, running throughout the Northeast. The highly successful promotion, based in Madison Square Garden, was built around such legendary stars as Bruno Sammartino, Superstar Billy Graham, and Bob Backlund. But Vince Sr. was getting old, and his son—the handsome, fast-talking announcer on his wrestling shows—was eager to make a serious impact.

Vince Sr. wasn't so sure about his son. He never wanted him to be a wrestler, and probably didn't want him to be involved much with the business at all. Plus, the young McMahon seemed to have some pretty grandiose ideas. Wrestling had always been a territorial business, with different groups promoting cards exclusively in "their" areas of the country. There was Roy Welch in Alabama; Nick Gulas in Nashville; Leroy McGuirk in Oklahoma; and Sam Muchnick in St. Louis, among over two dozen others. While promoters would sometimes venture into opposing territories, no one had ever attempted to do what Vince Jr. was planning on such a massive scale. Vince Jr. wanted to promote wrestling wherever he pleased.

Contrary to what most believe, Vince Jr. wasn't the first wrestling promoter to "go national." His father's Madison Square Garden cards aired on the MSG Network in the early '70s. When Ted Turner's Atlanta WTCG UHF station went up on satellite as the Superstation in 1976, it took Jim Barnett's Georgia-based promotion nationwide, airing two shows on the weekends: *Georgia Championship Wrestling* on Saturday nights, and *Best of Georgia Championship Wrestling* the following evening. The station quickly grew to serve 15 million people, and the wrestling show was the first program to draw over 1 million viewers on cable. The NWA promoters were leery of this, but Vince Sr. argued that it would be ridiculous for him to stop promoting in the Garden, and Barnett simply said that no matter what, his show still featured just Georgia wrestlers. Several years later, however, Turner requested that the name be modified to something less regional in scope, and therefore the show was changed from *Georgia Championship Wrestling* to *World Championship Wrestling*, which just so happened to be the name of a promotion Barnett had run in Australia. Cable, Barnett would later say, could not be stopped. And he was right.

In 1982, Vince Sr. finally caved and sold the World Wrestling Federation to his son. The deal, though, was that if Vince Jr. missed even one of his quarterly payments he'd lose the promotion back to Vince Sr.'s three original partners: Bob "Gorilla Monsoon" Marella (who eventually got a lifetime announcing gig out of it), Phil Zacko, and Arnold Skaaland. While many believe that Vince Sr. was never aware of his son's lofty plans, some feel otherwise. The sense was that even if Vince Sr. did know, he didn't believe that his son could pull it off. Shortly after selling the company, Vince Sr. was diagnosed with cancer, and he died a few months later.

Those who doubted Vince Jr. couldn't have been more wrong. Not only did he take the WWF national, he created a near monopoly for himself within five years of doing so. One of his first major offensive moves was to offer lucrative contracts to stars (and sometimes guys nobody in their right mind would consider star material) from other territories, most notably Verne Gagne's AWA. Vince had already offered to buy Gagne's promotion outright, but he'd been shot down. His next step, therefore, was to buy up all Gagne's talent, including his hottest star of all: a young, bleached-blonde muscleman named Hulk Hogan. Hogan ended up being the chosen one, and McMahon quickly moved his WWF title from his father's long-term champion Bob Backlund to the dastardly Iron Sheik. On January 23, 1984, Hogan beat Sheik in Madison Square Garden with his dreaded Legdrop of Doom, and Hulkamania took off.

Widespread TV was the next major step. In those days, many wrestling promoters got along swimmingly with their local TV affiliates. In many territories, the television people would air the programming for free and make money off the advertising. The wrestling people, meanwhile, would write shows to compel fans to go to the local arena and pay for tickets. In some territories—Memphis, for Jerry Jarrett, would be a good example—the TV stations would actually pay the promoters for the programming. Vince went from territory to territory and not only offered the station managers his slick TV tapes in place of their current, often poorly filmed local wrestling shows, but also offered to *pay* to get them on the air.

Further into his expansion, McMahon purchased Georgia Championship Wrestling for $750,000. As part of the deal, he got the coveted Saturday and Sunday 6:05 P.M. timeslots on TBS, where his plan, obviously, was to replace tapes of the Georgia wrestlers with tapes of his WWF superstars. The problem with this plan was that there was a vast in-ring difference between

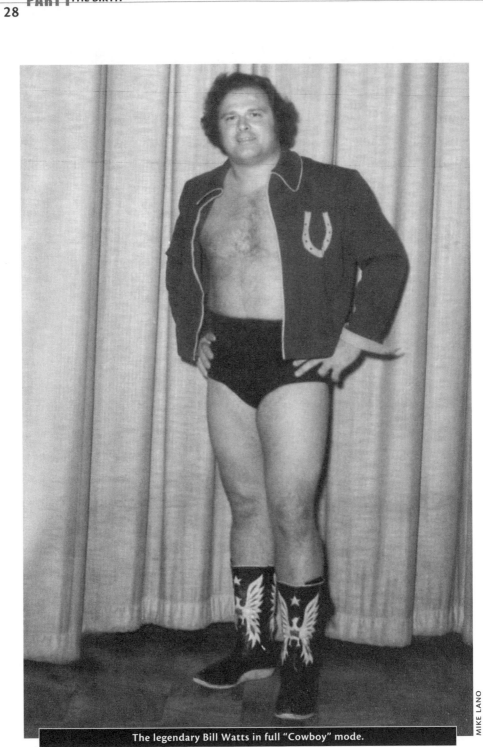

The legendary Bill Watts in full "Cowboy" mode.

MIKE LANO

the two products: the Georgia show featured an emphasis on in-ring action with talented workers, and the WWF show featured a bunch of one-sided "squash" matches that had already aired on the USA Network. When the switchover took place on "Black Saturday," July 14, 1985, over 1,000 fans angrily complained to the Superstation. Turner's response was to give Ole Anderson a 7:00 A.M. timeslot so that he could open up *Championship Wrestling from Georgia, Inc.* (which didn't last long). Then, the following year, he gave Bill Watts' *Mid-South Wrestling* a one-hour timeslot on Sunday, and agreed to finance him so that he could compete nationally against McMahon. Vince, who thought his purchase of *GCW* would give him an exclusive on TBS, was outraged. Turner, of course, disagreed, feeling that Vince had reneged on a stipulation in the contract that required him to produce a separate weekly program from an Atlanta studio. If Vince wasn't going to do it, well, someone else would. Thus began the two-decade war between McMahon and Turner.

What made things worse for Vince was that *Mid-South*, a tremendously well-booked and entertaining show, immediately started to destroy all of his programs in the ratings. Turner, who had promised to bankroll Watts, was ready to kick Vince off the station when Jim Barnett, a longtime promoter and a personal friend of Turner's, stepped in. Barnett negotiated a deal between Vince and Crockett Jr. that enabled Crockett to purchase the TBS slots for $1 million. Turner was ecstatic: not only was he rid of Vince, but he had also regained popular wrestling stars like Dusty Rhodes and the Four Horsemen. Vince was probably pleased to have made several hundred thousand dollars on the deal. Watts agreed to step aside, and on the final episode of *Mid-South Wrestling*, he put over Crockett's performers and said fans would get to see great NWA action from now on.

Heading up the top two promotions in the country, McMahon and Crockett continued to feud over the next few years. The smaller territories couldn't compete with the level of TV exposure these companies had, and subsequently, most died off. Among the promoters who didn't make it was Watts, who tried to go national but couldn't afford it in the end. He finally sold to Crockett for $4 million, although he only ended up with $1.2 million when all was said and done because Crockett, as it turned out, couldn't afford to go national either.

After buying Watts' company, which was known as the Universal Wrestling Federation at that point (you know, because the universe is bigger than the world—seriously, that's why it got the name), Crockett booked an ingenious invasion angle that consisted of having all his guys destroy all the UWF guys while making them look like total losers. Crockett was years ahead of his time, because like the WWF/WCW invasion in the summer of 2001, it was so ingenious that it made almost no money whatsoever and died a painfully quick death.

Crockett had many brilliant ideas, none of which would ever be learned from. He signed guys to huge guaranteed deals he couldn't possibly afford. He snubbed loyal fans by moving *Starrcade* (the NWA equivalent to *Wrestlemania*) out of the South for the first time ever, and did it in Chicago instead. He flew himself and the top stars around in an expensive private jet. And he allowed Dusty Rhodes to book the company into oblivion with cheap finishes that outraged fans. In fact, Dusty's penchant for having a babyface (or good guy) win a belt or match and then later reversing it on television became commonly known within the industry as a "Dusty Finish." Another Crockett moment of genius saw mid-carder Ron Garvin beat perennial champ Ric Flair for the world title. Although Garvin was a babyface, fans didn't see him as a man who should be beating the Nature Boy, and ratings plummeted from the 4.0 range to a 2.8—the fastest drop in history.

In late 1987, Crockett announced that the annual Thanksgiving-night *Starrcade* show would be broadcast for the first time on PPV on November 26. Like McMahon did with the first *Wrestlemania*, Crockett was betting his company's existence on this show's success, having run up some huge debts with all his crazy spending. McMahon, knowing the stakes were high for Jim Crockett Promotions, announced that he was going to be running a Thanksgiving-night pay-per-view as well: the first annual *Survivor Series*. Crockett didn't want to run head-to-head with McMahon, who was doing great pay-per-view numbers at the time, so he offered to move the *Starrcade* show to Thanksgiving afternoon. The cable companies were thrilled to hear this, since they expected wrestling fans to buy both shows and basically sit in front of their TVs watching wrestling all day. But Vince had other ideas. He announced that any company that aired Crockett's PPV would not be allowed to air *Survivor Series* or the next *Wrestlemania*. Since he was the established king of wrestling PPV at the time, and since *Mania III* had been such a huge financial success that it basically made the genre, all but five companies across the country chose to air the *Survivor Series* over *Starrcade*. Crockett was dead in the water before his show even aired.

Struggling to keep his company alive, Crockett planned his revenge. He booked his next PPV, the *Bunkhouse Stampede*, at the Nassau Coliseum, a building right in the middle of McMahon's home territory. Nobody is quite sure why he thought this was such a great idea, because his product had absolutely no history in the area, and it inevitably bombed at the gate, drawing just 6,000 fans and $80,000. But it got worse. McMahon had a plan of his own: to air the first-ever *Royal Rumble* (a modified battle royal in which new men enter the match at two-minute intervals) live from Hamilton, Ontario, on the USA Network, head-to-head with Crockett's PPV. The *Rumble* ended up doing an 8.2 rating, the highest number for any wrestling show in history on that network—and that includes the

Monday Night Wars. And, if all of that wasn't bad enough for Crockett, the *Rumble* was widely regarded as the superior show since Crockett's PPV, headlined by Flair versus Road Warrior Hawk, had yet another hackneyed Dusty Finish.

But Crockett was not yet done. His next idea was to run a free *Clash of the Champions* on TBS on March 27, 1988, head-to-head with *Wrestlemania IV*. This time, his plan was somewhat a success, as the *Clash* did a 5.8, and the Flair versus Sting main event ended up being the most-watched match in the history of cable television, peaking at a 7.8. *Wrestlemania IV*, on the other hand, was a miserable show headlined by Randy Savage, who beat Ted DiBiase to win the vacant WWF title.

Despite Vince having done exactly the same thing with the *Royal Rumble*, the cable industry was irate with Crockett and Turner for having the audacity to air a free show opposite *Wrestlemania*, despite the fact that *Mania* did 585,000 buys—the most in history. The problem was that the universe for PPV had doubled that year, and even though they set a purchase record, the feeling was that the show would have done substantially better without the competition. Wrestling companies were starting to make the bulk of their money through PPVs, and cable companies were also getting a nice slice of the pie (to the tune of approximately 60 percent of the gross!). Turner was told never to allow something like that to happen again.

Despite the *Clash*'s huge success, Crockett was informed shortly thereafter that his company was going broke. Despite his disastrous year, and despite the huge-money contracts he was paying off, and despite all his jet flying and limousine riding and kiss stealing and wheeling and dealing, Crockett was shocked by this revelation. He'd figured he would make huge money on PPV and through national advertising. Unfortunately, Vince had stomped all over his PPVs, and advertisers (just like today) thought only inbreds watched Southern pro wrestling and weren't willing to pay much for commercial time.

Turner got wind that things were bad and took an interest in buying. He had a soft spot in his heart for wrestling, as the success of Barnett's program years earlier had helped to convince him that he hadn't made a mistake and that his Superstation could indeed be a success. So, late in the summer of 1988, shortly after Crockett took out $600,000 in loans to make payroll, Turner purchased Jim Crockett Promotions for $9 million. While Turner didn't end up owning the entire NWA, he did own its biggest member and its biggest stars. The Crockett family was given a minority interest (they were bought out a few years later), and everyone in the family was given a job. This included Jim himself, who, after all his years in the business, became a consultant whose ideas were never used.

In the following years, audiences sat through the highs and lows of what would become World Championship Wrestling, thinking to themselves that as horrible as some of this was, at least with a billionaire like Turner bankrolling everything it couldn't ever go out of business.

For the early years of WCW's life under the Turner empire, the booking duties ping-ponged between two men: Dusty Rhodes and Ole Anderson. Amazingly, despite both having had successful booking runs in regional promotions in the past, neither man seemed to have any clue as to how to run a wrestling company on a national basis. Both had their own agendas, namely pushing themselves and their friends to the high-paying main event slots. And when things didn't go their way, they tended to act like little babies, doing things that did neither the company nor, ironically, themselves any good. A perfect example of this came in 1988, when higher-ups in the Turner hierarchy informed Dusty that blood was to be banned from the WCW television programs. Dusty, pissed at being told what to do, had the Road Warriors come out to the ring, grab a huge metal spike, hold him, and jam it into his eye. Suffice to say, Rhodes' orbital socket soon resembled a crimson version of Old Faithful. To the shock of no one—save perhaps Dusty himself—he was immediately fired.

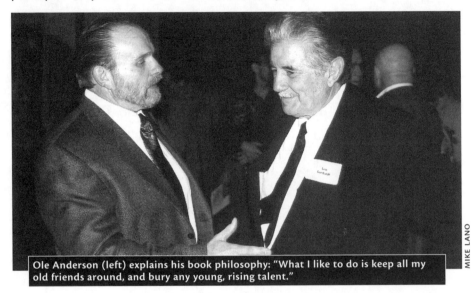

Ole Anderson (left) explains his book philosophy: "What I like to do is keep all my old friends around, and bury any young, rising talent."

MIKE LANO

With WCW no longer his home, Dusty looked north for employment, turning to Vince McMahon and the WWF. McMahon was more than happy to welcome him to the WWF. He even bought him some new outfits. And what outfits they were, with Dusty's flabby frame somehow squeezed into the tightest latex imaginable. Oh—and gigantic bright yellow polka dots! He was introduced to WWF fans through a series of asinine vignettes in which he delivered pizzas, cleaned toilets, and shoveled horse crap. See, that's the way a lot of folks in wrestling operate. You, the promoter, don't like someone in a rival organization. Circumstances arise in which that person is unemployed and in need of a job. Instead of simply denying him employment, you bring him into the company and completely humiliate him. Do the fans in the stands want to see this? No. Does it matter? No, because it's all about showing the guy you don't like who has the power.

The polka-dot outfits weren't the first time McMahon took a shot at Rhodes. In 1987, the WWF created a manservant character named "Virgil," so named because Rhodes' real first name was Virgil. If that wasn't childish enough, years later, when the WWF's Virgil jumped to WCW, he was renamed "Vincent" as a shot against Vince McMahon. Vincent/Virgil ended up making a career of spoofing folks, as later in his WCW tenure he was renamed again, becoming "Shane," an inside rib on Vince McMahon's son.

Dusty, after being made to look like a complete jackass in the WWF, returned once more to the Turner empire, this time to clean up the mess Ole Anderson had made in 1990. Who knows why anybody would think that rehiring him was a good idea, given his track record of pissing off upper management and booking himself as the star of the territory. But apparently WCW Vice President Jim Herd did, and Rhodes was back to take over booking early in 1991, just in time for the first PPV of the year, *Wrestle War*.

He came out flying, too, with one of his greatest creations: War Games. It was a ten-man tag match that placed two rings side by side and surrounded both with a steel cage. The participants entered the cage in two-minute intervals. A coin was tossed beforehand, and the winner of the toss would have the upper hand throughout the opening stage of the match, with a two-on-one, then a three-on-two, a four-on-three, and finally a five-on-four advantage. The match could not be decided until all ten men had entered, at which time the "Match Beyond" would begin. It was an ingenious concept, and it created some memorable bouts. *Wrestle War* was no exception, as top heel Sid Vicious nearly sent Brian Pillman through the roof of the cage before depositing him neck-first on the mat. If Dusty was looking to impress his bosses, old or new, he did just that in booking this showdown.

There were no American PPVs until May, but the company did put on a co-promotional show with New Japan Pro Wrestling in Tokyo called *Rumble in the Rising Sun*, featuring stars from both promotions. The event featured world champ Ric Flair dropping his title to Tatsumi Fujinami . . . kind of, sort of. The story line was that Fujinami pinned the champ, but this followed Flair being thrown over the top rope—grounds for a disqualification in WCW. It was not, however, grounds for a DQ according to New Japan, so Fujinami was recognized by that group as the new NWA World Champion.

This led perfectly into WCW's next domestic PPV, *Superbrawl*. The show saw Flair regain the title in a decent match, as well as a rare babyface versus babyface showdown between the most popular tag teams in the company: Sting and Lex Luger took on the Steiner Brothers in a match that absolutely tore the house down. Sadly, just as Scott Steiner appeared to be catching fire, he suffered a torn bicep that put him out of action for about a year. The only other notable match on the show featured El Gigante beating Sid Vicious in a match known to cause nightmares for anyone fool enough to watch it. Vicious skipped town immediately after this showdown, and left WCW without one of its biggest stars. Vicious was a loss for the company, but nothing could compare to the fiasco that took place in June, when one of the biggest wrestling cataclysms ever took place.

To explain how it all began, let's back up a bit and look at what had been going on behind the scenes between Ric Flair and WCW Vice President Jim Herd. Herd felt that Flair, at forty-two years old, was over the hill and ought to be replaced. He even went so far as to claim that Flair should cut his trademark bleached-blonde hair, wear an earring, and change his name to Spartacus. Perhaps most of all, however, he didn't care for Flair's contract, the highest-paying in the company. The animosity wasn't one-sided, however, as Flair didn't see Herd as anything more than a corporate suit. And indeed, looking at his employment history, that's exactly what he was: Herd had been a higher-up at Pizza Hut prior to his arrival at Turner. Obviously, the two businesses were radically different, and Herd had a tough time grasping some of the basic concepts of pro wrestling, including the notion that WCW fans would pay to see Ric Flair perform. Considering all of this, the fact that Herd offered Flair a contract renewal that basically cut his pay in half should have come as little surprise. Flair's response, inviting Herd to ram said contract up his rectum, wasn't exactly a shocker either. The two bickered back and forth for months, with Herd calling for Flair to drop the WCW title at seemingly every show, and Flair refusing to do so. In the end, Herd simply told Flair to hit the bricks without dropping the belt. The plan was that WCW would declare the title vacant.

All fine in theory, but unfortunately for WCW, Herd failed to realize that Ric Flair believed he owned the physical belt. Back in those days, the NWA Champion had to put down a $25,000 deposit to claim the title. Since Flair never lost the belt in the ring and never got his $25,000 back, he just figured the belt was his to do with as he pleased. He even went so far as to send the belt to Vince McMahon, who began showing it on his television shows. Manager Bobby Heenan claimed that the "Real World's Champion" was on his way to the WWF. Fans watching WWF TV at home were stunned to see this turn of events, and eager to finally see the long-awaited dream match: WWF champion Hulk Hogan versus WCW champion Ric Flair.

Herd may have breathed a sigh of relief when Flair left WCW, but once that belt showed up on WWF TV, chaos erupted within the entire company. Herd caught hell from everyone—from Turner officials to the wrestlers themselves. He immediately went into a full-blown panic and tried to lure Flair back into the company with offers of more money than he was getting from McMahon. Flair, having seen how WCW operated, said "Thanks, no."

Unable to get Flair himself back, Herd knew he damn well had to recover that title. WCW promptly filed a lawsuit that eventually forced Flair to send the belt back. It also set a legal precedent that would have a major impact on wrestling years later: the court ruled that a pro-wrestling belt was a valuable symbol for the promotion it represented, and if Flair continued to wear it on WWF TV, WCW could sue for damages. So the WWF tried to make a fake WCW belt for Flair to wear. Court wasn't happy. So WWF gave him a tag belt and digitized it on television. Court still wasn't thrilled. Finally, the WWF just had Flair win their version of the World Title, and scrapped the other version entirely.

To Herd, the Flair nightmare finally appeared to be in the past. In reality, it was only just beginning.

Herd's first order of business was to crown a new champion. A plan was set in motion to do just this at the upcoming *Great American Bash* pay-per-view from Baltimore. Both Herd and Dusty saw this as WCW's chance to start anew, not only with a new champion, but also with a new focus for the company. WCW really needed this show to be a success. Fans had not been happy with Flair's sudden disappearance from the promotion, and they made their feelings known with chants of "We Want Flair" at every venue. With a crowd already likely to be irritated, it was crucial that the *Bash* entertain fans to prove that WCW could succeed without Flair.

The show rushed right out of the gate with a scaffold match. For those of you who have never seen such an encounter, a scaffold match is pretty much just what it sounds like: a scaffold is erected above the ring, and the combatants attempt to knock each other down to the floor. This type of match is not only incredibly dangerous, with the workers dropping somewhere between fifteen and twenty feet from the scaffold, it's also pretty boring—after all, no one wants to get shoved off before they're ready to make the drop. The scaffold match was a feud-ender. First, build up a huge rivalry between two men and have them duke it out in conventional matches to no satisfactory conclusion. Then, with no other way to resolve the matter, have them square off in a match so dangerous that not only would the rivalry be settled, but careers could also be over at its conclusion.

It made little sense to open the show with the match, and even less sense to open it with a bunch of mid-carders like rapmaster PN News, a 400-pounder who would likely have collapsed not only the ring, but also the concrete floor underneath had he made the drop. Still, the four men did their best, tiptoeing around the platform and doing everything they could to not lose their balance. After about ten minutes of "action," the bell rang. Since no one had fallen from the scaffold yet, this appeared to be a major screwup on someone's part. But it wasn't. The match ended because one of the contestants had captured the other team's flag. This was a new rule, one that had never been instituted in a scaffold match before. Despite the fact that this had been advertised for weeks as a standard scaffold match, the rules were changed on the night of the show so that no one would have to take the fall. It was basically a bait and switch, an increasingly common theme in WCW shows. A few boos began to scatter through the arena.

Following the scaffold match fiasco, WCW carted out cartoonish characters—a wizard (Oz), a lumberjack (Big Josh), and a hooded executioner (Black Blood)—all of whom put on horrible matches. A showdown between longtime partners Ricky Morton and Robert Gibson disappointed, as did a goofy chain match featuring Sting and Nikita Koloff. The crowd, which had been presented a horrendous card thus far, was on the verge of turning not only against the show itself, but against the promotion as well. And they did just that during the main event of the evening: Barry Windham pitted against Lex Luger for the WCW World title.

Lex Luger had been a major player for the company since his debut in 1987. With his chiseled physique, many pegged him as Flair's inevitable successor. He had, after all, been chasing the WCW title for the better part of the past four years. When the card for the *Bash* was first announced, it was to be Flair defending the belt against Luger, and every fan in the country believed that Luger would finally step up to the big time and win the belt. When Flair left the company, it seemed obvious that Luger would be the next champion, although the fact that he never beat Flair himself would haunt Luger throughout his title run.

While it certainly made sense that Luger would be in the main event, the other half of the match was puzzling. There was no doubt Barry Windham had been a solid performer in both WCW and the WWF for years, but he was never a true-blue, main-event player. He had worked a few main events (generally against Flair) throughout his tenure, but for most of 1991 he was nowhere to be found. He had been buried in a silly feud with Brian Pillman, who was running around as the masked Yellow Dog—yet another goofy Dusty creation. He was nowhere near the title scene when Flair was champion, and the sudden decree that he was the top contender to the belt seemed preposterous. Fans simply didn't buy Windham as a contender because he hadn't been presented as one in years.

The match took place within the confines of a steel cage—probably a good thing, since fans had taken to throwing garbage toward the ring. Windham and Luger proceeded to "entertain" the fans with one of the most boring title matches in years. At this point, it seemed the crowd was just looking to release its frustration with the promotion. Random cries of "We Want Flair" began to build throughout the arena, finally culminating in a deafening chant that was clearly audible not only live, but also to everyone watching the PPV broadcast.

It wasn't over yet. In a moment of infinite wisdom, WCW did decide to book Luger to win the match, but not before heel manager Harley Race came out to help him. Yes, WCW turned Luger heel, the mind-set being that Flair was always a draw as a heel, so Luger should try to duplicate that act. It wasn't a bad idea in theory (although comparing Luger to Flair in any way was comically absurd), but turning him on a night when so much else was going wrong probably wasn't the best idea, since it sent the crowd right over the edge. Despite everything else they were forced to endure, the one thing fans knew they could always count on was a celebration at the end of the night with a babyface champion. Instead, Luger and Race hugged to the crowd's catcalls.

Presenting Luger with the belt was a problem in and of itself, since WCW was not in possession of the title at the time. To "solve" the problem, WCW took an old regional title (the Western States Heritage title, to be precise) and glued a plate that read "World Champion" on top of the embossed representations of Texas, Arizona, and New Mexico.

The situation was starting to resemble a riot. And that was the last thing WCW needed: not only was the promotion in no position to mend the bridge with Flair, but he was headed straight for their competition. The company had needed to turn things around when Luger was on top, and now they had to do it with Luger as a heel. So they did the only thing they could possibly do: they put Luger into a feud with Ron Simmons, a guy who had never been over and had competed primarily in tag teams throughout his entire WCW run.

Simmons was granted the next title shot on PPV at *Halloween Havoc*, live from Chattanooga, Tennessee. But before fans got the title match on that show, they were treated to an extra special bonus attraction: an abomination known as the Chamber of Horrors. The object of this ten-man cage match was to strap your opponent in an electric chair and pull the switch. You'd think grown men hitting each other with shrunken heads would be entertaining—at least in a morbid sense—but you'd be wrong.

The remainder of the card was just a series of squash matches, followed by the Simmons-Luger match, which did little to excite the crowd. There was, however, one noteworthy match: the debut of the WCW Phantom, who completely annihilated his opponent for the evening, Tom Zenk. Later in the show, the Phantom was unmasked, and was revealed to be "Ravishing" Rick Rude, one of the WWF's top heels for the past several years. It didn't make much sense not to at least promote Rude's appearance on the show—advertising his involvement might have generated a few last-minute buys. Still, the company had a new top heel on their hands, and this would come in handy as the calendar turned to 1992.

The year ended for the company with what had traditionally been their biggest show of the year, *Starrcade*. In the past, the show had featured the settling of feuds, and it was generally the showcase for the year's most important world title defense. This year, however, in an effort to change things, Dusty came up with the Lethal Lottery, in which randomly paired tag teams would square off against each other, and the winning pairs would take part in a big battle royal at the end of the night, the Battle Bowl.

The catch in this case was that the lottery picks were so bizarre it appeared for all the world that the draw was, in fact, random. It wasn't, but it might as well have been. The card became a weird mishmash of matches between guys who had no business being in the ring with each other. Fortunately, WCW did plot a proper ending to the night: the final pair ended up being Luger, still the world champ, and Sting, the man many fans saw as the top contender to the belt. Sting triumphed over Lex to set up the one match that WCW fans were actually interested to see.

The only problem was that now Luger wanted to get out of WCW, just like Flair had six months earlier. His dream of becoming WCW World Champion had become a nightmare, and he had no desire to stick around for more "We Want Flair!" chants. In early 1992, he basically vanished from the scene, and it was more than a bit anticlimactic when he dropped the title to Sting at *Superbrawl* on February 29.

Luger wasn't the only guy to depart. Jim Herd was also shown the door following a confrontation with his boss in which he demanded that Dusty be fired. Shockingly, Dusty was kept on, and Herd was fired—sadly before his desire to create a pair of hunchback wrestlers could come to fruition. Honest to God, that's one of the things he wanted to do.

Herd was replaced by Kip Frye, who had a novel approach to the task of turning the company around. It involved, believe it or not, the wrestlers themselves. His concept was simple: reward the men who did their jobs the best. In fact, he created a new bonus system in the company in which a $5,000 award was distributed to those who performed the best match on each pay-per-view event. Raises were also introduced. This led, amazingly enough, to workers suddenly being motivated in the ring, which in turn gave fans events worth watching.

It was something new, something wholly unexpected by the boys in the back. For years, they had listened to grizzled veterans and grumpy bookers like Ole Anderson telling them to shut their mouths and just do as they were told. Anderson, in particular, would basically try to get higher-priced young talent to quit so he could bring in his old pals at a reduced rate. Of course, this wasn't what the fans wanted to see, but that mattered little to Ole. He'd grown out of touch with the business, seemingly stuck in a time warp in which he and other geezers were still the belles of the ball. After years of being held down, it looked as though the younger guys in the company, such as Brian Pillman, Steve Austin, and Tom Zenk, were about to catch a break.

Just as things were starting to move forward, Frye suddenly quit, and it looked as though everything was going to end up right back where it started. Frye's successor was Bill Watts, late of the UWF, a tough former wrestler who was known as the "Cowboy" during his days in the ring. He had a good mind for the business, and gave men like Jim Duggan, Ted DiBiase, and Junkyard Dog their first real national exposure. He had run shows at the Superdome in New Orleans, drawing tons of money and creating a television show that drew insane ratings in Oklahoma and other parts of the country. Unfortunately, those areas were devastated by the collapse of the oil market in the mid-'80s, causing a severe economic depression. Folks were more worried about how they were going to feed their families than about what was happening inside a wrestling ring. The UWF had been devoured by WCW in 1987, and Watts had then taken a long sabbatical from the business.

Unfortunately, in his first few weeks in office, it became very apparent that Watts hadn't watched a single match since his company had folded. He was old school, damn it, and that's the way he liked it. Therefore, effective immediately, he was going to make WCW matches seem much more "legitimate." He did this via a bizarre series of rule changes that made little sense to anyone other than old-timers like himself.

For example, he immediately instituted a ban on all moves off the top rope. This effectively killed any Cruiserweight matches, which had begun to help differentiate WCW from other organizations. In fact, the 1992 showdown between Brian Pillman and Japanese sensation Jushin Liger at *Superbrawl* had been heralded by many fans as the best wrestling match on the entire planet. He also removed the protective mats that surrounded the ringside area. This was done in an effort to . . . hmmm . . . well, no one really knows why it was done. It could be argued that perhaps it was done to make the workers look tougher when they took bumps outside the ring. Watts had an affinity for legitimate tough guys—one of his favorite performers ever was Steve Williams, who once got busted open during an afternoon card and returned to work later that night with 108 stitches in his head. Why Watts would want to encourage such dangerous working conditions by removing the mats is anyone's guess, and it did little to drum up support for the Cowboy backstage.

The deemphasis of the Cruiserweight division led to a lot of bad blood between Pillman and Watts, which escalated when Watts told Pillman he was looking to cut his pay. Pillman, who was under contract, told Watts to shove it. Watts responded by stating that he would job out Pillman (make him lose all his matches) for the remainder of his tenure. "Fine," Pillman replied. "I'll be the world's highest-paid jobber."

Not that it mattered to Watts; it was apparent from the beginning that Watts cared little about what the boys thought of him. He cut payroll. He eliminated catering at events. He outlawed wives and families from visiting backstage with the wrestlers. And in an apparent effort to piss everyone off, he set forth a rule that forbade any wrestler to leave the arena until the entire show was over. Even the opening-match guys had to sit around for three hours until the final bell rang. In short, Watts was not popular among his employees.

It got worse when Watts brought in a new wrestler who was immediately pushed to the moon, despite having approximately zero talent and somehow even less charisma. Why would he do this, you ask? Because, silly,

Despite his Herculean physique, Erik Watts was pretty much detested both by fans and his fellow wrestlers.

JEFF COHEN

it was his son, Erik. Yes, just like Dusty Rhodes, who had pushed his son Dustin up the card despite his being totally unprepared, Watts fell into the trap of bringing up his untalented son and giving him more than his fair share of the spotlight. Wrestlers who had worked for years hoping to get a push were aghast at this turn of events. Not only were the workers unimpressed, but so were the fans—and they damn near booed poor Erik out of the building on a nightly basis.

One guy who did connect with fans, however, was Big Van Vader, an import from Japan. A 400-pound monster, Vader was booked as the top heel for the promotion, and he immediately began to lay waste to everyone in his path. No one could stop him, and within weeks, fans knew that only one guy had a prayer of doing him in: Sting. This was classic pro-wrestling booking, as the unstoppable heel faces the plucky, popular babyface champion. Even more shockingly, WCW didn't drop the ball with Vader, as he defeated Sting in a stellar match at the *Great American Bash* and established himself as a viable world champion both to the fans and to the boys behind the curtain.

After defeating Sting, Vader was inexplicably booked to drop the title to Ron Simmons, the guy whose feud with Lex Luger had failed to generate much interest the year prior. Actually, it wasn't completely inexplicable, as Watts thought that by putting the belt on Simmons and making him the "first black world heavyweight wrestling champion," he would be able to duplicate the success he had attained in his old Mid-South promotion with the Junkyard Dog. But while Dog was charismatic and adored by the fans, Simmons was merely passable on the mic, and garnered little reaction. It didn't help matters that he was booked in world title bouts with lifelong mid-carders like The Barbarian. A champion, after all, is only as good as the folks he beats, and the fans knew that beating a stiff like Barbarian meant nothing. With little fanfare, Simmons dropped the belt back to Vader in late December.

Watts' old-school ways were starting to get him into hot water, not only with the dwindling WCW fan base, but also with the Turner corporation. In particular, an interview he had done prior to his hiring in the *Pro Wrestling Torch* newsletter upset many within the organization, as he'd stated that he believed restaurant owners shouldn't have to serve blacks if they didn't want to. Obviously, this outdated thinking wouldn't be tolerated in a corporate entity such as Turner. Watts soon found himself in a confrontation with arguably the most famous black on the Turner payroll: all-time home-run king Hank Aaron. Although most in the wrestling community question whether or not Watts really did have racist tendencies, the fact that he was allegedly working on a tag team known as the Posse—featuring two black men in the guise of criminals being led to the ring by a rich white Southerner—did little to help the Cowboy's case.

Watts' style of running a promotion may have worked in the mid-'80s, but he seemed to have no clue about how to change with the times, nor any inclination to do so. (You may be noticing a trend with WCW bookers here.) But it wasn't just his wrestling philosophies that were outdated; Watts' people skills were lacking as well. He was used to being his own boss, not answering to a bunch of suits. Watts' temper was definitely not his ally, and it led to shouting matches with those who disagreed with his tactics. Finally, it became too much to bear, and the Cowboy rode off into the sunset, quitting before he could be let go, but not before he was able to pull of one final, huge coup.

By the end of 1992, Watts was in dire straits, and he knew there was only one man who could bail him out: Ric Flair. Yes, *that* Ric Flair. The same guy who had departed the company under the Jim Herd regime, the same guy fans had been chanting for since his departure. In an effort to boost WCW's sagging ratings, Watts decided to air classic Flair bouts, such as those with Ricky Steamboat and Terry Funk. It worked, and the ratings skyrocketed. TBS was ecstatic with the gains, so Watts went to them and urged them to try to bring Flair back.

Despite achieving success in the WWF in the form of a pair of world titles, Flair had become something of a second-tier player in the WWF. After dropping the WWF title to Bret Hart in Saskatchewan, Flair knew his days at the top were over for the time being, and that he could make an immediate impact in WCW if he returned. With WCW waving huge money his way, Flair went to McMahon and asked to be released. McMahon had always told him that if he was ever unhappy with his position in the company or wanted out, all he had to do was ask. And McMahon was true to his word, giving Flair his release and asking only that he put over one of his top stars, "Mr. Perfect" Curt Hennig, in a Loser Leaves Town match.

After that, it was time to go back home, back to his most loyal fans. And it was time to do everything he could to make the company competitive with McMahon's. Although Flair couldn't wrestle for several months due to a non-compete agreement with McMahon, he kept himself busy both on-screen, in a non-wrestling segment entitled "Flair for the Gold," and behind the scenes, eventually becoming the lead booker of the promotion.

Seeing that they were able to regain Flair convinced Ted Turner to open his wallet in an attempt to lure in more big names. It took nearly a half-million dollars to bring Sid Vicious back into the fold, a move many in the industry justified by the fact that he had main-evented *Wrestlemania* less than a year earlier against Hulk Hogan. They also signed "British Bulldog" Davey Boy Smith to an inflated deal—a bit puzzling, seeing as he had been a mid-carder (as half of the British Bulldogs tag team) for most of his WWF career. He had main-evented exactly one PPV—admittedly a huge success, as it drew over 80,000 fans to *SummerSlam* in 1992 at Wembley Stadium

Big Van Vader was a huge star in Japan, and quickly became WCW's top man. These good times wouldn't last for him, since when Hulk Hogan arrived in the company, he pretty much killed Vader immediately.

JEFF COHEN

in London. But that was the catch: he was a star overseas, namely in his "homeland," England. He'd never drawn in the U.S., where WCW was promoting all of its shows.

Not only did WCW begin to sign names, but at the advice of their PPV head, Sharon Sidello, they also began to film expensive skits in an effort to sell their upcoming shows. These weren't cheap-looking productions filmed with standard television equipment; they were professionally filmed, and they looked like honest-to-God movies. And why not? They had the Turner family behind them, and if anyone could make such a production look high-end, it would be them.

The only problem was that these skits were so horribly written and acted that the results were laughable, at best. Take, for instance, the showdown between Vader and his new nemesis, Cactus Jack (Mick Foley). The story line for this one had already been set up by Vader and Jack's knock-down, drag-out affair on *WCW Saturday Night*, the promotion's flagship show at the time. Vader slammed Jack's head into the concrete outside the ring, knocking the guy out cold. With a setup like that, Pro Wrestling 101 says to just replay the bump over and over so fans will see Jack as a sympathetic character to get behind. Instead, an overblown backstory was created, in which Jack had amnesia, believed he was a sailor, and was hunted down for weeks by a bogus news reporter.

Foley truly hated the amnesia angle. When he came back to the ring, he attempted to salvage things by claiming this was all part of an elaborate ruse to play mind games with Vader. However, even after he said these things on TV, the announcers continued to play up his amnesia. This despite him saying that he didn't have amnesia. Contradictory story lines such as this would soon become commonplace in the company.

Even though *Lost in Cleveland* (a mini-movie based on the amnesia angle) was a flop, WCW felt they were onto something, and set forth plans for their next cinematic epic. This one was for *Beach Blast*, in which Davey Boy and Sting were slated to take on Vader and Sid. Standard wrestling booking says that to promote a tag match with the biggest heels in the company facing the good guys, you'd film the bad guys beating the crap out of the babyfaces in the ring. This sets up a scenario in which Sting and Davey would be seeking revenge, but they'd appear to face insurmountable odds in getting it. After all, they'd just been laid out by the guys they were confronting, so how could they possibly win?

Instead, fans were "treated" to Sting and Davey Boy playing volleyball with orphans on an island—and this is a direct quote—"somewhere in the Gulf of Mexico." Vader and Sid showed up to crash the party (on a war boat, no less!) and challenged the good guys to outdo them in a clam bake. No, just kidding, they challenged them to a match at *Beach Blast*. In the meantime, an evil one-eyed midget named Cheatum (yes, as in "cheat them") planted a bomb on Sting's boat and blew it to smithereens as the heels had a good laugh.

Let's look at the two scenarios we've presented. Scenario one, in which the heels beat up the faces and leave them sprawled out in the ring, would have cost approximately $0 extra to film. Scenario two, the amazingly well-produced but equally amazingly poorly written and performed orphans/war boat/one-eyed midget/boat explosion route, wound up costing $80,000 (more than double the $33,000 PPV live gate). Both would likely have garnered the same results, as the buy rate for *Beach Blast* received no bump from the prior show, achieving a mere 0.5.

Having lost so much money, WCW was looking for someone new to take the reins. And so the company hired yet another new boss, this time former third-string announcer Eric Bischoff.

Bischoff had been in the industry for just a handful of years and had, in fact, been turned down for a job by the WWF in June of 1990. He'd learned the business from Verne Gagne, the man behind the American Wrestling Association, which, in its day, was a huge power in the pro-wrestling business, operating primarily out of the Midwestern region of the United States. The company, around since the 1960s, had become so established that they eventually were able to ink a television deal with ESPN, which gave them a daily show that reached millions of viewers.

The American Wrestling Association played host to countless wrestling stars, but not unlike Ole Anderson, Verne made sure the spotlight always shone brightest on himself and a handful of his closest friends. Eventually, that wound up biting him in the ass, as the unthinkable happened—he got old. So did his chums. Tired of their geriatric antics, fans made it clear that they wanted to see some fresh faces. Verne was stubborn, though, and stuck to his guns, allowing men such as Hulk Hogan, Jesse Ventura, and the Road Warriors to slip right through his fingers. Even on the rare occasion a newcomer was able to break through, said newcomer was usually a relative of one of the old guys, notably Curt, Larry Hennig's son, and Verne's own son Greg—a scrawny beanpole no one wanted to see in main events.

By the time Bischoff arrived in the AWA, the promotion was on its deathbed. Attendance at shows had dipped so badly that Gagne opted not to run any more live arena events, taping his shows in an empty warehouse instead. Seeing the writing on the wall, Verne's top stars fled for other promotions. Verne saw it too, but he decided to give his young apprentice one last shot to save the promotion.

Bischoff racked his brain, and came up with what he felt was an ideal solution: the Team Challenge Series. The idea was to divide the roster into thirds, making unlikely teams work together in a series of matches, with the winning squad taking a $1 million prize. This way, if someone should leave the company (which was happening on a near-weekly basis), his team could continue on without him. The matches themselves consisted of wacky gimmicks; the high point of the series was a match in which two men fought to retrieve a raw turkey placed atop a pole. Really. Shockingly, the Team Challenge Series did little to repair the damage that the company had suffered, and the AWA folded shortly thereafter.

Despite his abject failure, Bischoff had developed a taste for the business, and had learned much under Gagne's tutelage. After Vince showed zero interest in the guy, he turned to WCW and was eventually given a shot as an announcer on lower-end shows. Like a sponge, Bischoff soaked up every bit of wisdom he could—not only from the wrestlers and the booking team, but also from the production people. Bischoff was smart enough to realize that there was more to wrestling than just what went on inside the ring. This paid off for him big time; following the departure of Bill Watts, the company was looking for a new head honcho. At the time, many believed that the next boss would be Tony Schiavone, WCW's lead announcer at the time. Schiavone had, after all, been with the organization since before it was even known as WCW. He'd worked for Jim Crockett, not only as a wrestling announcer but also a baseball play-by-play man. If anyone was a lock for the job, many reasoned, it was him.

But it didn't happen. Instead, Turner reps liked what they saw in Eric Bischoff. He was young, he was handsome, and he was aggressive. He had new ideas. And, perhaps most importantly, he also seemed to have a more corporate mentality to him, with an understanding of marketing that they found very appealing. In short, he knew more than just pro wrestling, and he was a far cry from the crotchety old ring warriors who had preceded him. Ole Anderson would start yelling at a moment's notice . . . but Bischoff? No way. He was far too levelheaded, and perhaps for that reason more than any other, he was given the ball and told to run with it.

Despite the artistic and commercial failures of the mini-movie ventures, Bischoff saw the value of having more control over the product he was presenting on-screen. Therefore, the decision was made to forgo most of the arena television tapings and instead begin to record shows at MGM Studios in Orlando, Florida. This would have the twofold effect of lowering costs (as they could tape several shows at once), and allowing the promotion to "demonstrate" to fans at home who was really popular and who was really hated in its ranks. To that end, WCW began to screen the crowds at these tapings, specifically filtering out any hardcore wrestling fans, since they would likely have their own opinions on different characters, opinions that wouldn't jive with what the company wanted to present. For example, Marcus Bagwell was a babyface many hardcore fans didn't care for, so they'd boo him on his way to the ring. WCW didn't want any of that, so they had signs to instruct folks when to cheer or boo, just like a standard television show.

And just like a "normal" TV show, they were taping months in advance. Never before had this happened in wrestling, but to Bischoff's credit, the tapings likely saved the company many thousands of dollars, which no doubt pleased his bosses in the Turner regime. However, this also forced the company to plan in advance, because they would tape three months' worth of shows at a time. Therefore, any title changes the company had, such as those at live pay-per-view or live *Clash of the Champions* specials, were to be factored into the production of the show. For example, when the tapings began, Barry Windham was the NWA champion, but later in the tapings, Ric Flair was the NWA champion. The match where the belt switched was not filmed since the title change was planned for later on at the *Beach Blast* event. Not only that, but the tapings also made it clear that Flair would drop the title shortly after winning it to Rick Rude. This made for some major headaches for WCW, such as when news of the changes was leaked to the fans. That happened, of course. However, since the Internet was in its infancy, the only way fans really knew what was going to happen was through insider newsletters, and WCW didn't consider that a big enough issue to be of real concern.

No, the major dilemma was that once the filming was done, WCW more or less had to follow through with their title changes. They had done this once before, in the early months of 1991, when matches were taped with the Fabulous Freebirds wearing the tag belts despite the fact they hadn't even won them yet. In fact, the 'birds lost the belts to the Steiner Brothers, all before they'd even actually won them in the first place! It didn't matter, because things would play out in order on TV.

Since that scenario turned out fine, WCW felt that the Orlando tapings would as well, but there were some major issues. One of the biggest was that the National Wrestling Alliance found out about upcoming NWA title switches at the tapings. You see, since the formation of the NWA, the main governing body had to vote on all upcoming title changes and approve them. If a promoter wanted to put the NWA title on, say, Ronnie Garvin, the board would vote and say, for example, no, unless they'd lost their minds.

In 1993, WCW was still officially an NWA member, and all their belts were still technically being overseen by the NWA. Bischoff, however, ignored all the old rules and just started putting the belts on whomever he pleased. A huge argument erupted between both sides, and WCW eventually broke all ties with the NWA. However, they had footage of Rude with the NWA World championship bantering back and forth with Flair that they somehow had to factor into their programming. Since they could no longer promote the NWA World title by name and all they had was this big gold belt, they just started promoting matches for the "Big Gold Belt." It was a mess.

Another snafu caused by the tapings involved the WCW Tag titles. The Hollywood Blondes, Steve Austin and Brian Pillman, were to drop their titles to the Horsemen, Arn Anderson and Paul Roma. At the tapings, it was revealed that the Blondes would do this at the *Beach Blast* show, but at the last minute, WCW decided to keep the belts on Pillman and Austin. They could do this because there was still a live *Clash of the Champions* event at which WCW would have the belt change hands. All great in theory, until Pillman was injured prior to the bout and couldn't work the show. A makeshift "championship" team of Austin and Steve Regal (who had never worked with Austin before and had no ties to the Tag belts) defended—and lost—the belts to the Horsemen.

For all the problems being created, everyone felt as though the pendulum was on the upswing, especially with the biggest show of the year, *Starrcade*, on the horizon. The event was to feature a match that had never been presented before, one that fans were looking forward to and were therefore willing to pay for the right to view: Vader versus Sid Vicious, with the WCW World title on the line. Again, the MGM tapings revealed the course of events: Sid, with the belt around his waist, was portrayed as a hero.

This time, though, things really fell apart. During a tour of the U.K., a fight broke out between Sid and Anderson following a confrontation at a pub. Both had been drinking, and Vicious became boisterous, claiming that he was the future of the business and that Arn and his pal Flair were ancient dinosaurs. Arn did not take kindly to being compared to a brontosaurus. Just as the two men were about to come to blows, it was broken up, and Arn retreated to his room. Vicious followed shortly thereafter and knocked on his door, offering an apology in the form of a chair to Arn's head. The two went at it, with Sid allegedly grabbing a pair of scissors and stabbing Arn, puncturing himself in the process, too. The incident hit the U.K. papers, and you can just imagine how well that went over with the Turner hierarchy. The wrestlers themselves were livid at the event, as Arn was beloved, and Sid was . . . well, to be blunt, he was starting to be a total dickhead backstage. Finally, the decision was made to fire Vicious.

And therein was the rub. The man who was to lead the promotion into 1994 as champion—and who had already been taped doing so!—was history. A mad scramble ensued to determine just who would wind up with the main-event slot at the biggest show of the year against Vader, with Cactus Jack, Sting, and Rude at the top of the list. In the end, though, Bischoff listened to the crowds at the WCW events: "We Want Flair." Billed as a match after which he'd retire forever if he lost, an emotional Flair beat Vader before 8,000 fans paying $65,000 in Charlotte's Independence Arena to regain *his* title. Yes, despite being "too old" for Jim Herd three years earlier, and of no further use to McMahon or the WWF, Flair was once again the man.

It was a good time for all within the company. The happiness was short-lived, however, as Turner officials decided to look at the books to see just how well the company had done under Bischoff's leadership in the past year. No doubt his new style of promoting, along with his money-saving measures—like filming the bulk of WCW programming at MGM—would pay huge dividends when the financials came out.

But they didn't. In fact, the company was still losing money, and this was something Bischoff didn't want to be a part of; after all, if he could be the first man in WCW to actually turn a profit, he'd likely get even more power and money to do with as he pleased. They were close, so close, and he wasn't about to let *his* company slip away.

After a week or so of intense soul-searching, Bischoff decided that the one thing WCW lacked was mainstream media attention. If they could just be accepted as the WWF's equal, the company would be set. Had they lost money? Yes, Mr. Turner, we have. But we can make it back, tenfold. We just need a bit more time, a bit more money. We need to capture the attention of the casual fan, and I've got just the guy to do it. You've probably even heard of him: Hulk Hogan.

Now *there* was something Ted could buy into: the biggest star the business had ever seen. With Turner's blessing, Bischoff, with a major assist from Ric Flair, who knew Hogan from their WWF days together, set out to catch the biggest fish in the pond and bring him home to Uncle Ted. The timing was perfect, because Hogan had left the WWF earlier in the year, following a blowup with Vince McMahon over the way he was being booked. Hogan felt that he should still be the focal point of the company—the champion. McMahon disagreed, preferring to focus on younger guys such as Bret Hart and Shawn Michaels, believing they would connect with a "new generation" of fans. The two got into a bitter argument following Hogan's title win at *Wrestlemania IX*, as McMahon wanted Hogan to drop the belt to Hart and "pass the torch" in the process. Hogan, stuck in his 1980s mind-set, refused, saying Hart was way too small. Instead, he put over the enormous Yokozuna at that year's *King of the Ring* PPV, then disappeared from the company to pursue acting and wrestle the occasional big show in Japan.

But there was room for Hulk Hogan's star to shine in WCW—if he wanted to be the top dog in the promotion, well, that was just fine. Hogan had, after all, drawn more money than anyone else in the history of the business. Just ask him; he'd tell you so. The only stumbling block was that Hogan wanted *so much* money—a contract larger than any WCW had ever offered before. Bischoff didn't care. It was Hogan or bust, and after convincing higher-ups in the company—namely Ted Turner himself—of this, he got his wish.

//

Upon Hogan's arrival, WCW had an entirely different look. The old Center Stage Theater—the longtime taping location for *WCW Saturday Night*—had been completely renovated. According to a source who worked for WCW at the time, "Center Stage used to be a rathole in the grossest part of town in Atlanta. Then, the first day Hogan came in, they put purple curtains up everywhere so you couldn't see how shitty it was. That very same day. Went from coffee and water and Gatorade to fruit and all sorts of food. In the old days, when wrestlers walked out, they used to come out under the seats, from the bleachers. You're kind of ducking a little bit to not hit your head. So they put curtains up everywhere to hide things and try to make it look better than what it really was."

\\

WCW's Hogan era began on June 11, 1994. His arrival was celebrated with an elaborate parade (complete with confetti!), and sure enough Hogan was booked as the number-one contender and set his sights on current WCW champ Ric Flair (who had to turn heel as soon as Hogan arrived). Hogan easily conquered Flair at *Bash at the Beach*, selling out the Orlando Arena and doing a colossal 1.02 buy rate for the company, one of its largest ever.

Bischoff breathed a sigh of relief. His investment had paid off, and the fans were really starting to buy WCW as a true alternative to the WWF. Maybe he could catch Vince. No, no maybes about it—he WOULD catch Vince, and even surpass him. Hogan was able to convince Bischoff that he held the key that would take WCW to the top of the mountain: his friends (all of whom, coincidentally, needed big paydays). So Randy Savage, Jim Duggan, "Earthquake" John Tenta, Honky Tonk Man, Jimmy Hart, and countless others were brought into the fold. Longtime WCW employees like Steve Austin, Vader, and Mick Foley were thrown into the background so as not to steal the limelight from Hogan and his pals.

"I was thrilled to be there, don't get me wrong," recalls John Tenta. "Hulk really went to bat for me. But I was amazed by just how much money that company blew. Hogan would tell me about how he and Bischoff would go out for sushi, and spend $1,000 in a single evening. They didn't care. It wasn't their money, it was Turner's."

And then there was Ric Flair, the man who had done everything he could to repair WCW following his stint in the WWF. Bischoff quickly realized that there was no way Hogan and Flair could coexist at the top of the WCW mountain, so Flair was asked to job to Hogan one more time in a "retirement" match at *Halloween Havoc*. The event was a huge success, drawing a record gate for WCW and another buy rate around 1.0. Things were only looking better for the company as they headed toward *Starrcade*, which was to feature a showdown between Hogan and longtime lackey Ed "Brutus Beefcake" Leslie.

But something funny happened on the way to the event. The fans, who had been so hot for the Hogan-Flair showdowns, seemed to suddenly lose interest in what Hogan was doing. And when the buy rates came in for *Starrcade*, the company was stunned. At 0.6, it was 40 percent lower than what they'd done for *Havoc* just two months earlier. Obviously, Ed Leslie was no Ric Flair.

There was a bit of a rebound in the opening months of 1995, when Hogan was moved into a feud with Vader. It just made sense, since Vader had been the top heel of the company for the better part of the previous three years. The two battled it out both at *Uncensored*, a goofy card featuring all gimmick matches (which did a 0.96), and at *Bash at the Beach* (0.82). It should be noted that the *Bash* show took place on a real, live, honest-to-goodness beach, which resulted in a gate of zero dollars.

With business otherwise once again looking promising, Bischoff and Turner had yet another meeting, and this time Ted had a question. Why, he wondered, were they not beating the WWF if they had Hogan, Savage, and all the other top stars? Bischoff, panicked at being put on the spot, blurted out: "We need prime-time TV." He knew they'd never get it.

Shockingly, this man (Ed Leslie) did little to stir either fans' interest or ticket sales.

Turner, however, paused. Moments later, he turned to his television supervisor, telling him to give Eric two hours on TNT every Monday night.

In other words, WCW would be competing directly against the WWF's flagship show, *Monday Night Raw*.

Bischoff was stunned. He had just been given the go-ahead to fight Vince McMahon mano y mano, and now he had to deliver the goods. This all seemed like madness, and those within the wrestling side of the company pleaded with Bischoff to somehow get Ted to change his mind.

Bischoff, though, knew something that no one else did: WCW could beat McMahon by changing wrestling forever.

Which is pretty much exactly what *WCW Monday Nitro* did when it debuted on Turner Network Television the night of September 4, 1995—a week in which *Raw* was not-so-coincidentally preempted. The years-old formula of wrestling shows consisting primarily of squash matches flew right out the window. In its place were big-name versus big-name showdowns, something reserved for pay-per-views in the past. Shocking happenings, such as Lex Luger suddenly defecting from the WWF, began occurring on an almost weekly basis. Fans soon learned that if you missed *Nitro*, by God, you could miss a lot, and it became *the* show to watch on Monday nights.

On top of that, it was all 100 percent *live*, a fact that Bischoff flaunted *live*, as he had made himself the top announcer on the show. He had learned from his experience in Orlando just how damaging taping in advance could be, and he set out to teach that very lesson to McMahon.

"If you're thinking about changing the channel, don't bother," Bischoff advised viewers one evening when *Raw* was planning a Shawn Michaels versus Sid main event "Shawn beats the big guy in the main event with three superkicks." Yes, he was giving away the results of the pre-taped *Raw* live on the air! No doubt McMahon nearly had a heart attack upon hearing that. It was completely unheard of, and utterly unfathomable.

But Bischoff was there to fight. He knew that McMahon wouldn't take things lying down, so he had to get as many shots in as he could and change the rules, just as Vince himself had done to the smaller promotions like the AWA years ago. One way Bischoff did this was by having a monitor installed underneath his announce table so he could see what was taking place on *Raw* while *Nitro* was going on, and change his booking plans on the fly. The boys in the back didn't like it, since it gave them little time to prepare for matches, but it gave Bischoff an edge in this war. He could change things up, whereas McMahon couldn't because his shows were in the can. It was a huge tactical edge in WCW's war with the WWF.

And it really was a war. Bischoff made no bones about taking pot-shots against McMahon; he knocked not only the WWF talent, but even McMahon himself. Bischoff brought in as many top WWF stars as he could, many of whom were happy to bash their former employer. WWF Women's champion Debbie "Madusa" Micelli, foolishly fired by Vince without ever being asked to lose her title in the ring, went so far as to show up on *Nitro* the following week with the belt and promptly throw it in the trash for all the world to see. In many ways, this was a war between the two promotions, but it also quickly became a personal issue between Bischoff and McMahon. It was a fight, and during the opening round Bischoff didn't just throw the first punch—he kicked McMahon in the ass, then turned around and kicked him right square in the balls. McMahon, stuck in a time warp just like all those regional promoters he put out of business a decade earlier, never saw it coming. And in an incredibly hypocritical moment, like those same promoters, he cried foul.

But nothing Bischoff did during the first six months of the battle meant nearly as much as what happened on the May 27, 1996, edition of *Nitro*. That's when Scott Hall, formerly known as Razor Ramon in the WWF, took the stage and proclaimed war on WCW.

And thus the battle was truly and fully on.

"You want a war? You got one!"
—*Scott Hall to Eric Bischoff,* Monday Nitro, *May 27, 1996*

CHAPTER 2

1996: The War Begins

From the time WCW and the WWF first emerged as the two major leagues of professional wrestling, fans had debated who would win in a showdown between the two. Many knew that the whole business was in fact pre-determined, but it was still fun to contemplate the awesome matchups that would take place should the two companies ever compete under one banner. In fact, many wrestling magazines seemed to stay in business by publishing at least one article detailing interpromotional "dream matches" each month. Every fan hoped to see, once and for all, which of the two organizations was truly superior.

So when Scott Hall appeared for the very first time on *Nitro*, it should have come as no shock that the fans suddenly sat up and took notice. His debut certainly was unique. In the past, promotions typically released video packages to detail a wrestler's imminent arrival. These would establish just who the character was, what his motives were, etc., to create a "buzz" before he ever stepped foot in the ring. With Hall, however, WCW concluded that everyone knew who he was, since he had been an integral part of the

WWF's upper card for the better part of the past three years. Therefore, no packages were produced, and nothing was ever mentioned.

No, Scott Hall just showed up one night on *Nitro* and grabbed the promotion by the balls.

The night was May 27, 1996, a night which, for many reasons, was a turning point in the history of wrestling. It just happened to be the week that *Nitro* made a huge jump, expanding from one hour to two. Since *Raw* ran from 9-10 P.M., Bischoff decided to run *Nitro* from 8-10, giving the show one full unopposed hour to build up the second hour as a must-see. Turner was happy because the show in the 8-9 slot, *Thunder in Paradise* (which, ironically, featured Hulk Hogan in a leading role), was doing miserable numbers. In exchange for the programming, Turner agreed to pay WCW $2 million per year for the added hour. Because attendance at WCW live events had started taking off months earlier due to a Randy Savage versus Ric Flair (who was unretired again at this point) feud, this additional revenue meant that the company had reached a new milestone: for the first time in history, it turned a profit.

It was on this occasion, as *Nitro* expanded to fill its new timeslot, that the Scott Hall deal unfolded. During the midst of a mid-card match featuring Mike Enos and Steve Doll (that's right, and for historical purposes it should be noted that, aside from Hall's appearance, this show totally blew), Hall jumped the rail from the stands and grabbed a microphone. It looked for all the world like a completely unscripted event, and immediately fans began to think something was up—after all, here was this big WWF star invading *Nitro*! Those fans were even more suspicious when Hall made his way to the ring and began to speak.

"Hey, you people know who I am. But you don't know why I am here. Where is Billionaire Ted? Where is the Nacho Man?" The mystery continued to build as Hall hunted down the announce team, including Eric Bischoff himself. "Bischoff, you got a big mouth. You started it, now we're going to finish it!" He also mentioned that he wasn't alone, and that he'd have a "big surprise" for all of WCW the following week. "You want a war?" Hall asked. "You got one!"

WCW got one all right. A real-life war with the WWF that resulted in a real-life lawsuit filed by McMahon's company on June 20. The suit cited, among other things, unfair competition (with regard to WCW's portrayal of this as an interpromotional angle—ironic, given WWF's portrayal of Ric Flair in 1991), trademark infringement (Hall looked and spoke too much like Razor Ramon for their tastes), unfair competition (WCW had allegedly claimed on its 900 Hotline that WWF was ready to file for bankruptcy—a stretch, but this was the year in which WWF was closest to going under in its entire history), and defamation and libel (for an incident in which the power went out at *Nitro* and Bischoff implied that "the competition" might have had something to do with it).

WCW didn't care. The following week, Hall delivered on his threat, as Kevin Nash, who had competed as Diesel in the WWF, made his debut. Not only was Nash a former WWF champion, he was also the man around whom McMahon had developed his most recent marketing campaign, the "New Generation," the idea being that Nash was fresh, while the guys in WCW like Hogan and Savage were yesterday's news. Like Hall, Nash began to berate Bischoff and WCW as a whole.

"You've been out here running your mouth for six months!" Nash bellowed. "This is where the big boys play? What a joke!"

The implication was clear: Bischoff had taken shot after shot at the WWF on *Nitro*, pulling stunts like announcing the results of the taped shows and mocking their top stars. Now, here were two of the WWF's biggest names confronting Bischoff about his actions and threatening to dismantle WCW to its very core. In a stroke of what can only be described as genius, the words "WWF," "Razor Ramon," and "Diesel" were never mentioned. Indeed, the loudest words were unspoken. On top of all this was the irony of WCW throwing the WWF's entire series of "Billionaire Ted" skits. The skits, in which elderly actors played knock-offs of Hogan ("The Huckster") and Randy Savage ("The Nacho Man"), did little more for the WWF than to further stir interest in the WCW product.

Everything led to the *Great American Bash* PPV, an event so shockingly great from both in-ring and booking standpoints that many fans went as far as to call it the greatest U.S. pay-per-view of all time. Right before the main event, Hall and Nash showed up again and interrupted the proceedings, to a bigger reaction than almost anyone else on the show. In fact, the crowd began to chant "Diesel! Diesel!" Amazingly enough, neither man had even been named by the promotion at this point.

After berating Bischoff once more, Hall and Nash made their demand clear: a three-on-three match for the upcoming *Bash at the Beach* PPV. Bischoff agreed, and Hall asked who WCW's three men would be. Bischoff wouldn't say, so Hall punched him in the stomach, doubled him over, and sent him into the waiting arms of Nash. Nash then lifted Bischoff high into the air and powerbombed him off the stage and through a table below.

The crowd went absolutely crazy. Armageddon had arrived: the WWF was here, and they were taking out WCW from the very top!

Before we continue, it must be said that the manner in which WCW initially booked Hall and Nash was nothing short of phenomenal. The whole idea behind drawing money in wrestling is actually pretty basic: create a match that fans want to see and, more importantly, one that they're willing to pay to see. If fans perceive that one side has zero chance of winning, they won't want to see the bout. After all, the outcome of such an encounter would be predetermined (which is ironic, since all pro wrestling is predetermined). It's also crucial that the two factions are perceived as equals: if a main-eventer takes on a lower-card guy, fans will likely reject the match. When Hall and Nash made their debuts, they were treated as something very out of the ordinary; in fact, they were made to look absolutely dominant. They were a huge threat, not only to this wrestler or that wrestler, but also to the entire company of WCW as a whole.

Never before had two men simply come into a company and acted like it was their personal playground. It was called an "attempted hostile takeover," and by God, that's just what it was. During matches in which they weren't involved, the announce team would talk about them, fearing what might happen when they showed up. These "outsiders" were such a threat that not only was everyone on the alert, but at one point the announce team even had armed guards to protect their positions. It's one thing to KO a guy in a wrestling ring—it's another altogether to be so dominant and intimidating that security guys with GUNS are required.

This was a threat WCW took very seriously. The only way to fight guys who were the tops in the WWF was to use their own main-eventers. In fact, on the very first night that Hall showed up, none other than Sting came out to defend WCW's honor. It made sense, as Sting was often viewed as the promotion's franchise player. Unlike nearly everyone else in WCW, he'd never left the company, and had remained true to WCW through all of its ups and downs. If anyone could block this WWF onslaught, it would be the Stinger. But he'd definitely need backup, and in this case, he got it in the form of two of WCW's other top stars, Randy Savage and Lex Luger.

So Team WCW was set, but leading up to *Bash at the Beach*, one question remained: who would Hall and Nash (now dubbed "the Outsiders") have as their mystery partner? Indeed, one of the biggest selling points of the PPV was the chance to see just who the third guy was. Although "mystery partner" angles almost always turn out to be complete flops in wrestling, the fact that WCW had delivered two monumental surprises in the appearances of Hall and Nash convinced fans that WCW would unveil another huge name. Right up until the ring introductions, the question remained: who was the third man?

///

There were several schools of thought as to just who would wind up as Hall and Nash's mystery partner, both in the minds of fans and behind the scenes. Since Hall and Nash had just jumped ship, and it appeared that McMahon was having problems holding onto his talent, one theory had yet another WWF main-eventer jump ship: Bret Hart. And since it was known that Bret was unhappy with his current position in the WWF hierarchy, he seemed a likely third man. In reality, Bischoff wouldn't begin negotiations with Bret until months after the *Bash*, so it was never going to be him.

\\\

As the crowd craned their necks toward the entrance ramp, Michael Buffer made the introductions. But something wasn't right—only Hall and Nash made their way toward the ring. The announce crew immediately cried that this was unfair, and this really said something—after all, shouldn't the WCW announce crew have been happy that it was now a handicap match? Apparently not, as Tony Schiavone, practically in tears, screamed, "They've got to tell us who the third man is right now!" His announce colleague, Bobby Heenan, countered, "They know what they're doing. They're keeping us on the edge of our seats and making our palms sweat!" They sure were; they had the entire crowd and all those watching at home antsy about what the hell was going on.

Gene Okerlund made his way to the ring and demanded to know where the third man was. Hall, channeling the Puerto Rican accent he had used as Razor Ramon, retorted, "You know, Scheme Gene, you know too much already. All you need to know, little man, is that he's here and he's ready." Nash followed up and proclaimed: "He's here all right, Gene, but we're enough to handle it here right now."

He was right. Nash and Hall began a complete dissection of the WCW crew, knocking Luger out of the match almost immediately. This furthered speculation that perhaps Luger would reemerge as the third member. That wasn't in the plans, however. And just in case fans at home hadn't caught on that Nash and Hall were bad news, the announcers began to beg for a third guy to come out, so that team WCW would once again have a three-on-two advantage! They needed the help, too, as the Outsiders beat the ever-loving crap out of Sting and Savage. Note to wrestling promoters: *this* is how you book strong heels. Finally, Sting was able to make the tag to Savage, and the crowd went insane. One low blow later, though, Savage was once again down.

Just as things began to look most bleak, WCW's biggest star hit the aisle: Hulk Hogan. As he came down the ramp, the fans cheered—WCW was finally saved!

Hogan surveyed the ring. Hall and Nash had dropped to the floor, leaving Randy Savage alone in the ring, flat on his back. Hogan looked around the ring nervously, and glanced momentarily at the crowd. No doubt, Terry Bollea had serious reservations as to what his wrestling persona was about to do. For the first time in over a decade, and for the first time since he had taken the nation by storm as Hulk Hogan, he was about to become a heel.

The third man had arrived.

Hogan dropped the leg across Savage's throat. Sting came back in to make the save, but was promptly thrown out. Again and again, Hogan nailed Savage, stopping only to high-five his new friends. The wrestling world had its new number-one heel. And WCW was about to take off into the stratosphere.

Gene Okerlund hit the ring once more to find out what the hell had just happened. Hogan launched into a tirade: "Mean Gene, the first thing you need to do is to tell these people to shut up if you want to hear what I got to say. The first thing you got to realize, brother, is that this is the future of wrestling. You can call this the New World Order of wrestling, brother!" And thus the group had its name.

What about its motives? "These two men right here came from a great big organization up north. And everybody was wondering who the third man was. Well, who knows more about that organization than me, brother? I made that organization a monster. I made people rich up there. I made the people that ran that organization rich up there, brother! And when it all came to pass, the name Hulk Hogan, the man Hulk Hogan, got bigger than the whole organization. And then Billionaire Ted, he wanted to talk turkey with Hulk Hogan. Billionaire Ted promised me movies, he promised me millions of dollars, and he promised me world-caliber matches. As far as Billionaire Ted, as far as Eric Bischoff, and as far as the whole WCW goes, I'm bored, brother!"

Fans began to get irate, and hurled trash into the ring. What began as a paper cup here or there had become a flood of garbage that washed over Hogan, Hall, and Nash. In fact, the entire area was becoming less like a wrestling ring and more like a landfill confined by ropes and turnbuckles.

Hogan continued: "As far as I'm concerned, all the crap in this ring represents these fans out here! For two years, for two years, I held my head high! I did everything for the charities, I did everything for the kids, and the reception I got when I came out here, you fans can stick it, brother! Because if it wasn't for Hulk Hogan, you people wouldn't be here! If it wasn't for

Hulk Hogan, Eric Bischoff would still be selling meat from a truck in Minneapolis! And if it wasn't for Hulk Hogan, wrestling wouldn't be here!"

Tony Schiavone concluded the telecast with these words: "We have seen the end of Hulkamania . . . Hulk Hogan, you can go to hell! Straight to hell!"

//

At this point, the New World Order name was here to stay, despite commentator Larry Zbysko's best efforts to call them the New World Odor. That Larry, he was a damn clever man.

\\

It was a long time coming, both for Hogan and for the fans, who had grown bored with the goody-two-shoes image that Hogan had used for so many years. Indeed, a handful of fans had already been booing Hogan in his appearances leading up to the turn, and now they were given carte blanche to scream their lungs out against the guy. Hogan, having seen his popularity decline, was truly at a career crossroads. Being a bad guy wasn't something he wanted to do, per se, but Bischoff had made an excellent argument: as a babyface, Hogan had worn out his welcome, but as a heel, he would be at the top of the cards once more.

It was a good argument, but Bollea was still undecided. He had strong reservations about leaving behind what was a secure (though not as profitable as it had once been) role as wrestling's number-one good guy. He was already starting to wane as a babyface . . . what if he flopped as a heel? Bad guys didn't sell T-shirts, and they didn't take starring roles in movies. In fact, as a heel, Hogan had never main-evented wrestling shows, either. Although none but the hardest of hardcore fans knew it, Hogan had started his national career as a heel for the World Wrestling Federation in 1979, wrestling under the tutelage of evil managers like Fred Blassie and taking on fan favorites like Andre the Giant. In fact, his first babyface turn came by accident, as he was supposed to debut for Verne Gagne's AWA on August 9, 1981, as a heel, but for whatever reason, the fans went wild for him.

By the middle of 1996, Hogan had few options. His WCW contract would be due after two more PPVs, and he had no leverage left. He had tried one of his usual tricks months earlier, and it had backfired. The NBA playoffs were coming up, so he left to film a movie. Of course, the playoffs wreaked havoc on *Nitro*'s ratings, and his plan was to come back and say the reason they were down was because he was gone. There was a flaw in his plan, however. He was gone too long, and when the playoffs ended, *Nitro* returned and started doing better numbers than when he'd been main-eventing every week. So, less than two weeks before the *Bash*, Hogan decided to take the gamble and turn heel.

The gamble paid off. Hulk Hogan, bad guy, became the talk of the wrestling industry. His career was instantly rejuvenated, giving WCW a huge shot in the arm. Fans who hadn't been following the business suddenly wanted to know just what could have caused such a catastrophic turn of events. The following night on *Nitro*, Hogan launched into yet another tirade, echoing his sentiments from the previous night and adding that if the fans didn't like what he had to say, they could "stick it."

Anyone involved in wrestling—especially promoters and bookers—should take note that even when things appear to be taking off, nothing happens overnight. All the angles that WCW booked in mid-1996 certainly increased casual fan interest in the product. This interest, however, did not immediately turn the company's fortunes around. In fact, despite all the awesome hype leading up to *Bash at the Beach*, the show actually did *fewer* buys than the same PPV the year prior (0.71 versus 0.82). *Nitro* ratings were up, but that was slightly deceptive, partially owing to the addition of an unopposed first hour. And house show business, legitimately up a whopping 125 percent, was the result of the Flair versus Savage feud that had started earlier in the year, and had nothing to do with the nWo.

With Hogan, Hall, and Nash running roughshod over WCW, it became apparent that the entire promotion would begin to rally together as a group to fight this invasion. The Giant—WCW World champion at the time—stepped up to the plate to defend WCW's honor, in addition to the title. This was a major turning point in the early formation of the angle, since the Giant had been a heel right up until Hogan's heel turn.

And indeed it was all of WCW against the New World Order, as the invaders began to assail anyone and everyone within the company with a series of sneak attacks, spray-painting their victims with an "nWo" tag. One such attack saw the near–seven foot Kevin Nash launch five-foot-two Rey Mysterio Jr. into the side of a truck like a lawn dart. Arn Anderson of the Four Horsemen was also injured during the beatdown, showing that the nWo didn't care who was a face or heel on the WCW side of things; all were enemies to them. Everyone, from legends like Ric Flair to opening-match guys like Brad Armstrong, stood united against the nWo's onslaught.

To stand up to such numbers, it was clear that Hogan, Hall, and Nash would need to bring in more members. And so came *Hog Wild*—an annual PPV event emanating from the Sturgis motorcycle rally. The matches took place in the middle of a field of thousands of drunken bikers, whom WCW did not charge to attend the event. In other words, the gate was zero dollars. Despite this lack of revenue, the company would hold the event over the next several years, primarily due to the fact that Eric Bischoff was such a huge motorcycle enthusiast. On this occasion, commentators

Dusty Rhodes and Tony Schiavone, dressed to look like a pair of gay biker lovers, opened the program, proclaiming that WCW had stumbled upon new evidence that the nWo was growing, and that their numbers would increase by at least one man by the end of the evening.

The show itself was rather boring and bland, aside from a women's match featuring Madusa Micelli, who had made quite a name for herself a year or so earlier when she showed up on *Nitro* and threw the WWF Women's title into the garbage. On this night, Micelli took on Bull Nakano from Japan. Nakano was quite the sight, a 200-plus-pound brute of a woman with hair sticking up two feet from her forehead. She looked like the world's most brutal Japanese porcupine. But she was a fantastic in-ring competitor, and the two had some really good matches. Micelli and Nakano had previously had a heated rivalry in the WWF when Micelli, hoping to boost the status of women's wrestling (which had never been taken seriously in the U.S.), urged McMahon to bring in some of Japan's top stars. McMahon, however, thought Micelli would be better served by taking on the 350-pound Rhonda Singh, whom he dubbed Bertha Faye, queen of the trailer park. Madusa was more than happy to get out of the WWF when she had the chance.

Playing to the xenophobic nature of pro-wrestling crowds, especially those containing thousands of (likely inebriated) bikers, the *Hog Wild* encounter saw the two fight for the right to smash their opponent's motorcycle. It should be noted that Bull's manager was the diminutive walking Japanese stereotype, Sonny Onoo, who would later file a lawsuit against WCW for racial discrimination. This despite his claim that he'd ride his bike "like a kamikaze" during this match. Anyway, despite the best efforts of Nakano and Onoo—who unfortunately did not attempt a suicide mission with his Honda—Madusa got the duke and took a sledgehammer to the bike to the cheers of the crowd.

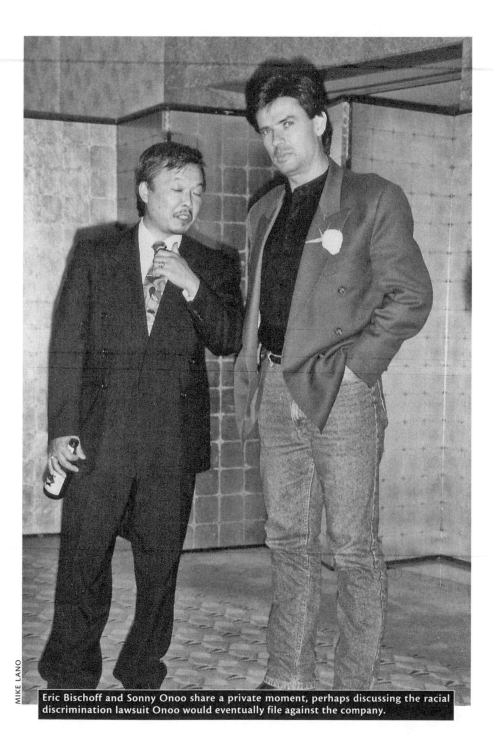

MIKE LANO

Eric Bischoff and Sonny Onoo share a private moment, perhaps discussing the racial discrimination lawsuit Onoo would eventually file against the company.

Heading into the main event, the New World Order had yet to reveal any new members. At least not officially. During the Outsiders matchup against Sting and Luger, it looked as though Luger would get the submission victory over Hall. However, referee Nick Patrick accidentally-on-purpose clipped Luger's knee, allowing Hall to roll him up for the pin. This would lead to a loooong angle during which Patrick would become the "official" official for the group. However, at this point, Patrick was not officially a heel, and the nWo still hadn't bolstered its ranks.

Again, in the main event, it looked as though Giant had things in hand, until Hogan walloped him with the title belt, leaving the big guy flat on his back for the next fifteen minutes. They must have replaced the gold with lead. Metallurgic inconsistencies aside, the win gave the nWo their first championship, and Hogan took the spotlight atop the card once more. Out came longtime Hogan lackey Ed Leslie, the man of a thousand horrible gimmicks. Fans had last seen him as The Bootyman, a character who shook his ass at the camera to the delight of no one and used the high knee (get it, as in "hiney"?) as his finisher. Since the *Hog Wild* event fell on Hogan's birthday, Leslie, in an effort to suck up to the Hulkster, brought out a cake. Hogan thanked Leslie, then proceeded to have the Outsiders beat the crap out of him. What an ingrate. They then proceeded to spray-paint the World title belt with the initials "nWo" as the announce squad once again cried foul.

It was around this time that the New World Order began to air vignettes on WCW shows. These were filmed entirely in black and white, and featured all manner of bizarre camera tricks and sound sampling. It looked as though someone had filmed it with a half-dozen shaky hand-held cameras, all of which had faulty zoom lenses. At the end of each of these segments was a black-and-white message that simply read: "The preceding announcement has been paid for by the New World Order." It was completely unlike anything the wrestling world had ever seen, very cutting edge, and so out there that fans immediately paid close attention.

In fact, fans paid close attention to just about anything the group did at this point. They did interviews in which they'd say things that almost appeared to be shoot (or "real-life") comments, which no one else in the industry was doing. They interrupted matches, threatened announcers, and basically had the entire promotion on the run. More than anything, though, they did exactly what they said they'd do. They'd claim they would win belts, and then they did. They'd say they'd beat people up, and then they did. And, most importantly for the company, they were adding viewers. With the nWo invasion as the focal point of the promotion, the ratings for *Nitro* began to pull away from *Raw*, generally beating the competition by a full point. They were nearing 4.0 at the time—far and away the best ratings *Nitro* had ever achieved.

Seeing that the New World Order had fans on the edges of their seats, it was decided that the time had come for them to add more members. Following an attack on his stablemates in the Dungeon of Doom, Giant came down to the ring, apparently looking for revenge against Hogan and his crew. However, in a moment that made absolutely no sense from a story line standpoint, Giant turned on his team and joined up with the nWo (the reason this made no sense was that Davey Boy Smith was supposed to be the fourth guy, but the day he was scheduled to jump ship from the WWF, he instead re-signed a five-year contract). Even though the members of the nWo were technically the heels, fans cheered like crazy for the Giant turn, mostly because the four so-called "bad guys" were overcoming incredible odds and were on their way to destroying eight top WCW names.

During the Giant's official induction into the group, Scott Hall, acting on a goofball impulse, asked if Andre the Giant was really this Giant's dad, referring to a pathetic angle a year earlier in which WCW had claimed that as fact. Visibly upset at Hall's sudden ad-lib, Giant shot Hall a deadly glare and replied, "Don't go there."

Shortly before Giant's turn, Ted DiBiase had shown up at *Nitro*, sitting in the crowd. He would eventually act as a mouthpiece of sorts for the New World Order. This story line made a bit more sense. Furthermore, since DiBiase's character in the WWF was that of the Million Dollar Man, it was explained that he was the benefactor who enabled the group to bring in high-priced talent and air commercials on WCW television. The group had member number five.

Member number six turned out to be a very shocking turn, as WCW's number-one guy turned against his company: Sting. But it wasn't really Sting, and it was the beginning of a tremendous angle that would set the stage for the most successful PPV in WCW history. Ironically, though, the very first angle they shot in this story line was such a turn-off for fans that approximately 700,000 people immediately switched channels.

The angle began on the September 9, 1996, *Nitro*. The nWo's familiar black limo was waiting in the parking lot as Lex Luger chased after the group. Out of the car and into the murky night came Sting, who, with the help of the rest of the group, proceeded to pummel Luger. This made little sense, as Sting had been the most vocal against the invaders and had, in fact, begged Flair and Anderson to join himself and Lex Luger to take them on in the upcoming War Games match at *Fall Brawl*. Team WCW seemed to be in a shambles. After all, if Sting was now on the other side, who would defend WCW's honor at War Games?

Aside from the War Games match, the most notable aspect of *Fall Brawl 1996* was the incredible number of outstanding matches on the show.

Not only did Chris Jericho make his WCW PPV debut against Chris Benoit in a fantastic bout, but Juventud Guerrera, Chavo Guerrero Jr., Super Calo, Rey Mysterio, and Diamond Dallas Page all had incredible outings as well. It proved to be a formula for which WCW PPVs would become known: fantastic undercard matches followed by main events featuring big names that weren't so great as far as wrestling action was concerned. And when Sean Waltman—in the WWF as the 1-2-3 Kid—joined the nWo as Syxx (you know, because he was the real sixth member since Sting hadn't really joined), the group found itself with a talented worker to help carry the load in their main-event matches.

Waltman was actually set to debut at *Hog Wild* after the WWF agreed to give him a release from his contract. However, WCW's plans to debut him kept being thrown into disarray when the WWF repeatedly "forgot" to send him his release papers. Strangely, his journey back to the WWF years later would also be due to his getting stuck in the middle of a political game.

While the main events were largely bad in the ring, it would be a mistake to say they were lacking in drama. Never mind that the drama often made absolutely no sense. Indeed, the War Games match had everyone glued to the action, with the question now reversed: who would team with Flair, Luger, and Arn to take on the nWo? The question was seemingly answered in an interview immediately prior to the War Games main event, in which the real Sting appeared before his former teammates and pleaded innocence. "All I've got to say is it's not me, it wasn't me, Lex!" It was never explained why Sting waited six days to have this talk with his pals as opposed to calling them immediately to explain that it wasn't really him who attacked them. Luger, Anderson, and Flair didn't believe him, and so, like total idiot babyfaces, the group headed down to ringside by themselves to take on Hall, Nash, Hogan, and their partner, who turned out to be . . . Sting.

But of course, it wasn't the real Sting again, it was the imposter. The crowd picked up on that fact immediately, even though the announce crew didn't. Minutes later, the real Sting hit the ring, and the announce crew figured it out. However, the rest of Team WCW just stood back and watched the real Sting go to work, apparently stunned by his actions. After laying out the entire nWo, he turned to Luger and yelled, "Is that proof enough for you right there?" He then proceeded to flip Luger off and leave the ring. Stunned by the real Sting's departure, Luger fell prey to the bogus Sting, and the New World Order scored yet another win. To cap off the night, Randy Savage—another good guy who was supposed to be getting the next title shot at Hogan—was completely obliterated by the nWo, giving the impression that he had no chance.

As for Sting, a story line in which he felt that he had been betrayed by both WCW and the New World Order was developed. He changed his look entirely, trading in his trademark Sgt. Pepper–style ring jackets for a long black trench coat. Gone too was the spiky blonde hair and the outgoing demeanor. In their place was a silent, almost ghostly figure who closely resembled the lead character in the movie *The Crow*. He would hang out in the rafters and silently observe the proceedings. Each week, the commentators would question his loyalties, using such clues as the color of his makeup to indicate whether he was nWo or not. He didn't do interviews, and he didn't wrestle, yet he remained arguably the company's hottest commodity.

Not only did ratings soar, but events also took an almost entirely different direction. Throughout the fall, WWF and WCW became engrossed in the biggest bidding war in wrestling history over the services of Bret

Hart. WCW wanted him to come in as the savior of the company for huge matches with Hogan and his cronies. The WWF did not want to lose him. Both sides made huge offers virtually unheard of in the industry: WCW put a three-year, $2.8 million contract on the table, while the WWF offered him a twenty-year deal worth an estimated $12 million total. Ultimately, he signed what he figured was going to be the last WWF contract of his career. As it later turned out, it was, but not in the way he'd expected.

This was not the only major signing. Hogan re-signed a lucrative three-year deal with the company after claiming that WWF was willing to offer him $5 million per year to jump ship. Nobody really believed it except those who were in a position to call his bluff. Roddy Piper also signed a deal to come in and re-create his mid-'80s feud with Hogan. While he could barely move after having undergone hip surgery, it was a smart move by WCW since the *Nitro* audience skewed much older than *Raw* and drew an audience that remembered all these big stars from when they were younger.

And that audience was growing. On August 26, *Raw* was preempted for the U.S. Open tennis tournament, and the *Nitro* built around the Sting angle did an unopposed 4.3 rating, by far its biggest number in history. Things were starting to happen.

It had been five months since the beginning of the New World Order angle, and they were on an absolute tear. WCW was made to look totally inept, as Hall and Nash won the tag belts and Giant won the United States title—all in short order. At *Halloween Havoc*, a show with a record-setting $94,000 in first-day ticket sales, WCW put Savage up against Hogan in an effort to regain the WCW World title. But, unlike their encounters in WWF (which were phenomenal), this time the match pretty much sucked, likely due to the fact that both guys were starting to get up there in years, and it showed.

Despite being at least a decade past his prime, Roddy Piper entered WCW as one of its top babyfaces. He main-evented three pay-per-views in the span of twelve months, which, despite the matches being very bad, drew huge money.

MIKE LANO

And speaking of Father Time, he appeared in human form as "Rowdy" Roddy Piper to end the show.

"So you're bored, are you?" Piper began. "I've come here to break your monotony! I am not here to represent the WCW, the NWA, the SPCA, the SOB—although I can be one SOB when I want to be! I'm just as big an icon in this sport as you are, Hogan! Do you know what bothers you? I am the only guy you've never been able to beat."

Although that wasn't entirely true, the stage was set for *Starrcade 1996*: Hogan versus Piper. But before that could take place, Eric Bischoff came out on *Nitro* and stated that, for reasons he could not get into, the Hogan versus Piper showdown would not, in fact, take place. Quizzed by the announcers as to the reason, Bischoff stormed off the set. Bischoff claimed that despite his best efforts, Piper was not returning his phone calls or e-mails asking him to sign the contract to face Hogan. Something wasn't adding up. Soon enough, Piper cornered Bischoff in the ring. The nWo then jumped Piper and revealed its newest member: none other than Bischoff himself!

There were several reasons why Bischoff became the on-screen leader of the nWo. The first, and most important, was that *Raw* had moved an hour earlier to an 8-9 P.M. timeslot. Knowing they now had to promote a killer hour of *Nitro* to keep fans from tuning in to *Raw*, Eric's idea was to split the show in half: hour one would be an nWo show, and hour two would be the WCW show. People were reacting more to the nWo at all the shows, so Bischoff figured nWo versus *Raw* would be better than WCW versus *Raw*. He also wanted to make sure that he was on the air doing commentary at the same time Vince McMahon was, because he took great delight in driving Vince crazy week after week from thousands of miles away. And, of course, being a TV star with the hottest heel group in wrestling sure sounded like fun.

Bischoff the character was given leadership in the story lines of the New World Order. From that perspective, it made sense, as who else could orchestrate all these ex-WWF guys coming in, or give the invaders so much leeway to get away with things that they reasonably had no right to do? And make no mistake about it—Bischoff was excellent in his role. His smug, arrogant attitude had already alienated some wrestling fans, and he now had the opportunity to be as all-out annoying as he wanted to be.

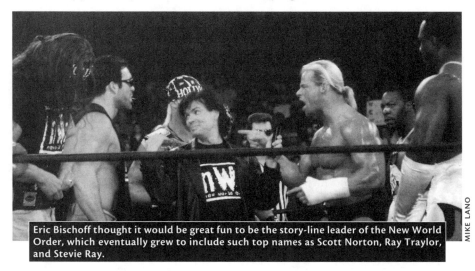

Eric Bischoff thought it would be great fun to be the story-line leader of the New World Order, which eventually grew to include such top names as Scott Norton, Ray Traylor, and Stevie Ray.

MIKE LANO

His first order of business was to give WCW wrestlers a chance to join the most prestigious and elite organization the wrestling industry had ever seen, via a membership drive for the New World Order. Effectively, he was telling the entire roster that they were either with them or against them. This led several WCW mid-carders—Big Bubba, Scott Norton, Michael Wallstreet, and others—to jump ship and join the heel conglomerate. It could—and will—be argued that this was the first huge mistake Bischoff made with regard to the booking of the New World Order story line. Before, the nWo consisted of top-tier guys in the industry. Now, it was being watered down considerably as wrestlers who had been nowhere near the top of the card gained easy entry into the previously elite group.

The next PPV, *World War 3*, featured an overbooked and confusing sixty-man, three-ring battle royal. On the show, Hogan and Piper had yet another confrontation in which Hogan informed the world that Piper was really just an old man with a plastic hip, going so far as to lift Piper's kilt and show the entire world the scar from his hip-replacement surgery. After dubbing Piper "Pegleg Pete," Hogan signed the contract for the *Starrcade* match, a contract that, according to story lines, Piper himself came up with. Keep that in mind; it's important later on. Then the nWo beat the crap out of Piper once more, although this time Piper was able to regain his feet and hobble to the back on his own. The rest of the show was rather uneventful, with Giant winning the battle royal for a shot at Hogan at some undefined point in the future.

The contract signing set up *Starrcade*, which had traditionally been WCW's biggest show of the year. And, much like the PPVs that immediately preceded it, it had really good mid-card action from the usual suspects like Dean Malenko, Chris Benoit, and Eddy Guerrero. In one of the first wins for WCW since the formation of the New World Order, Lex Luger pinned the Giant after Sting snuck down to ringside and whispered something in Luger's ear. He also left behind his now-trademark baseball bat, which Luger used to waffle the big guy and score the pin.

The main event, of course, was the lure of the show. Despite the fact that both guys were way past their physical primes, Hogan versus Piper had tremendous appeal, especially to more casual fans of WCW. Those fans likely remembered their wars from years past—namely the first *Wrestlemania* and the various MTV bouts they had leading up to it—so the nostalgia factor was kicking in big time. And, to be fair, the booking leading up to the match was very strong as well, with both men playing their roles to perfection: Hogan was really beginning to peak as an insufferable bully heel, while Piper did a super job as the never-say-die babyface.

While the build-up was good, the match itself was not. It was becoming apparent to even his most ardent supporters that Piper's best days in the ring were long past, and Hogan, despite the novelty of his being a bad guy, didn't look much better. The two men hobbled around the ring as best they could, trading slaps like a couple of sissies. Piper finally cut loose with a comical punch-kick offense, and Hogan countered with scratches. Suffice to say this was a far cry from what fans had witnessed earlier in the evening from the superb mid-card action. The crowd fell silent following the inevitable nWo run-in, but Piper was able to get rid of the Giant and locked Hogan in a sleeper, the oldest of old-school moves. Hogan's arm dropped three times, and referee Randy Anderson called for the bell.

The crowd was stunned. How long had it been since someone had won a match with a sleeper hold, for God's sake? It didn't take long, however, before they realized that Hogan had been beaten, and they leapt to their feet. As the crowd celebrated, everyone waited for the gold to be strapped around Piper's waist. It never happened, though, because the match was inexplicably a non-title affair. Since Piper himself came up with the contract (we told you that would be important), we hereby nominate Roddy Piper as the dumbest babyface of 1996. But we also must decry WCW for promoting a match that was clearly designed to look like a title affair. WCW had given its fans a bait-and-switch on their biggest show of the year; one that some would remember right to the bitter end.

Booking aside, the show would have to be considered a complete and total success. It drew a 0.95 buy rate—higher than any other show the entire year—and it nearly doubled the buy rate of *World War 3* just one month prior. The company also celebrated yet another victory in the Monday night wars, demolishing *Raw* by a margin of 3.51 to 1.64—an amazing accomplishment considering that on the first Monday night of the year, they had lost the battle 2.61 to 2.52.

There was absolutely no denying that the company was on an incredible roll, delivering buy rates and ratings the likes of which WCW had never seen before. Bischoff had the formula, he had the stars, and, perhaps most importantly, he had the one matchup that everyone was dying to see. And he was going to make them wait to see it for an entire year, building up not only the anticipation, but also the inevitably enormous buy rate.

Yes, he had the whole world in his grasp, and as hard as it was to believe, 1997 was only going to get better.

PART II
The Rise

"Hulk has control over what he does. We don't mind, because obviously he is doing it right. It helps us...we need help."

—Terry Taylor, WCW Booking Committee Member, 1997

CHAPTER 3

1997: The Waiting Game

If 1996 taught Eric Bischoff anything, it was that the New World Order was the future of his company. That much was made clear from the ratings and the buy rates, both of which had skyrocketed following the launch of the angle. The numbers did not lie. Attendance was up 43 percent over 1995, gates were up 87 percent, and buy rates for PPVs—where the company made the bulk of its money—were closing in on that. In fact, the very first *Nitro* of 1997 drew 10,034 paid—a brand-new record—and this came a week before the Chicago show shattered that number with over 17,000 fans paying $189,206. The nWo had brought them to the Holy Land, and nowhere else would the spotlight shine brighter than this.

No longer was WCW beneath Vince McMahon's mighty World Wrestling Federation. No, now they were on more or less equal ground, and having come this far, there was no way they were turning back.

Although the New World Order was a strong contingent, the fact remained that they were a bunch of bad guys. And in wrestling, bad guys are only draws if they have a strong babyface to confront them. Although the rest of WCW was often made out as a bunch of buffoons, one guy had not yet been booked to look like a total idiot: Sting. The man who had been the franchise of the company from almost the moment it became WCW, Sting was viewed by fans as the one guy within WCW who could conceivably compete with and defeat these invaders.

To Bischoff's credit, he knew that in order to maximize revenue from the inevitable battle between Sting and Hogan, this could be no ordinary feud (in those days, feuds generally played out over a couple of months). The plan was to make this one of the slowest-building feuds ever—a long, drawn-out affair lasting over a year. By building the feud up to December's *Starrcade*, WCW's biggest show of the year, fans would be lined up to pay to finally see Sting take down Hogan. The only remaining question was whether or not Bischoff would actually stick to his guns and keep Sting out of action for twelve months, or if he'd get antsy for the big payday and rush the match to pay-per-view.

In order to allow the match-up he wanted, Bischoff felt he had to focus the company almost entirely on the New World Order. Never was Bischoff's game plan more obvious than during the first PPV of the year, *Souled Out*, or to be more precise, *nWo Souled Out*. This show was designed to be a showcase for the group; it wasn't promoted on-air as a WCW event, but as a New World Order event in which WCW wrestlers would show up and get their asses kicked. The idea was to see if a pay-per-view could be marketed and successfully sold solely under the New World Order name. If this could be done, it stood to reason that at some point in the future, Bischoff could begin to run more than one PPV a month, thereby doubling the revenue these events generated. It seemed well worth the gamble to give it a try.

The show opened in a manner most bizarre, as Bischoff, Sean Waltman, Scott Hall, Kevin Nash, and the rest of the group circled the arena riding atop garbage trucks. Say what you want about him, but even the most jaded skeptic has to give Bischoff points for originality: certainly no pay-per-view in the history of pro wrestling had begun in such a manner. Even the set pieces on the show were unique. The standard bright and gaudy WCW sets were vacant, and in their place was a dark, industrial look from which it appeared no color could escape. The entrance was black, the ring apron was black, the ropes were black, and the turnbuckles were black. Aside from a few white nWo logos splashed around the arena, everything was black. In addition, the group's trademark camera tricks were in full effect, with static blacking out the picture at random intervals. The bizarre camera angles likely had first-time viewers wondering if they were watching wrestling or an old episode of the '60s *Batman* TV show. It was totally bizarre and completely different from anything else the wrestling world had ever seen. This was definitely not your ordinary, run-of-the-mill wrestling pay-per-view event. This was new; this was different. This was a New World Order pay-per-view.

If anyone needed evidence that the nWo was starting to become severely watered down at this point, they need look no further than the *nWo Souled Out* PPV. Hogan, Nash, and Hall, the original nucleus trio of the group, had been joined by Waltman, DiBiase, and Bischoff shortly thereafter. Rounding out the ranks were Buff Bagwell, Scott Norton, Masahiro Chono, Mike "Virgil/Vincent" Jones, Ray Traylor, Elizabeth, a fake Sting, and about twenty other scrubs, all of whom tried to push each other out of the way in a vain attempt to occupy more of the television screen. It was almost an omen of what would come later in the year.

In addition to the matches, the show also featured a Miss nWo contest, as middle-aged women straddling Harley-Davidson motorcycles proclaimed their love to the New World Order. It was neither erotic nor comical, but more like what would happen if your mom had a pageant with her friends and they all said they wanted to grope Kevin Nash. Doesn't sound like a good time, does it? The fans in the arena weren't amused, and immediately began to chant "Boring," as Bischoff himself began to mack on the scag biker chicks onstage.

In between his make-out sessions with the skanks, Bischoff, taking center stage on a podium above the entrance ramp, began to preach the message of the New World Order to the crowd. His statement was clear: WCW sucks. It was a familiar rallying cry, one that was repeated over and over again to the point that no one watching the show could miss it. And even if they did ignore Bischoff's rantings, the presentation of WCW at the event would certainly sway their opinion. The WCW wrestlers who were not on the show were shown sitting in the crowd like common fans, a band of outcasts who couldn't cut it with Bischoff's rogue coalition. Even the handful of WCW wrestlers who participated in the show looked like losers: they had no music, no pyro, and they were introduced by a monotone voice in a very mocking manner. The nWo, meanwhile, were given grand entrances with music and lighting as the announcer declared their superiority. The point was clear: the WCW guys were pathetic, and no match for the New World Order.

Despite the fact that the angle had given the promotion new life, the fact remained that the New World Order, as cool and hip as they might be, were supposed to be the bad guys in the story. All the mockery of WCW seemed to sap the very life out of the crowd, as they sat quietly throughout the majority of the show, seeming neither upset nor particularly thrilled by the outcome of any of the matches. Of course, those outcomes involved the New World Order winning almost every bout, generally with the help of evil referee Nick Patrick. The few wins WCW was able to rack up were generally due to match stipulations in which the referee didn't come into play, such as a ladder match in which Eddy Guerrero (billed as the "Mexican Jumping Bean" by the ring announcer—a line that surely wouldn't offend anyone) was able to yank down the U.S. Heavyweight belt suspended above the ring. The atrocious main event saw yet another nWo debacle, as Hulk Hogan pinned the Giant (who had joined and then left the group in the span of less than six months) following a beat-down by nearly every member of the group.

Was the *Souled Out* experiment a success? In a word, no. The buy rate was a mere 0.47, the lowest since the start of the New World Order angle. The show took place in Cedar Rapids, Iowa, before a crowd of around 5,000—yet another sellout, but since the building was so small, the take was under $70,000, and a major disappointment. In short, everything was about half of what the previous pay-per-view, *Starrcade 96*, had generated.

The company decided to go back to the successful *Starrcade* formula for the next show, *Superbrawl 7*, this time pitting Hogan against Piper in what was very clearly billed as a World title match. To promote the event, Piper was filmed in a bizarre series of vignettes in which he was locked away inside Alcatraz. Following the conclusion of the main event, fans probably wished that they too had been locked in solitary confinement.

To be fair, however, the company had once again gone back to the blueprint they had followed to make *Nitro* a must-see show: they'd feature great matches prior to the blockbuster show-selling—albeit generally bad—main events. Bouts featuring men like Dean Malenko, Eddy Guererro, Waltman, and Chris Jericho opened the show, bringing the fans to life. The undercard was as solid as ever, due primarily to the fact that Bischoff continued to spare no expense when it came to bringing in talent. Through raids of either the WWF, ECW, or Japan, Bischoff had brought in an amazing array of outstanding talent from around the globe. From 1996 to 1997, newcomers like Jericho, Juventud Guerrera, Rey Mysterio Jr., and countless others tore up the ring.

WCW would need the fresh young talent, as it was slowly becoming apparent to everyone (save those in charge) that guys like Hogan and Piper just couldn't deliver in the ring as they once could. Try as they might, the two stumbled through yet another horrible main event. This time, Piper once again appeared to win the belt, but this was overturned when Randy Savage turned his back on WCW and put Hogan's foot under the rope, thus negating the title change. As all this was going on, Sting just watched silently from down the entrance ramp, then slowly turned and walked away. The slow burn would continue.

Despite the bad main event, the show was able to rebound slightly from the depths to which *Souled Out* had taken the company, scoring a 0.75 buy rate and drawing almost $200,000 at the door from the 13,324 in attendance. It was a move in the right direction.

WCW immediately took that money and spent it, announcing that they had just signed a huge star for *Uncensored*, their next PPV: Dennis Rodman. It didn't matter that Rodman wouldn't be able to actually wrestle on the show due to the fact that it was the middle of the NBA season. Bischoff knew that with the media covering the basketball bad boy at his every turn, WCW would get instant exposure, and a ton of it, if he could somehow sign him to do a couple of shows. It was also rumored that Vince McMahon was looking to do the same, so it should come as no surprise that Bischoff was willing to do anything to once again stick it to Vince and the WWF. McMahon had offered the "Worm" $1 million for two dates, so Bischoff outbid him to the tune of nearly $2 million for three dates.

Uncensored once again epitomized the company at the time, with young guys like Ultimo Dragon coming in for great matches with Mexican luchadors like Psicosis. For once, though, the main event of the evening was actually pretty good, largely due to the fact that they crammed nine guys into the ring in a three-way, which the nWo obviously won when Rodman and Savage interfered. In the story lines, this win gave Hogan's organization the right to challenge for any title anytime they so desired. However, as the group celebrated, Sting rappelled from the ceiling, baseball bat in hand, and lay absolute waste to Nash, Hall, and Savage. As the crowd went nuts, Sting slowly raised his bat and pointed it at his target: Hogan. Finally, Hogan got into the ring, and Sting obliterated him as well. It was unquestionably the biggest response any WCW star had gotten since the birth of the New World Order, and it seemed impossible to believe that Bischoff could hold off on delivering this match on PPV for another nine months.

The buy rate, though, showed that Bischoff was on the right track, as it wound up at just under 0.9 (which WCW trumpeted far and wide as having beaten that year's *Wrestlemania*, which scored a 0.77). It was apparent that Bischoff could and would hold off, as the following PPV, *Spring Stampede*, featured neither Sting nor Hogan. Instead, the main event was a showdown between Savage and Diamond Dallas Page. The event was largely forgettable, and largely unwatched, drawing a low 0.58 buy rate. However, even with a weak lineup, the company was still hot enough that it sold out in advance, drawing 8,356 fans paying $107,115. Indeed, selling out shows in advance was becoming a trend—a trend, ironically, that would end up hurting the company in the long run.

To his credit, Bischoff didn't panic and hotshot the Sting-Hogan show-down to the next show. Instead, he continued to do *Nitros* in which Sting would silently and methodically stalk Hogan and the New World Order from the rafters. In a business that is well known for getting the big payday as quickly as possible, it is absolutely amazing that Bischoff stayed his course. Indeed, even after the next show, *Slamboree*, did a similar 0.60 buy rate, as did the follow-up to that, *Great American Bash,* Bischoff was resolute in his plan. In short, his was precisely the type of patience the company would not show in subsequent years—and this would eventually cost them dearly.

By this point, business was really starting to pick up. Tickets went on sale in April for the June 9 *Nitro* at the Fleet Center in Boston and set a new first-day record with 10,000 sold for $170,000. House show business was also through the roof. In fact, by mid-1997 they were doing *triple* the business they had done in 1995. It didn't seem to matter what anyone did; everything the company touched was turning to gold.

One of the primary reasons that WCW house show business was so hot at the time was due to the awesome work of Zane Bresloff. Bresloff not only promoted WCW events, he was also the man behind the promotion of *Wrestlemania III,* for which the WWF claimed to have jammed 93,000 fans into the Pontiac Silverdome. Years later, Bresloff himself would admit that the number was realistically 78,000.

The next show featuring Hogan was *Bash at the Beach,* which had become something of a gala event for WCW. Hogan had not only made his debut at *Bash at the Beach* in 1994; he also did the legendary heel turn to form the New World Order there in 1996. The 1997 version of the show was also going to give the fans something memorable, as Dennis Rodman would not only be present at the event, but *wrestle* as well. Because basketball season was over, the Worm now had the green light to actually get in the ring, and he would team up with Hogan to take on WCW mainstays Lex Luger and the Giant.

WCW certainly couldn't be blamed for focusing the promotion of the event on the Rodman match, as he was all over the place in 1997. He had just won the second of three consecutive NBA world titles with Michael

Jordan and the Chicago Bulls, he was just about to release a best-selling autobiography, *Bad as I Wanna Be,* and he was a constant media magnet due to his bizarre behavior both on and off the court. In short, Dennis Rodman was a hot property.

A hot property and, because of his real athletic ability, Rodman was a surprisingly decent wrestler in his very first real match. Some even went as far as to call him the best wrestler of the four that evening. (This was not high praise; the other three in the tag match were Hogan, Giant, and Lex Luger). Hogan did most of the in-ring work, if you can call stalling for the first five minutes of the showdown "work." After about seven minutes, Hogan finally tagged in Rodman, and the crowd held its breath to see just what the Worm would bring to the table. Rodman strutted around the ring, sunglasses on, and eventually locked up with Luger. And then it happened: he armdragged Luger! Yes, he was able to execute one of the most basic maneuvers in the history of pro wrestling. The announcers went hysterical, acting as though a successor to Frank A. Gotch himself had finally been discovered. Rodman posed for the crowd, took off his sunglasses, polished them, and then put them right back on. Fortunately for WCW, Luger was somehow able to regain his breath, and not only arm-drag Rodman twice, but also Hogan twice for good measure as well. The pro-WCW announce team celebrated, proclaiming, "Welcome to WCW, where the big boys play!"

Hogan and Rodman weren't foiled yet, however. Rodman once again locked up with Luger and threw him into the ropes. As Luger came to-wards him, Rodman—get this—leapfrogged him. Though this exact same sequence of maneuvers had been done in almost every single match of the last twenty years, the announce team nearly had a heart attack: "That's no rookie we're watching! He's been tutored by the best!" Tony Schiavone even claimed that Rodman was showing, and this is a quote, "flashes of brilliance." Despite the "brilliance" of such high-impact moves as leapfrogs and armdrags, the nWo was defeated when Luger managed to get a submission win over Hogan.

Although the Rodman match was a total and complete fiasco from a technical wrestling standpoint, the show did a decent number: 0.78 with a $150,870 gate. It wasn't the number WCW was hoping for, but the momentum was definitely building. The ratings for *Nitro* continued to move upwards as Luger's chase for Hogan's championship took center stage. The night after *Bash at the Beach*, *Nitro* scored a 3.5 rating. Three weeks of promotion later, a three-hour *Nitro* special (it was the 100th episode) scored a whopping 4.34, and the title bout, in which Luger dethroned Hogan, scored an amazing (for the time, at least) 5.2 rating. Obviously, the success of the show inspired Bischoff to present more three-hour programs in the future.

The Luger win set the stage for the next pay-per-view, August's *Road Wild* (a lawsuit filed by Harley-Davidson forced them to drop the "Hog"), the annual money pit from Sturgis. Not only did the event once again produce its famed zero-dollar gate, it also had to be somewhat of a disappointment, as the buy rate came in at 0.65. This was well below expectations, especially since the Luger-Hogan feud had been generating such good numbers in the Monday-night ratings.

But there may have been an even more damaging effect on the company in this show, although one much less noticeable than could be computed by tallying gate receipts and buy rate numbers. This was the simple fact that, when push came to shove in big matches, the New World Order never lost. At *Road Wild*, this was proven during the Steiners versus Outsiders (Hall and Nash) match for the World Tag championships. The Steiners had been around WCW for years, and even though they'd had a brief run in the WWF, they were considered to be a true "home team" talent. The pair had been babyfaces during their entire time as a tag team, and so they, along with Sting, were seen as the saviors of the company. The number of wrestlers that fans bought as being on equal ground with the New World Order was slim, with only Luger, Sting, the Steiners, and maybe the Giant viewed as guys who could legitimately hang with Hogan and his cronies. In order for this belief to be perpetuated, however, these men eventually had to be given wins over their adversaries.

In Luger's case, such a win happened, albeit very briefly. The Steiners didn't even get that much. Despite the fact that they had been chasing Hall and Nash for almost a year, they left *Road Wild* without the tag belts yet again. Keep in mind that not only had they been feuding with Hall and Nash all this time, there was even a vignette filmed in which the evil duo ran the Steiners' car off a road. Rick and Scott didn't file charges because in the wacky world of pro wrestling, the only way to get true revenge for attempted vehicular manslaughter is to take your opponent's title belt.

The Steiners were scheduled to take the belt, but in the end, it didn't happen. Hall and Nash went up to Bischoff backstage at the PPV and said the frequent title changes were hurting the drawing power of the belts. Therefore, they argued, they should retain against the Steiners. Bischoff assented. The irony of all this was that Luger, who had just won the WCW title six days earlier at *Nitro*, didn't get to retain, and dropped the belt instead to Hall and Nash's good buddy Hogan. The next night on *Nitro*, Luger was hardly mentioned at all. This upset more than a few of the boys in the back.

It wasn't just Luger and the Steiners—others were being held down as well. The Four Horsemen, led by Ric Flair—the man many fans considered to be the very epitome of WCW—were also made to look bad at every opportunity. Despite having been made out as Hogan's whipping boy since his 1994 arrival at WCW, Flair still commanded the respect of many loyal

WCW fans, specifically in the Carolinas, a longtime hotbed for the company. Hogan and Nash didn't particularly care for Flair or for the reaction he was garnering from the crowds there, so at seemingly every live *Nitro* that took place in the region, they would take shots at Flair and how old he was, or better yet, they'd simply leave him lying in a broken heap. To make a long story short, since Hogan, Nash, and Hall basically had total say on their characters (Hogan had complete creative control written into his contract), they made Flair look like an idiot time and time again in front of his hometown fans.

And never did Flair or his Horsemen look more like total idiots than during the *Nitro* that took place on September 1, 1997. A week earlier, the *Nitro* in Columbia, South Carolina, had destroyed all previous ratings records (thanks in part to *Raw* being preempted for the U.S. Open tennis tournament), doing a 4.97 rating for a show built around area legend Arn Anderson's announcement of retirement due to serious neck surgery. The plan for the following week was pretty straightforward. The show would be presented as a tribute to Arn, but halfway through, the nWo was going to do a skit making fun of Arn's tremendous speech the week before. All the fans would be outraged. Then, at the end of the skit, the Horsemen would run out and clean house as Anderson stood smirking on the ramp.

This never happened. Instead, the nWo did the parody, and there was no retaliation, as Nash got the whole Horsemen run-in nixed. Flair, outraged, refused to go out for an interview later, saying it would kill the Horsemen off even more to do so without having attacked the nWo earlier. Arn was so upset he nearly quit the company, not so much because of the content of the skit, but because of the fact that his family watching at home was devastated by it (the skit touched on Arn's alleged alcoholism, and his reaction to this was made worse by the fact that his mother had died of the disease when he was very young).

The parody set up *Fall Brawl*, which took place deep in the heart of Flair Country: Winston-Salem, North Carolina. Before a crowd of almost 12,000 rabid Horsemen fans, Flair was once again booked to take the loss, as new member Curt Hennig (who had been nominated by Arn as his Horseman replacement just weeks earlier) turned on the group and gave yet another win to the New World Order. At this point, it was beginning to appear that no one could ever compete on even ground with the nWo.

Bischoff didn't care about the backstage squawking of men like Flair, since business was going through the roof. *Nitro*, which at the beginning of the year was averaging ratings in the low threes, was suddenly and consistently doing in the fours. The September 8 show was a huge success, doing a 4.27 to *Raw*'s 2.15 (the biggest margin in history up to that point). Shows were selling out left and right (the weekend of September 4 was the first in history in which the company grossed over $1 million on house show revenue alone), and PPV buy rates were climbing. *Halloween Havoc*, in particular, was a massive success. Despite the fact that the show was headlined by yet another horrendous Piper-Hogan match (the third in the last nine months), it drew a gigantic 1.1 buy rate, drawing 12,457 fans and a $297,508 gate. On the bright side, the Rey Mysterio Jr.–Eddy Guerrero mask versus title match (which Rey won, although he had been scheduled to lose until just minutes before the show started) was WCW's best match of at least the past five years. As good as business was for that show, the next PPV, *World War III*, was even better, drawing 17,128 fans and $407,831 at the gate.

Who the hell cared about wrestlers pissing and moaning when WCW was making this much jack?

Not only were they making money, but Bischoff was about to stumble upon yet another success, one that would ensure the health of WCW for years to come: Bill Goldberg. The former Atlanta Falcon turned Power Plant trainee debuted on the August 22 *Nitro* in a 2:24 win over Hugh Morris. Afterwards, he simply held up a single finger, as if to say, "That's one." He didn't say a word, and in fact wouldn't for almost a full year after his debut. By the time the show was over, most had probably forgotten the match—ironic, given that he'd soon become one of the company's most unforgettable stars.

WCW had everything going for them, and it was about to get even better: Bischoff would soon sign the hottest free agent in the history of wrestling. And when he did, it would no doubt be the final nail in the coffin of Vince McMahon and the WWF.

Although Bischoff had amassed the greatest array of talent the wrestling world had ever seen, there was one guy he'd been after for years and had been unable to get: Bret Hart. Bischoff had badly wanted to bring Hart in during the summer of 1996; he knew that if he could somehow grab not only Hall and Nash, but also Hart, it would truly appear that every top star from the WWF was coming to WCW. Unfortunately for Eric, McMahon was able to convince Bret to stay, and signed him to that twenty-year deal mentioned previously.

There were a lot of questions regarding that contract, most specifically how could McMahon afford to pay it? Bischoff knew—beyond a shadow of a doubt—that the WWF was in severe financial straits; the company had lost $6 million in 1996, and things weren't looking to improve that drastically for 1997. Pushing WCW castaways like Steve Austin and Mick Foley, who'd been unceremoniously discarded by Bischoff himself? Bischoff figured the WWF didn't stand a chance.

As if he needed any more proof to support his theory, the rumor mill had once again begun to rumble about problems developing between McMahon and WWF champion Hart. Those rumors were confirmed when

Hart, with the blessing of McMahon himself, contacted Bischoff to see if the possibility existed to accept the contract he'd declined a year earlier. Bischoff no doubt trembled with glee as Bret told him the story: McMahon claimed he could not afford to pay the promised monies to Hart. In fact, Vince had told Bret that the company was in "financial peril." In Eric's mind, this translated to "Bret Hart is once again a free agent, and the WWF is dead."

This was a joyous moment for Bischoff. By signing Hart, not only was he getting one of the greatest wrestlers of all time, but he was also taking away one of the few remaining WWF draws. Just as he had been able to do with Nash and Hall, he would leave fans' jaws on the floor by bringing Bret to *Nitro*. After all, he wasn't just a huge star for the WWF—he was their WORLD CHAMPION, for God's sake. At this point, Bischoff realized that as bad as he thought things were going for Vince, they had to have been much, much worse than even he could have ever possibly dreamed.

One of the provisions of Bret's twenty-year contract with the WWF was that he had reasonable creative control of his character. Therefore, as champion, he had the right to decide whom he'd lose the belt to and when he'd do so. For months, a very real rivalry had developed between Bret and one of McMahon's other favorite performers, Shawn Michaels. Michaels, who also had a great deal of power backstage, seemed to take delight in pissing Bret off at every turn. One time, he even went so far as to allege—on air, no less—that Bret was in the midst of an extramarital affair with popular WWF diva Sunny. This infuriated Hart (not to mention his wife), and it led to an infamous backstage fight between the two men that ended with Shawn temporarily quitting after a huge chunk of hair was pulled out of his scalp.

As Bret's WWF contract approached expiration and his WCW debut loomed ever nearer, he and Vince began to discuss scenarios to get the title off of him. The next WWF PPV was the *Survivor Series* in Montreal, and Vince suggested that Bret should drop the strap to—you guessed it—Shawn Michaels. Shawn had first won the belt from Bret a year earlier in a sixty-minute Iron Man match at *Wrestlemania*, and injuries (both real and fake), fights, and other problems kept the big rematch from ever taking place. At first, Bret exercised his creative control and refused, stating that he'd rather "blow his brains out" than lose to Shawn. One of his main gripes was that, several weeks earlier, Shawn had told both him and McMahon that he wasn't going to do any more jobs to anyone else in the promotion, and that included Bret.

If that was going to be Shawn's attitude, Bret figured he'd just "return the favor" and refuse to lose to Shawn. On the Wednesday before the Montreal *Survivor Series*, Vince called Shawn up and once again asked if he'd lose. Shawn got to talking about it with his good buddy Hunter Hearst Helmsley (Triple H), and Hunter was appalled, arguing that Shawn would be a fool to agree to lose to a guy who was on his way over to the competition. So Shawn called Vince back and said losing the match was a no-go. As soon as Bret heard that, he said if Shawn wasn't going to lose to him in Montreal, then he wasn't going to lose to Shawn anywhere under any circumstances.

A few days later, Bret changed his mind. That Friday, his lawyer sent the WWF a letter stating that Bret was willing to drop the belt to anyone in the company as long as it didn't happen in Canada. Since his WCW contract didn't start until December 1, there were several places where he could lose the belt, including the house shows the following week in Youngstown, Ohio, on November 13, in Pittsburgh on November 14, or at Madison Square Garden on November 15. And, he said, if Vince wanted to do it on PPV, he'd drop the belt in a four-way at the December 7 show in Springfield, Massachusetts.

Vince noted that Bret's WCW deal started on December 1. Bret said that wasn't a problem, and convinced Eric to hold off on his WCW debut until December 8. Upon hearing this, Vince said fine, Bret could win via DQ (thereby not making Shawn look bad) in Montreal, then lose the belt in the four-way in December. But then Vince changed his mind *again*, saying word had gotten out that Bret was leaving, and it was therefore imperative that he lose the title before *Nitro* the night after *Survivor Series*. After all, Vince reasoned, even though Bret couldn't show up on *Nitro* until after December 1 for legal reasons, if Bischoff went on TV and even *mentioned* that he'd signed away his champion, the WWF would be dead.

Bret said he'd call Bischoff and get him to hold off on the announcement. Unfortunately, Eric was off hunting in Wyoming, and Bret couldn't reach him. Vince suggested he drop the belt at the house show in Detroit the night before Montreal. Bret again refused, saying that the match between himself and Michaels was too big to trivialize, and that to do it right, he had to go into Montreal as the champion. If Vince wanted him to lose it later that week at a house show, he reiterated, that would be fine.

Sunday was fast approaching, and nobody could decide on a finish, which had Bret on edge. Vince argued that it wasn't fair for him to refuse to lose. Bret said it was fair, as Vince himself had put the creative control clause in his contract. They argued about what the "reasonable" part of "reasonable creative control" meant. Finally, just hours before the PPV, they met backstage. Vince asked Bret what he wanted to do. Bret said he wanted to leave with his head held high, and then the next day on *Raw*, he'd vacate the belt and, without burying the company (i.e., making Vince or the WWF look bad) in any way, and tell the fans that he was leaving. Vince acquiesced, and the plan was set for Shawn to lose via DQ when Degeneration-X (Shawn's group) and the Hart Foundation (Bret's group) ran in.

During the match, Shawn put Bret in Bret's own finishing maneuver, the sharpshooter. Bret was told beforehand that he would reverse the move, which would lead to another series of near falls. This never happened. Instead, referee Earl Hebner—a longtime close friend of Hart's who had actually sworn on his children's lives before the show that he wouldn't fast-count him—simply called for the bell. The timekeeper, who wasn't in on what was going to transpire, was initially confused about what to do. Thankfully, McMahon himself came down to ringside to offer the following helpful advice: "RING THE FUCKING BELL!" And so Shawn was now the champion, and Bret, as he'd later state countless times, was "screwed."

It became known as the most famous double-cross in wrestling history. Bret had been with his former employer for fourteen years, missing only two shows in that time, and he'd done everything he could to help the WWF. Callously, they'd turned their backs on him. It was a moment that would live forever in the minds of all those who saw it; a memory reinforced by the footage replayed over and over on WWF television in an effort to make fans believe that Vince had done the right thing.

This should have helped WCW (since Bret was about to be all over both programs), and hurt the WWF, which had blatantly screwed over a very popular star. But the wrestling business is a uniquely peculiar world. As it turned out, McMahon—who really just hoped the whole story would die, having no desire to play a major on-screen role—suddenly became the biggest heel on WWF television. This ultimately led to an everyman versus everyboss feud between him and the company's biggest babyface star, Steve Austin. This rivalry turned out to be a springboard for the company's fortunes, which subsequently skyrocketed to the point that Vince became a certifiable billionaire.

And what of Bret Hart? Heading into WCW with such momentum, it seemed absolutely impossible that the company could somehow screw this up. There was no question that something huge would be lined up for Bret come the next big PPV blockbuster, *Starrcade*.

But prior to that event, Bischoff had something else to take care of. He decided to try doing another show entirely based around the nWo. Apparently nothing had been learned from the *Souled Out* fiasco in January, so serious thought was now being given to handing *Nitro* over to Hogan and his heel contingent. In early 1998, plans were on the drawing board for a two-hour Thursday-night show on TBS, and Bischoff's grandiose idea was to eventually split the company so that there would be a WCW show and an nWo show, thereby making the WWF—get ready, because he really believed this—the number-three promotion in America.

Thus, *nWo Nitro* got a trial run, with results that were either shockingly disastrous or shockingly predictable, depending on your viewpoint. The show opened with the nWo b-squad's arrival and their immediate demand that the production crew tear down anything with the WCW logo on it. Every sign, every banner, even the gigantic metal "WCW" were all laid to waste. In their place were custom-designed *nWo Nitro* banners and set pieces. Just to show that this wasn't designed as a one-time shot, a spiffy new video opened the show. Everyone involved was to be aligned with the New World Order, from the wrestlers to the announcers, right down to the ring crew.

Although the entire group glad-handed each other and went on about how wonderful they all were, the night truly belonged, of course, to Hulk Hogan. The majority of *nWo Nitro* was less of a wrestling show than it was a celebration of the life and times of Terry Bollea, complete with a twenty-minute segment in which Bischoff gave Hogan presents like giant banners and motorcycles featuring his image. He even dropped down to one knee and placed a ring (in the shape of the WCW World title) upon his finger. It looked for all the world like he was either going to propose to the Hulkster or blow him mid-ring. Maybe both.

Although all this posturing no doubt pleased Bischoff and Hogan, those watching at home didn't share the love. With *Starrcade* (set to deliver arguably the best-promoted match in the history of the company) just days away, you'd have thought that this *Nitro* would have drawn incredible ratings, possibly the highest-ever for the company. Not only did that not happen, but the show actually dropped almost a full point from its average, and the original plan to air *nWo Nitro* on a weekly basis was permanently scrapped. The elaborate sets, the shirts, the video production—it all amounted to nothing more than a colossal waste of money.

To Bischoff, though, it was just a failed experiment. Sure, they had lost a few bucks on the sets, and the ratings had sagged slightly. But wasn't it worth the risk? What if it had worked? And really, what did it matter? The biggest show of the year, *Starrcade*, was coming up, and it was the one show that every single wrestling fan in the country was going to line up to see. Not only would Sting versus Hogan finally happen, but Bret Hart would also be making his first ever appearance on a WCW PPV as a special referee for an Eric Bischoff–Larry Zbyszko match.

Huh?

In a move that was puzzling to, well, everyone (including Bret himself), the hottest commodity in pro wrestling was not going to appear as an in-ring competitor, but rather, as a referee. The bout between Zbyszko and Bischoff was to determine the fate of *Nitro*: should Larry win, *Nitro* would remain under the control of WCW. If Bischoff took the bout, the world would be "rewarded" with *nWo Nitro* each and every week. The big question leading up to the match was whether Bret would side with the nWo or with WCW. In other words, Bret Hart, the man who was WWF champion until less than two months earlier, the man the company was paying almost $3 million a year, the man who had just competed in the most shocking and noteworthy bout in decades, was nothing more than a pawn in the never-ending WCW versus New World Order battle. It was the start of what would be a long, confusing tenure for Hart in his newfound home.

Much of Hart's difficulty had to do with career politicians like Hogan and Nash, who played Bischoff like a fiddle, getting out of doing jobs to protect their spots high atop the card. And when Bischoff wouldn't cave in to their demands, they'd simply take their ball and go home. Such was the case at *Starrcade*, when Nash was scheduled to take on—and lose to—the Giant. However, that afternoon, Nash, suffering from indigestion, called the office and said that he seriously believed he'd had a minor heart attack. Nobody backstage believed the story, since Nash had been saying he wouldn't lose to Giant for months, and it had become a running joke. Fans instead saw Scott Hall trash-talk the Giant; then he took a chokeslam during an interview. Yes, not only did Nash get out of doing the job, but the obvious replacement match, featuring Hall against the Giant, also didn't take place!

Shockingly (or not, considering the men involved backstage) almost none of the nWo members lost their matches at *Starrcade*. Even career scrubs like Mike "Vincent/Virgil/Whatever" Jones went over top WCW guys like the Steiners. Lex Luger, WCW champion just four months earlier, wound up on his back for a three-count in a losing effort to Buff Bagwell. It was all very strange, because this had been built up as the ultimate WCW revenge show, the show in which the New World Order would finally get their comeuppance from the good guys.

In fact, one of the only bouts in which the nWo was defeated was in the co–main event of the evening, the Bischoff-Zbyszko contest. Yes, on the biggest PPV in the company's entire history, Bischoff booked his match as one of the main events. To show he was a team player, however, he wound up losing when Hart decided to side with WCW, thereby saving the world from repeated viewings of *nWo Nitro*. And even in that match, Bischoff wasn't pinned, nor did he submit—Bret just kind of awarded the bout to Zbyszko due to . . . well, no reason in particular.

It could, of course, be argued that all of the goofiness on the show really didn't matter, because at the end of the day, the fans were really there to see the match WCW had been building for over a year: Sting versus Hogan. Sure, those fans may have been let down by the evening's proceedings, and maybe they'd even lost some faith in WCW. But it didn't matter, because now, finally, Hulk Hogan would get his ass kicked by Sting.

However, this being Hogan, that didn't happen.

Hogan strutted down the ramp in his usual cocky manner, playing his air guitar and eventually ambling over to confer with Nick Patrick, the evil referee assigned to the bout. The two chatted for a moment in a manner far removed from the standard overt pantomimes of the wrestling business. In fact, it almost looked as though Hogan and Patrick were double-checking to make sure they had certain spots laid out within the match itself. Weird.

After having descended from the rafters in a breathtaking manner for the better part of the past eighteen months, this time Sting simply walked down the aisle, stopping to glance at the crowd momentarily, then resuming his journey. He then slowly climbed into the ring. It was as if this were just another run-of-the-mill match on another run-of-the-mill show.

Nick Patrick stood between the men, and explained the rules. Hogan and Sting locked eyes, and then it happened: Hogan shoved Sting. Sting responded by slapping Hogan in the face. It was on. Hogan slowly circled Sting, and the two locked up. The crowd came to life, chanting "Hogan sucks." It was obvious they were desperate to see the Stinger KO this arrogant asshole once and for all.

And the crowd kept waiting for that to happen. And waiting. And waiting.

It never happened. In fact, Hogan began to dominate the bout, with Sting only scoring a few minor moves here and there. A headlock spot was worked for over two minutes as the life began to drain from the crowd. Hogan took Sting outside the ring and worked him over, throwing him into the guardrail and then choking him out with his boot. He threw Sting back in, cupped his hand to his ear as he had done so often in his career, and bounced off the ropes, landing his signature finishing move, the Legdrop of Doom.

Hogan covered Sting. Patrick dropped down, and started his count.

One.

Two.

Three.

Sting didn't kick out.

No, he did not kick out. The man who had stalked Hogan and his evil band for over a year had just failed miserably in a match one year in the making.

Patrick raised Hogan's arm in victory as the once-rabid crowd sat in stunned silence.

The WCW announcers scrambled for an explanation. They claimed that Patrick had issued a fast count and that Sting hadn't really lost. Problem is, it wasn't a fast count. Bret Hart ran down to ringside and grabbed the ring announcer. Over a muffled house mic, Bret claimed, "This isn't going to happen again" (in reference to the infamous Montreal finish where he himself had been screwed out of the WWF title). Most in the crowd didn't even hear what Hart had said, and they looked angry and confused.

And Sting, the savior of WCW, was still flat on his back in the ring.

After a brief skirmish, Hart flattened Patrick and tossed Hogan back into Sting, who had finally come back to life. Sting nailed Hogan with a Stinger splash; then he locked on his finishing maneuver, the dreaded Scorpion Deathlock. The crowd waited for Hogan's hand to slap the mat, the so-called "tap out" that would signal his submission. It didn't come, and instead, Bret Hart told the timekeeper to ring the bell, the story being that Hogan had said "I quit" (a fact that no microphones picked up). The belt was awarded to Sting as WCW wrestlers filled the ring in a joyous celebration.

And as the wrestlers and the fans celebrated, so did Bischoff. All his hard work, all his patience, it had all paid off big time.

Starrcade 97 was, without question, the biggest money-maker WCW had ever produced.

17,500 fans.

A $543,000 gate.

An incredible 1.9 buy rate, meaning nearly $6 million in revenue.

And the beginning of the end.

"I read somewhere if something is working, don't try to fix it. Our ratings are high, our arenas are selling out, we can't keep merchandise in inventory. You're right . . . there must be something wrong with Nitro.*"*

—*Eric Bischoff to a fan asking why* Nitro *was so repetitive in a Prodigy Chat, April 17, 1997*

CHAPTER 4

1998: Momentum Is Money

The March 9, 1998, edition of Monday *Nitro* was the ninth consecutive sellout for World Championship Wrestling. In addition to those nine sellouts, the company had already sold out the following eleven shows as well. Never before had they sold out twenty venues in a row.

That was not the only good news. Business, as compared to 1997, was through the roof. Attendance in January averaged 8,023 paying fans per show, an increase of 49 percent from the year prior. Gates averaged $157,019 for the month, an increase of almost 150 percent. And the *Souled Out* pay-per-view in January, which drew just a 0.47 buy rate the year prior, pulled a 1.02, an increase of over *173 percent*. That, of course, meant a revenue increase of over 173 percent as well.

The company was skyrocketing. However, the lesson of the year was not learned until much later; sadly, many in wrestling never learned it at all.

The lesson is that when things are hot in pro wrestling, promoters can do no wrong. Booking can be horrible, matches can suck, story lines can make no sense, TV shows and pay-per-views can be letdowns, wrestlers can be falsely advertised, and none of it matters. Because it's hot, fans are going to spend money on the product. Of course, any damage done during this period eventually takes its toll, but to promoters who live only for Tuesday-morning Nielsen television ratings, the only thing that matters is the moment. Unfortunately, a few years later, WCW would learn the other half of this lesson: when things are bad, promoters can do nothing right.

There has always been a theory that the wrestling business is cyclical. A superstar or an act takes off and gets incredibly hot for a period of time; then things cool off, and eventually things get really hot again. It seems that no one ever has bothered to stop and ask why; it was just accepted. Today, the explanation is fairly obvious to anyone *outside* the wrestling industry.

First, a wrestling star catches fire. There is not necessarily any rhyme or reason as to how or why this happens. Sometimes a guy comes along and the company knows from day one that he's going to be it; the Rock was a perfect example of this. There were WWE officials who predicted that he would be the biggest star in the business by the year 2000 after his very first professional match. He actually beat that estimate by a couple of years. There are also guys nobody saw coming who got over because they just happened to be in the right place at the right time with the right gimmick. "Stone Cold" Steve Austin, probably the biggest star in wrestling history in terms of drawing money, was a good example of this.

If a star really takes off, he can turn an entire company around. In fact, Austin turned the World Wrestling Federation around to such a degree that they went from losing $6 million in 1996 to grossing $456 million a few years later, making Vince McMahon a legitimate, honest-to-God evil billionaire. But, as the old saying goes, nothing lasts forever.

Eventually, even the brightest star starts to cool. There is absolutely *no* avoiding this. Sure, he might still be popular, and if he's a big enough star, like an El Santo in Mexico, he may become iconic. But he's not going to sell millions of dollars worth of tickets and pay-per-view buys forever, especially against the same old foes he's wrestled a hundred times before. Worst-case scenario, if he's pushed too hard for too long, the fans may actually turn against him, making him more of a liability than anything else.

In a perfect world, the company would use the still-super-hot star to create another huge superstar, a successor of sorts. Unfortunately, to do this correctly, the successor has to be booked in such a way that he appears to be a true successor. That means he has to win a lot of matches, and eventually decisively beat the big star.

Perhaps you can see the dilemma.

Promoters have rarely been able to bring themselves to replace their bread-and-butter before it's too late. They see him making extraordinary amounts of money for the company, and they cannot fathom tinkering with the formula in any way. Wrestling promoters are notoriously short-sighted; as noted earlier, they live for the moment—for the sound of the cheering crowd, for the following day's ratings, for that next buy rate. They don't have the long-term vision to see that unless things stay fresh, the decline in fortunes can be just as swift, and sometimes even faster, than the ascent.

There is an old saying, popularized by Bret Hart in Paul Jay's excellent documentary *Wrestling with Shadows*, that promoters ride a wrestler like a horse until he can't go any more; then they put a bullet in his head. Inevitably, they ride that horse until he's long past the point of drawing big money, and then, when things start to decline, they panic. The panic breeds inept and hotshot booking, the decline speeds up, and it finally gets to the point where the company is so cold that, in the eyes of the fans, it can do nothing right.

Of course, to those inside the wrestling business, especially those who've booked their promotions into a cold period, this is absurd: wrestling is simply cyclical; there's no reason for it. And if there *is* a reason, well, it certainly has nothing to do with anything they have or have not done.

Once the decision was made to create *Nitro* to go head-to-head with *Raw*, Eric Bischoff created a winning formula that helped the company take off. He put huge marquee matches such as Hulk Hogan versus Lex Luger on free TV to build the audience. He bought up all the big-name talent available and put them on TV as often as possible. He used working agreements with promotions in Japan and Mexico to bring in talented performers from around the world and expose them to a new audience. The show basically had it all: big names, great talent, and good matches. If you wanted to see established superstars like Hogan and Sting, you could watch *Nitro*. If you wanted to see great wrestling matches with mat technicians like Dean Malenko and Chris Benoit, you could watch *Nitro*. If you wanted to see crazy highspots from Mexican luchadors, you could watch *Nitro*. It was the best of all worlds, and the company caught fire.

Things were clearly reaching a peak in early 1998. However, for every dollar made, it was as though the WCW made another stupid mistake. And for every million they made, they made one huge mistake that would help cost them everything in the end.

The biggest mistake of all was that nothing changed. Ever. At first, that doesn't sound so bad; they made more money in one year than the money they'd lost in all the previous years put together—why change anything?

The answer, of course, is that nothing is forever.

Those big stars? Some of them were old. Plus, those that were old in 1995 were now three years older. Some couldn't wrestle a good match to save their lives, and some, sadly, could barely even move. The nostalgia was gone, and now that all the big marquee matches had been used up, fans were anxious for something new. That something new, you'd think, would come from the guys on the undercard, who were having all those great matches three years earlier.

The good news is that those guys were still having great matches. The bad news is that they were having the same great matches with the same guys they were wrestling in 1995. As great a match as Rey Mysterio versus Juventud Guerrera was, fans could only see Rey give him a huracanrana so many times.

In essence, *Nitro* looked the same in 1998 as it did in 1995. When you have several hours of first-run television every single week, three years might as well be three decades. And anyone who follows the television industry knows that no weekly television program featuring the same characters—no matter how hot it is at the peak—lasts forever.

In early January, two major television changes took place, both ultimately for the worse. First, after internal pressure from TBS, WCW created a new two-hour program to air every Thursday night, *Thunder* (originally, it was going to be an nWo show, but that idea went out the window when *nWo Nitro* bombed). Bischoff was largely against the idea, realizing that not only would it likely oversaturate the market (which it eventually did, though not at first), but it would also possibly take a chunk out of *Nitro*'s numbers. The estimated $12 million TBS paid the company for the show helped to change his mind.

The downside to the addition of *Thunder* from the boys' perspective was that, all of a sudden, they had fifty-two more dates on their schedule for the year. One of the perks of working for WCW back in the day was that you could make better money than in the WWF and work fewer dates. Now, with another TV program and more house show dates, the road schedule was getting harder, and the guaranteed deals meant that the wrestlers were pretty much doing those extra dates "for free." This didn't exactly go over too well.

Amazingly, no one in charge of WCW had any idea whether the debut episode was going to be two hours or three until just a few days prior. It ended up going three hours and fifteen minutes, which threw the rest of the TBS schedule into disarray. Although it was more of a laid-back show, compared by some to *WCW Saturday Night*, it ended up drawing what was alleged to be the highest debut cumulative rating in cable TV history: a 4.0. To give you an idea of how hot WCW was at the time, the January 15 *Thunder* drew a 3.7 rating despite the fact that a satellite malfunction destroyed the picture quality and caused the entire show to be virtually unwatchable (as opposed to years later, when the show was unwatchable regardless of whether the picture was good or not).

The second major change took place on January 26, as *Nitro* was also overhauled and given an additional hour, making it a three-hour program. If four hours of WCW weekly weren't enough, fans were now given *five*. Over at *Raw*, the WWF was building towards *Wrestlemania XIV*, and appearing in some capacity on television most weeks was the man who would be the guest enforcer in the Shawn Michaels versus Steve Austin WWF title match: Mike Tyson. As a result, once *Nitro* ended, many viewers were jumping over to *Raw*. Instead of moving the two hours head-to-head (*Nitro* was airing from 8-10 and *Raw* from 9-11), the decision was made to have *Nitro* go an extra hour permanently (they'd experimented with a few three-hour shows in late 1997), therefore keeping the high unopposed first-hour rating to add to their cumulative total.

Alongside all the additional television time, the year started out with yet another new record: 26,733 fans and a $510,610 gate for a January 5 show at the Georgia Dome. It was highlighted by a classic interview between Bret Hart and Ric Flair, in which Hart said that if Flair (who was still the top ratings draw in either company) had a problem with him calling himself the best there is, was, and ever will be, he could do something about it. Some thought it was too early to be booking this match, but the crowd was clearly clamoring to see it.

Bret versus Flair took place at the first PPV of the year, *Souled Out*. The event, largely considered a success, drew a sellout 5,087 fans to Dayton's Hara Arena to witness Luger beat Savage in a horrible main event. Worse yet, they had a chance to have a great headliner with Hart versus Flair, but at the last minute, this match was moved up to the semi-main position. The reason Luger and Savage went on last was that Hulk Hogan did a run-in afterwards, and of course, he couldn't do a run-in on a semi-main. The buy rate for the show ended up being on par with many of the Hogan-head-lined shows, largely due to the hype for what ended up being an excellent Flair versus Hart match.

And how did WCW reward these two men for having such a great match, drawing such great ratings, and popping such a great buy rate? They ended the feud cold-turkey and took Flair off TV for several weeks. The reasoning was that too many people were cheering for Flair, and they wanted him to be a bad guy. If the people couldn't play along and boo him, then they would be punished with his absence. (Ironically, later in the year, when Bret was getting a strong babyface reaction despite being booked as a heel, he too was removed from television.)

In addition to the horrific main event, there was almost another disaster at the PPV as Giant landed on his head after Nash attempted to give him a powerbomb. The two had done the spot successfully in February of 1997, but a year later Nash was physically weaker, having suffered a knee injury. Giant had put on what looked like about 100 pounds through various means, most of which involved consuming massive amounts of pizza and milk. Nash got him about halfway up, then dropped him right on his neck. Thankfully, Giant was OK. WCW Commissioner J.J. Dillon later announced in story line that because of the incident, the powerbomb was now banned. Of course, the ban affected everyone in the company except Nash, who used it regularly and began to get over as a rebellious babyface because of it. At first, he'd be "fined $150,000" and "arrested" every time he did it, but eventually the bookers completely forgot about it, and the angle was dropped.

Hogan was all over TV. Some found this strange, since he allegedly was not under contract at the time. The belief of many backstage was that this was the latest political move by arguably the most brilliant strategist in wrestling history. Hogan, making around $5 million per year, knew WWF wouldn't offer him anything close to that, especially since they were already investing millions in Tyson for *Wrestlemania*. So, using the creative control written into his contract, he booked himself on TV until he was pretty much indispensable, then started to float rumors around that he was about to jump ship to the opposition. It worked, and not only did he get re-signed for his $5 million, but he got a $1.5 million bonus as well. Some would argue that, from a business perspective, WCW would have been foolish not to re-sign him, as an untelevised January 31 house show that he worked against Sting drew 18,759 fans and $325,154 at the gate, a new company record.

As if anyone needed a sign of just how hot the company was at the time, Sin City Productions began work early in the year on a porn video called *Nude World Order*. When the porn industry takes note, you can be sure you're onto something.

Not only was the company doing incredible numbers at the box office, but the ratings continued to soar as well. In fact, the ratings war seemed more futile than ever for the WWF as the February 2 *Nitro*, headlined by Hogan versus Savage for the nine millionth time, did its second highest rating in history, a 4.93 to *Raw*'s 3.45. This was the most impressive number of all time up to this point, because the previous record, a 4.97 on August 25, 1997, was set on a week in which *Raw* had been preempted for tennis, giving *Nitro* full access to the entire wrestling audience.

In the midst of all these incredible numbers, tragedy struck. On February 14, Louie Spicolli (Louis Mucciolo), who had just turned twenty-seven and was starting to get a push in WCW as a Chris Farley-like nWo lackey, died of a drug overdose. Spicolli, who took as many as thirty soma pain pills daily, had washed down twenty-seven with some alcohol. He was found dead in his home at 8:55 A.M., facedown in his own vomit. It wasn't his first overdose; in fact, in 1996, while working for the WWF, he'd collapsed after taking fifty-five somas and was in critical condition for two days. Disturbingly, he'd told friends just days before his death that he was concerned that the drug use in the company was getting out of control. The following Monday, *Nitro* opened with a tribute for him. His close friends on the show weren't allowed to mention him at all. The only person who did bring him up was Larry Zbyszko, with whom he'd been feuding. Zbyszko said that there were a few things he'd like to say, but out of respect for the family, he'd keep his mouth shut. Yes, a guy really died, but because there was a wrestling war to fight, WCW wouldn't even allow Zbyszko to get out of character to acknowledge it. Backstage, there was some shock and sadness, but overall, it was business as usual. In fact, to show just how brazen some wrestlers in WCW were, Dr. Joel Hackett, who had prescribed the pills to Spicolli, was flown into San Francisco for that weekend's *Superbrawl* PPV.

Before 12,620 fans at the Cow Palace, the *Superbrawl* PPV was yet another sellout with yet another sub-par main event. Sting beat Hogan to win the held-up WCW title, but he'd been killed so dead by the *Starrcade* booking that it was way too little way too late. Worse, he couldn't even make it a clean win, as Randy Savage had to hit Hogan with a spray paint can prior to the finish. Once again, Sting came out looking far inferior to the almighty Hulkster, and fans were starting to catch on to that fact. If that wasn't bad enough, the usually great undercard wasn't so great, although

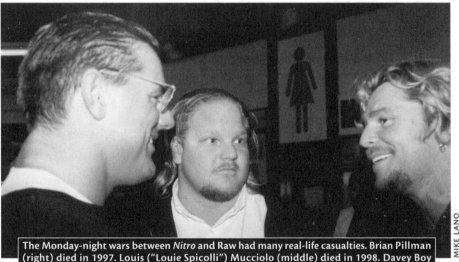

The Monday-night wars between *Nitro* and *Raw* had many real-life casualties. Brian Pillman (right) died in 1997. Louis ("Louie Spicolli") Mucciolo (middle) died in 1998. Davey Boy Smith (left) died in 2002. None reached the age of forty.

MIKE LANO

DDP versus Benoit and Chris Jericho versus Juventud Guerrera were both very good.

The latter match was the subject of a lot of controversy. Guerrera, real name Anibal Gonzalez, was the son of famous Mexican wrestler Fuerza Guerrera. In Mexico, the pro wrestler's mask (a symbolic take-off of the masks worn hundreds of years earlier in Aztec rituals) is considered almost sacred, and to lose it is normally a very big deal. The biggest superstar in the history of the culture, El Santo, never unmasked after he took on that persona, and he was even buried with it on. Because of the long tradition, which started when Salvador Lutteroth's family opened up the Empressa Mexicana de Lucha Libre (EMLL) promotion in 1933, major mask versus mask or mask versus hair matches continue to sell out huge buildings such as Arena Mexico.

WCW, however, didn't care about all that tradition stuff. After all, this was the United States of America, where wrestlers did not hide their faces. Guerrera, Bischoff explained again, just wasn't marketable with the mask on. When Guerrera was first approached about losing his mask, he—along with his father and all the other luchadors—was appalled by the suggestion. Bischoff swore that they would make a huge deal out of it, building it up over a long period of time with a series of major angles to make the match really mean something. The big push ended up with a loss to mid-carder Billy Kidman, a win over lower-mid-carder El Dandy, a loss to Jericho at *Superbrawl*, and, ultimately, the sale at the merchandise stand of his and Mysterio's masks a year later.

It wasn't like the luchadors were the only upset mid-carders. Eddy Guerrero, frustrated with both the mask situation and what he saw as a complete lack of upward mobility, tried to quit. Bischoff not only told him no, but yelled at him for even considering it. Later, Eric apologized. He was not sorry enough, however, to give Eddy his release. Dean Malenko wanted to know when Bischoff was going to keep his word and let him book a Cruiserweight tournament. Bischoff, tactful boss that he was, replied that Malenko, Guerrero, Juvie, Mysterio, Benoit, and the like were all great workers, but none of them put asses in the seats.

Their unhappiness was of no concern to Bischoff, who, on the morning of February 17, was overjoyed to learn that the previous evening's *Nitro* (which ran unopposed as the Westminster Dog Show preempted *Raw*) had done a 5.10 rating—yet another brand-new record. Better yet, it was widely considered to have been a great show, despite the fact that the booking was headache-inducing, and Hogan's old buddy Ed Leslie—now known as "E. Harrison Leslie"—was introduced as the newest nWo member, further watering down the once-elite faction. Not only was *Nitro* again breaking its own records, but Eric also had a great card in mind for the *Uncensored* pay-per-view on March 15 in Mobile, Alabama: Hogan versus Savage in a cage, Sting versus Scott Hall for the WCW title, Luger versus Scott Steiner, and Giant versus Nash. Sure, it was the same old largely horrible workers on top, but it didn't matter—it was considered a top-billing marquee.

On February 17, Randy Savage was named Real Man of the Year by the *Harvard Lampoon* for exuding "universal manliness." Welcome to 1998.

The next week, *Raw* and *Nitro* drew a combined 8.60 rating for shows that saw, on one side, the "baddest man on the planet" Mike Tyson join the cutting-edge Shawn Michaels–led Degeneration X (DX) faction and, on the other side, the 100 zillionth nWo run-in DQ. Fans were anxious for WCW to do something dramatically different and creative like, say, a clean finish, but WCW saw no reason to do that. After all, their show did a 4.81, and Vince's show only did a 3.80. They beat the WWF by a *whole point.* There was no reason to change anything.

Backstage, things continued to spiral out of control. The luchadors, suddenly informed that they would no longer be able to take bookings in Mexico on their off days, were more upset than ever. Most had been making good money collecting paychecks from both WCW and independent groups south of the border. Once the decree was made, some ignored it and took bookings anyway, while others began to trade ideas on ways to get fired.

The company's deal with New Japan Pro Wrestling also fell apart. For years, the two sides had been trading talent back and forth. Usually, it was to WCW's advantage. New Japan would send over one of their big superstars like Masahiro Chono, while WCW would send over talent like Robby Rage, who was unknown not only in Japan, but also in the U.S. Obviously, the international talent spiced up WCW television, and in fact, Keiji Muto (as the Great Muta) was one of the company's huge stars of the late '80s.

The deal fell through mostly because Eric went on one of his now-trademark power trips. New Japan had an nWo stable, and Bischoff decided to enforce a contract stipulation between the two sides that enabled him to choose who could and who could not be considered a member. Keep in mind that there wasn't one casual fan in the United States who would have had any idea who was and was not in New Japan's nWo stable. The point was that Bischoff had the power, so he was going to use it. As if that wasn't bad enough, he started trying to enforce which guys could even *team up* with nWo guys. It also didn't help when word got out in Japan that Bischoff had gone behind New Japan's back in an attempt to strike up a deal to send wrestlers to a show run by its competition, All Japan Pro Wrestling.

That was hardly Eric's only power play of the month. Back home, he was having problems with Hall and Nash, who were upset that they were being moved down in the pecking order in favor of Hogan and his new best friend, Randy Savage. Bischoff decided to show them who was boss in a very brash manner: he fired, via overnight courier, their best friend in the company, Sean Waltman, a.k.a. Syxx. Worse, Waltman was on the shelf at the time, healing a broken neck. Amidst quite a bit of fanfare, he ended up quickly signing a deal to return to the WWF. To fans watching at home, it appeared that a big WCW star had suddenly decided that the WWF was really the place to be. To disgruntled WCW wrestlers, especially the smaller guys, it suggested that if they jumped ship, they might also get a big push right out of the gate. Waltman was given a raise of almost $100,000 more than what he had been making in WCW, and this sent the message that the WWF was willing to pay top dollar to be competitive.

Hall and Nash, meanwhile, were outraged over the firing and wanted to quit. Eric reminded them that they were under contract until 2001 and couldn't appear anywhere else before then. So they stayed, but that didn't stop them from going on TV and acting unprofessionally. In one interview, Hall told fans that he was no longer allowed to say "Hey Yo!" On another occasion, he told Giant, "That's your cue" over the house mic. He was not reprimanded, and he took note of this fact. Later that week, Nash got into a loud argument with Hogan backstage, actually telling him to his face that he wanted his spot. Hogan said he wasn't giving it up, brother.

While Bischoff was likely stressed about everything, his worries only ran so deep. *Nitro* did a 5.7 quarter that week for a Sting and Savage and Giant versus Hogan and Hall and Nash match, killing *Raw*, which did a 3.3 for a quarter built around Austin and Tyson. Better yet, the following week the show aired unopposed again and did a 5.58 composite, destroying the previous record of a 5.10. The final quarter, featuring Sting and Luger versus Hogan and Savage, also crushed the previous week's record with an enormous 6.6. Eric felt like the king of the world.

At least, until *Uncensored*, which you'll recall had that great big marquee lineup. The undercard was again below average, although Jericho versus Malenko and DDP versus Benoit versus Raven were very good. Giant versus Nash sucked. Sting versus Hall sucked. And Hogan versus Savage was an atrociously bad cage match—even by WCW standards—that included run-ins by Sting and E. Harrison Leslie and didn't even have a finish. To the amusement of some hardcore fans, *Uncensored* at least lived up to its reputation of being the worst PPV WCW presented each year. But the issue that was becoming clear to anyone but those running the company was that, in spite of the sold-out crowds, record-breaking ratings, and amazing buy rates, they were putting on bad show after bad show.

WCW was so hot in 1998 that it affected world commerce. When THQ announced that they would no longer produce WCW's wildly successful video games, their stock dropped $8 per share on the Nasdaq. Amazingly, a full 25 percent of THQ's titles had been WCW-related.

The March 23 *Nitro* was notable for being the true dawn of the Bill Goldberg era, an era that should have set the company up for long-term success since he was about to become the company's most popular wrestler. The idea, devised by announcer Mike Tenay, was incredibly simple: Goldberg did not lose, and the commentators would play up his winning streak. Not only did this ensure that his eventual first loss would mean a great deal (and it did, but unfortunately for all the wrong reasons), but it also gave fans something to keep track of—a statistic of sorts in a fake sport that really didn't have any. In fact, fans got into it to such a degree that signs featuring simply a stat, "76-0," for example, began to appear on *Nitro*. The fragile egos backstage definitely took note of his increasing popularity.

In addition to Goldberg, WCW also had another star tailor-made for success, ironically as the result of an in-ring tragedy: Buff Bagwell, who had been injured earlier in the year taking a top rope bulldog. The injury was so bad that when it happened, everyone broke character and rushed to his aid. Doctors later told Buff that he was just three inches away from that worst-case scenario, and that he'd nearly died twice due to complications. After undergoing double fusion neck surgery the next day, in a near miracle, he was told that he'd probably be able to return to training within six months. In his return to Nitro, Bagwell came out in a wheelchair for a face-to-face meeting with the man who broke his neck, Rick Steiner. He told Rick that it was an accident and forgave him for what happened. The people cheered. The other half of the former Steiner Brothers tag team, the heel Scott, then came out and hit his brother with a chair. Bagwell stood up, apparently to make the save, but then jumped Rick and tore his shirt off to reveal, that's right, "nWo." In that instant, not only was the next potentially huge babyface star flushed down the drain, but a real-life neck injury was turned into a cornball wrestling angle. What should have been a new birth for Bagwell's major-league career ended up being the beginning of its end.

But it was something outside the company that month that changed WCW's fortunes forever. On March 29, Steve Austin beat Shawn Michaels to win the World Wrestling Federation Championship at *Wrestlemania XIV*. Austin's rise to the title immediately affected the ratings war. Despite winning handily in the ratings war just weeks earlier, *Nitro* was barely able to edge out *Raw* the following evening, 4.19 to 3.79. In fact, had *Nitro* not taken the lead in the last half hour, *Raw* would have won. The WWF's show was built around Sean Waltman's debut as a member of DX. In a pretty revolutionary segment, he ran down Hogan and Bischoff before he added, "And I got something else to say. Kevin Nash and Scott Hall would be standing right here with us if they weren't being held hostage by World Championship Wrestling. And that's a fact, Eric Bischoff!" With that one interview, DX was pushed over the top as being more revolutionary than the now-stale nWo that, over the past few months, had added such prestigious members as mid-carder Brian Adams and everyone's favorite flabby geriatric, Dusty Rhodes.

The following week, the ratings battle was even closer, with *Nitro* doing a 4.61 to *Raw*'s 4.43. Head to head, both shows did an 8.99 combined rating, a brand-new record. And the segment in which Austin, as WWF champion, came out on *Raw* to confront Vince McMahon did a 5.6, another new record. In the same quarter, *Nitro* did a 3.9. In fact, of all the quarters, *Raw* won four, *Nitro* won three, and one was basically a tie. Bischoff was sweating.

And then, the next week, everything hit the fan.

For the first time since May 27, 1996, *Raw* beat *Nitro* in the head-to-head ratings battle, ending an epic eighty-three-week winning streak. *Raw*, built for two hours around a supposed McMahon versus Austin singles match that never ended up taking place, drew a 4.63 to *Nitro*'s 4.34. The final few minutes also did a 6.0 quarter, the highest in history for *Raw*.

Bischoff went nuclear.

Frustrated beyond belief, he was looking to take his anger out on someone, and that someone wound up being Ric Flair, the man fans identified with WCW more than any other. Flair, who hadn't been used on TV for months, missed the *Thunder* event on April 9 in which he was supposed to re-form the Four Horsemen. He claimed that he'd given the company plenty of advance notice that he was going to attend his son Reid's AAU freestyle wrestling championships at the Pontiac Silverdome that same day. Unfortunately, advance notice was useless in WCW because the shows were often booked literally at the last minute (the term "literally" is not being used facetiously—there were times when the shows were still being written *while they were on the air live*). Flair never knew he was supposed to be at *Thunder* until three days before the show, at which point he wasn't about to change his plans.

Bischoff came completely unglued, verbally tearing Flair apart in a backstage meeting at *Nitro* on April 13 (which, ironically, had been deemed Ric Flair Day by the city of Minneapolis), then filed a $2 million lawsuit against him for "playing havoc with the script of the wildly popular productions" and "disrupting WCW's ability to introduce its planned story line, causing significant loss of time, money, and effort by WCW."

On the bright side, Reid won first place in his division.

While the temporary loss of Flair did hurt the company, WCW had an ace in the hole, as Goldberg was really starting to catch fire. His segments on *Nitro* were becoming the most highly rated, and his merchandise sales were beginning to skyrocket as well. It appeared that they truly had a fresh, hot commodity that fans were willing to pay to see.

In their efforts to push Goldberg to the moon, however, WCW made some critical mistakes. Ever since the announcers had mentioned that he was 60-0, fans with way too much spare time had begun to keep track of his winning streak. These fans were so hardcore that they even kept track of his untelevised house show wins. It was fun to see fans so interested in a character, especially one that WCW had created from the ground up. Of course, since WCW created it, they also had to ruin it. One week, announcer Schiavone's number didn't jive with the number the hardcores had. Then, the next week, it was even farther off. As it turned out, in a lame effort to make his streak appear more meaningful, the company had started to add imaginary numbers to the total. This had the exact opposite of its intended effect, as once fans figured out that the streak number had become fiction, all those signs fans had been bringing to the arenas trumpeting Goldberg's record disappeared. Worse yet, WCW was so happy to hear fans chanting Goldberg's name that they decided to pipe in some fake "GOLDBERG!" chants to make it seem like the fans were making even more noise. For whatever reason, though, the *Nitro* TV directors apparently weren't clued into this, because soon shots began to appear of the crowd sitting there with their mouths closed amidst loud "GOLDBERG!" chants. Again, once fans figured out the chants were being piped in, they stopped chanting so much.

WCW had a problem at the Augusta, Georgia, house show on April 30. The main event was scheduled to be Flair versus Hennig, but with Flair being out indefinitely and Hennig being, well, just not there, fans were very upset. So upset, in fact, that hundreds of them demanded refunds. After thinking over several scenarios, the decision was made to do a last-minute change and have Chris Benoit beat Booker T to win the TV title. It worked; the fans were over-joyed. So the decision was made to do it again the next night. And then again, and again, and again. The belt changed hands four times in four days at the house shows, going from Booker to Benoit to Booker to Benoit to Booker again. Every night, the fans went crazy as they watched something special happen right there in their hometown. But then on Monday, when Booker T showed up to lose the belt to Fit Finley on TV, the announcers never mentioned anything about the house show title changes. They just ignored them, and to all the casual fans watching around the nation, it was as though nothing had ever happened. It also sent a very strong message to all those previously overjoyed fans in Norfolk, Greenville, North Charleston, and Savannah: you don't count, and if anything happens in your little hick town, it won't be acknowledged on TV because it's not important. If they hadn't already done enough to kill business in those areas, this was another nail in the coffin.

But Bischoff wasn't really concerned about any of these small issues; he was still too obsessed with conquering the WWF in the weekly ratings war. By this point, word of Bischoff's increasing mental instability had reached Vince McMahon, who decided to have some fun by doing everything in his power to drive Eric completely over the edge. He had his hooligan group DX "invade" the Norfolk Scope where *Nitro* was being presented. Of course, the WWF guys couldn't get into the arena, so the invasion merely consisted of them talking to fans and telling WCW to "suck it." A week or so later, the

WWF sent DX and a film crew to Smyrna, Georgia, for another "invasion," this time of WCW headquarters. Unfortunately, WCW headquarters were private property, so Nick Lambros called the cops and actually claimed that "twenty-five guys" were "attacking" their offices. The cops showed up and told DX to hit the bricks. Their next stop was CNN Center, where they claimed they wanted to interview Ted Turner. The problem here was that the camera crew was now terrified and wouldn't film anything except them standing around in the lobby doing crotch chops and chatting with fans. This was even lamer than the previous invasion, but, once again, fans wanted reality, and that's what they were getting.

That evening on *Nitro*, Bischoff hit the ring to reveal his master plan for revenge. It was ingenious in that mad-scientist-losing-his-mind sort of way. He entered the ring literally shaking with rage and recited a speech that he'd given many times in the past, almost word-for-word, to folks backstage:

Vince McMahon, this is for you. I'm coming to your backyard this Sunday. That's right, Worcester, Massachusetts. Got a little PPV thing going on, and I got a hell of an idea, just a hell of an idea. You want me? I'm going to be in your backyard. Consider this an open invitation, Vince McMahon. You show up at *Slamboree*, it'll be you and me in the ring. How about it, Vinny? But I want to warn you people right now. If you think Vince McMahon has got the guts to show up, don't buy this PPV, because I guarantee you he's not man enough to step into the ring with me. But I'll be there, Vinny Mac. I'll be waiting for you. And I'm going to knock you out. See you there!

The fans in attendance, understanding the reality of the challenge, cheered Eric as a babyface. The WWF's response on *Raw* two hours later was to have announcers Jim Ross and Jim Cornette cry about it, and to have Waltman come out and tell Eric to suck it. A few days later on WWF.com, Vince issued a statement calling Eric's move a cheap ploy to increase PPV buys. "Therefore," he wrote, "I will not appear at Turner's next PPV as invited. However, if Mr. Bischoff is hell bent on fighting me, then such a fight can be arranged at any time, in any parking lot in the country; void of television cameras, photographers, and public announcement."

Eric wasn't finished. That Thursday on *Thunder*, he cut not one, but *two* promos challenging Vince. He also read a real-life legal letter that Vince's attorney, the famed and terrifying Jerry McDevitt, had sent to him, threatening him for what it claimed was a cheap bait-and-switch to try to get fans to order the PPV. In a true story, McDevitt claimed that when Bischoff told the fans that the match wasn't going to take place he was actually insinuating that it was, because in wrestling, when a person says something isn't going to happen, it's usually a sign that it is. Sadly, this never went to court—it would have been very interesting to see a judge and jury's reaction to that statement. They also aired a Bischoff training video on *Thunder*, which was comical because he was really training quite hard for an imaginary fight.

And imaginary it was. Bischoff came to the ring at *Slamboree* and had Michael Buffer introduce Vince. Of course, there was no Vince. So Bischoff had the referee count the imaginary Vince out and award him the match. The deal had more than run its course, so it came off as being incredibly stupid.

Just weeks after the whole childish "Vince McMahon versus Eric Bischoff" program took place, WCW took their complaints a step further by filing an unfair business practices countersuit against the WWF, a suit almost identical to the one the WWF had filed against them in 1996 after Hall and Nash jumped ship. The suit, like that of the WWF, was mostly frivolous, claiming that Vince and his crew had done mean things like saying all their wrestlers were old (and this was hilarious, because on several occasions when announcer Jim Ross made such claims, elderly men like Gerald Brisco, Pat Patterson, and Vince himself were involved in matches as he spoke). They did have one good point, however: that the WWF had falsely claimed on several occasions that WCW was giving away free tickets, when in reality the shows in question were legitimately sold out. When DX invaded the Scope, the WWF even went so far as to digitally insert a graphic on the marquee claiming that tickets to the show were still available (yes, they went to these absurd lengths for a corny skit). "In the professional wrestling business," the suit read, "the giving away of free tickets to an event on the day of the show is a response to a failure to sell out the venue, and it reflects badly on a promotion, suggesting that an insufficient number of fans were willing to pay to see the show." Coincidentally, on *Nitro* that evening, Schiavone claimed the *Raw* show in Hampton was not sold out when, in fact, it was.

At the time of the latest WCW-WWF lawsuit, the company found itself being sued by one of its workers as well. In June, prelim wrestler Bobby Walker filed a lawsuit against the company claiming racial discrimination, saying WCW told him point blank that he was being hired as a token black man, and that he always had to lose. Never mind the fact that there were ten times the number of white guys who were asked to always lose by WCW. Another one of his points was that he made a lot less than many of the white performers, including—he actually said this—Ric Flair. The suit was eventually thrown out. As absurd as this whole thing sounds on the surface, another suit filed by Sonny Onoo dragged on for five years, and numerous minority wrestlers jumped on the bandwagon. When Onoo's suit was finally settled by Time Warner (long after WCW had ceased to exist), it was said that the guys filing suit made out like bandits.

In the midst of all the lawsuits and childish behavior, WCW signed three big names: Dennis Rodman and Karl Malone would help generate mainstream interest, and the artist formerly known as the Ultimate Warrior would help to launch them into another universe.

Rodman was a friend of Hogan's, and Dallas Page was in tight with Karl Malone. The idea was to bring them in for a match at the *Bash at the Beach* PPV in July in an attempt to generate mainstream publicity—hopefully similar to what Mike Tyson's appearance at *Wrestlemania* had done for the WWF. It worked better than anyone had likely imagined. Rodman first appeared on the June 8 *Nitro* after skipping out on a Chicago Bulls practice session without bothering to tell anyone, for which he was subsequently fined $10,000. Keeping with his bad-boy persona, he teamed up with Hogan as "Rodzilla" to put the boots to Page, setting up Page and Malone versus Hogan and Rodman for the PPV. The angle got tons of publicity nationwide, as many of the major sports shows and evening newscasts aired footage of the incident.

Meanwhile, the company was making plans for their next huge show, a *Nitro* at the Georgia Dome on July 6. By early June, they'd sold over 20,000 tickets and were closing in on a $1 million gate. As the date drew nearer, Hogan the wily veteran came up with a plan. Aware that all the Turner bigwigs would be at the show, he offered to take Goldberg on in a non-title, non-televised match in which Goldberg would get the win and send the folks home happy. All the company execs, seeing the huge house, would obviously assume that Hogan drew it, and his standing as WCW's top dog would be cemented.

As the show approached, however, the decision was made to change the match to a televised title match. This was due almost entirely to the fact that *Nitro* had been losing the ratings war, and Bischoff was obsessed

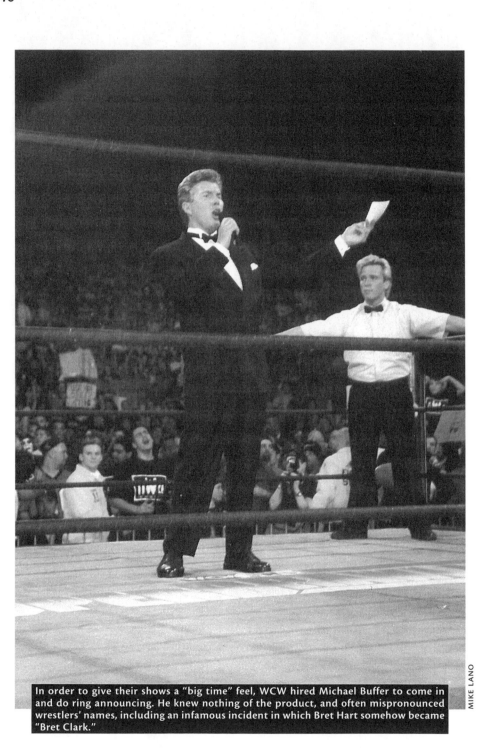

In order to give their shows a "big time" feel, WCW hired Michael Buffer to come in and do ring announcing. He knew nothing of the product, and often mispronounced wrestlers' names, including an infamous incident in which Bret Hart somehow became "Bret Clark."

MIKE LANO

with beating McMahon, even if only for one week. With Hogan taking on Goldberg, there was absolutely no way he could lose the night.

Make no mistake about it: July 6 should have been a pivotal day in wrestling history. It was on that day that Bill Goldberg—less than one year into his professional career—beat Hulk Hogan clean in the middle of the ring to win the WCW World Heavyweight championship. Internally, the sense was that this was the beginning of a new era for the company, and that Goldberg could be the answer to Steve Austin as a super draw. The ovation he received when he won the belt was among the loudest anyone had ever heard. The TV rating spoke volumes as well, as the quarter-hour for the title change set a cable wrestling record: a 6.91 with 5,054,000 homes tuning in, helping *Nitro* win the night 4.93 to 4.00. And Bischoff no doubt smiled widely on Tuesday morning when the ratings came in.

But something was lost in that ratings win: money, and lots of it. The first-ever Goldberg-Hogan match, which could have drawn millions of dollars on pay-per-view, was aired free on *Nitro* instead, owing almost entirely to the fact that *Raw* had kicked their ass the week before. Instead of showing patience, as he had with the Sting-Hogan bout, Bischoff allowed very lucrative business to be pushed aside because he wanted to brag that *Nitro* had won a week in a ratings war that he cared about more than any of the fans watching at home did. The title change, also a last-minute decision, effectively put the kibosh on several story lines that Hogan had been involved in that could have led to lucrative matches with Bret Hart and Kevin Nash.

There was actually worse news than that, too. WCW drew 41,412 fans—the biggest crowd in its history—to the Georgia Dome to see the match. At the time, it was the fourth-largest crowd ever to watch a wrestling show in the U.S. You'd think that WCW would brag about this, and likely even add to the figure, as it had always been common practice in the business to slightly exaggerate attendance numbers. Instead, however, they inexplicably *subtracted* 1,500 fans, announcing 39,919. Yes, WCW became the first promotion in wrestling history to claim a less impressive number than what they actually drew.

It gets even worse than that. When they first announced Hogan versus Goldberg locally, they only sold about 2,000 extra tickets. Realistically, the company was still hot enough at this point that very few, if any, of the wrestlers could actually be considered ticket-sellers. Instead, the name "WCW" itself sold tickets, usually on the very first day, before a card was ever announced. The mainstream wasn't aware of this, however, so Hogan decided to manipulate it so that it would appear that he did, indeed, sell tickets pretty much on his own. Therefore, he suggested the idea of doing the match live on TV and switching the title. After all, if the match was televised, it would look like he drew the house, whereas if it wasn't, someone else would get credit for the new company record. And that would be completely unacceptable.

Hogan had one major demand: that when "the time was right" to beat Goldberg, he would be the guy to do it. Because he agreed to drop the belt with a clean pinfall loss in the first place, there weren't any problems with this scenario. He also, as usual, had a few diabolical tricks up his sleeve, to be revealed over the next several months.

At the time the Goldberg-Hogan *Nitro* went down, no one really examined Hogan's motives or the long-term impact the title bout had on the company. Instead, everyone was looking ahead to *Bash at the Beach 1998*, in which Hogan and Rodman beat Page and Malone after E. Harrison Leslie interfered. The show was a shining example of the good and the bad that go along with using celebrities. On the bright side, the match got WCW a ton of mainstream publicity, with everyone from *Sports Illustrated* to *USA Today* sending reporters to cover it. Plus, Rodman and Malone proved to be successful draws, as the show did the best WCW buy rate since *Starr-cade*—an estimated 1.5 for almost a $7 million gross. For promoters who only look at the bottom line, that number alone was enough to convince them that they'd made a great decision.

That's where the good news ended, however. Malone was very professional, and for a guy in his very first pro-wrestling match ever, he was more than acceptable. Rodman, on the other hand, showed up in the infamous "no condition to perform." You could argue that at least he showed up, because he'd blown off basketball practice to attend *Nitro*, and blowing off a wrestling show to attend, well, a party or something probably wouldn't

Hollywood Hogan chokes Karl Malone with the same ferocity he'd use to strangle the career of Bill Goldberg.

have shocked anyone. In fact, he'd disappeared for several hours the day of the show, and when he showed up in whatever condition he was in, the company was actually thrilled because they had thought he wasn't going to show up at all. In the ring, he was beyond horrible, screwing up moves left and right and actually falling down on several occasions. Then he tagged out, stood on the apron, and put his head on the turnbuckle, apparently falling asleep. Luckily, that was the best role for him. Hogan had also shown up and demanded *forty-five minutes* for the match—approximately forty-four minutes longer than any of the four, with the exception of Page, could realistically have wrestled and remained entertaining. Everyone, from the fans to the sports reporters who may or may not have ever watched a full wrestling show in their lives, knew it was an in-ring disaster. It should probably also be noted that despite no-showing the last *Nitro* before the PPV, showing up in a questionable state of mind, and doing nearly nothing in the match, Rodman still later sued the company for $550,000, claiming they defrauded him in contract negotiations.

In light of all the publicity Rodman had been generating, WCW started to go overboard with celebrities, adding Kevin Greene (actually a pretty decent wrestler given his level of experience) to the semi-main event. The idea was to tag him with Goldberg to face Hennig and Giant. There was no logical reason for doing this, other than to waste a bunch of money on a guy who wasn't going to add one single buy to the show. Of course, this would be neither the first nor the last time *that* happened.

However, Greene's paycheck was nowhere near as large as the one WCW was about to write. On July 17, the company came to terms with their next huge mainstream superstar, Jay Leno of the *Tonight Show*. Yes, *that* Jay Leno. If that wasn't sufficiently absurd, Bischoff spent an estimated $75,000 to construct a mock *Tonight Show* set so he could act as host of his own "talk show" during *Nitro* and bury Leno. The first time they did this segment, it was so successful that it caused countless thousands of viewers to immediately switch channels to *Raw*. Eric, perhaps noting that Rodman and Malone meant nothing for TV ratings but did huge PPV numbers regardless, decided to keep doing the segments despite their enormous turn-off factor. This resulted in a string of some of the worst first hours of *Nitro* in history. The original plan was to bring Leno, a huge motorcycle fan, in for a match at the annual *Road Wild* biker rally pay-per-view in Sturgis. So not only were they bringing in a non-athlete to compete in a worked athletic event, but they were also spending all that money to bring him in for a free show, meaning they wouldn't be making hundreds of thousands of dollars at the gate to help offset the cost of bringing Leno in. Obviously, they were hoping that all the free *Tonight Show* publicity would result in thousands of new viewers buying the PPV.

In July, the one-year anniversary of Bill Goldberg's first-ever win, the one that launched the famous streak and catapulted him to stardom, took place on *Nitro*. To commemorate the occasion, Goldberg—the company's World champion, remember—never once appeared on the show.

Both shows set a new ratings record the following week, with *Raw* doing a 4.84 and *Nitro* doing a 4.72 for a combined 9.58 rating in 7,060,000 homes, meaning that approximately 10.5 million fans were watching wrestling at some point during that evening. This was the only good news for WCW, as Schiavone announced that their show, which actually drew almost 20,000 fans to the AlamoDome, had drawn only 13,000. Meanwhile, the *Raw* show, which drew 12,000, was billed as having drawn 18,000 by Jim Ross, so everyone figured the WWF had the better night. To make matters worse, those who watched *Nitro* witnessed one of the most atrocious shows in its history, a show in which, over the course of three hours, exactly nineteen minutes were devoted to actual in-ring pro wrestling. In fact, there was one match in the entire first hour, which ran less than two minutes. Meanwhile, Bischoff did another *Tonight Show* segment that went almost twenty. At the top of the hour, starting the head-to-head battle with *Raw*, WCW presented a true mat classic, Scott Norton versus Jim Neidhart, which went sixteen seconds. No, that's not a typo—sixteen *seconds*. Come to think of it,

MIKE LANO

WCW was a dream job for Scott Hall, who was paid handsomely to never show up to work. Sadly, WCW did not use this tactic with Kevin Nash, whose absence may have done more to help the company than harm it.

though, it was superior to those two going sixteen minutes. They replayed the entire horrible Page and Malone versus Hogan and Rodman match from the PPV, essentially telling everyone who bought it that they were stupid for doing so and had wasted their thirty bucks. The main event featured Page beating Hogan when, yep, the nWo ran in. Still, Bischoff argued, the bout served its purpose by pushing the *Road Wild* PPV.

In legal news, Scott Hall was arrested for allegedly getting intoxicated and groping a fifty-six-year-old woman outside a hotel in Baton Rouge, Louisiana. Time for a pop quiz. WCW was so outraged by Hall's behavior that they

- (A) suspended him without pay;
- (B) suspended him with pay;
- (C) turned the entire thing into a long-running angle in which Hall would come out on TV "pretending" to be drunk or wasted, stumble around in the ring, crash cars (in real life, he crashed five that year), and throw up on people.

Hopefully, after reading this far, you won't be shocked to learn that the answer was C.

Although the show confirmed that the celebrity magic was gone, doing around a 1.0 buy rate (with the zero dollar gate), the main event actually turned out to be better than anyone had any right to expect. The main reason was that Hogan did not ask for forty-five minutes this time, plus he and Page had figured out that the best course of action was to have the non-wrestlers do almost nothing. In fact, five other matches on the show were worse than this one, partly because those five matches were among the worst five of the entire year from any company worldwide. Steve "Mongo" McMichael versus Brian Adams, in particular, set a new standard for bad matches.

Upon closer inspection, the bad matches were realistically the most minor of the mistakes the company made in presenting this show. One of the larger issues was the fact that Goldberg, the WCW champion, mind you, was once again in the semi-main event of the show. One could have argued that at *Bash at the Beach*, it was fine for the World champion to work second-to-last, because the semi-main was a huge media event. However, Goldberg ended up working second-to-last on this show as well in a nine-man battle royal that absolutely nobody cared about. While logic suggests that a new challenger would eliminate Goldberg and lay claim to his belt, instead, not only did he win, he did so decisively, finally eliminating Giant in a dominating fashion with a spear and jackhammer. There he was, the WCW World Heavyweight champion, standing there with no challengers, no future programs, and playing second fiddle to—that's right!—Hulk Hogan.

He wasn't about to get any more of the spotlight, either. On August 17 in Hartford, Connecticut, right in the middle of WWF Country, former WWF champion the Ultimate Warrior made his WCW debut, pretty much out of nowhere. Actually, literally out of nowhere: his gimmick was that he could appear and disappear at will in a cloud of smoke.

Before we continue, we need to note that none of the following is being made up. This all actually happened, presumably because someone theorized that it would make fans buy tickets and PPVs.

Prior to his arrival, WCW couldn't hype up Warrior's return like they probably wanted to because they were tied up in a legal battle over what they could call him. It was pretty clear that "Ultimate Warrior" was out of the question, since the WWF had that one trademarked (and you should have seen Eric's face when, on the August 24 *Nitro*, Hogan accidentally said "Ultimate Warrior"). Just plain old "Warrior" seemed to be OK, though, mostly because that's what Jim Hellwig, the man who played the Warrior character, had legally changed his name to. The WWF didn't even want him to wear his face paint, but he claimed he'd worn it when he worked in Texas as the Dingo Warrior at the start of his career.

At the Hartford show, he was scheduled to talk for six minutes, but he ended up rambling on in a pretty much incomprehensible manner for almost twenty, and the entire show had to be rearranged live as a result (not that this was anything new for *Nitro*). It should be noted that the aforementioned ramble was by far the best interview of his entire career. The gist of his speech was that he was back, and he wanted to face Hogan again in an epic rematch from their first battle at *Wrestlemania VI* in 1990. In a comical moment, Warrior said that beating Hogan was no big deal, which kind of made one wonder why he would want to have a rematch with the Hulk. The interview was, as expected, a huge ratings draw: nearly seven million fans lost eighteen minutes of their lives watching it.

Warrior allegedly signed a $1 million deal to work roughly three shows per month, which of course had the locker room in an uproar as nearly everyone else was making a hell of a lot less to work a hell of a lot more. And everyone but Eric Bischoff seemed able to predict exactly what the future held: Warrior would have a shelf life of about, oh, five or six weeks, and then it would be all downhill from there. These people were sadly mistaken. His shelf life for his WCW run was actually about three weeks.

///

The week of August 24 was the stuff of legend. The two shows set a new combined ratings record: 9.72 in 7,169,000 homes. Meanwhile, on ABC, the debut of *Monday Night Football*, featuring a Green Bay Packers versus Denver Broncos preseason Superbowl rematch, did a 9.5. Realistically, because network TV is in more homes than cable, football actually beat wrestling 9.3 million homes to 7.2 million. However, it soon became "common knowledge" (read: "urban legend") that pro wrestling was so hot that it was regularly beating *Monday Night Football* in the ratings. Even at its peak, this was never really the case.

Short-term, though, Warrior was generating numbers. And it was beginning to look like another major ratings draw was coming back too, as Ric Flair, after being gone nearly six months, would likely return at the *Nitro* show in Greenville, South Carolina, on September 14. The WWF hadn't made him a serious offer due to their legal battles with WCW, plus some within the company had been very vocal in expressing their belief that Flair was too old to come in and headline against Austin.

Among those who argued against bringing Ric Flair back to the WWF was a young man by the name of Hunter Hearst Helmsely, who said outright in a radio interview that Flair should just retire. This was the same Triple H who, five years later, would end up best buddies with the still-active Flair on WWE television, and would, in fact, write the foreword to Flair's autobiography.

With *Raw* preempted for the annual U.S. Open tennis tournament, WCW's good fortune continued: *Nitro* drew a 6.03 in 4,485,333 homes, setting a new record for cable. Never mind that nearly seven million people witnessed yet another instalment in a seemingly endless series of hideous programs, this one headlined by Sting and Luger beating Hogan and Hart via countout. Afterwards, Warrior appeared in his cloud of smoke, a cloud now capable of making horrible wrestlers like Ed Leslie and Brian Adams faint, and good wrestlers like Bret Hart vanish into thin air. Let us reiterate that this was designed to be compelling, not comical. Goldberg, the World Heavyweight champion, again worked the semi-main, successfully defending his title against Kevin Nash's original tag team partner, a man named Al

Greene who hadn't wrestled in what seemed like decades. Exactly how Al Greene became the number-one contender to the World championship remains to be ascertained.

September 14 saw a battle of the ages, as both sides put on pay-per-view–caliber television shows with marquee matches and major character turns. From a wrestling standpoint, WCW presented one of its best TV matches of the year with Billy Kidman winning the Cruiserweight title from Juventud Guerrera. From a marquee standpoint, Goldberg's first-ever bout with Sting was a hugely anticipated match-up. On the other channel, WWF turned both Rock and Mankind babyface, Undertaker made a strong heel turn, and Steve Austin faced Ken Shamrock for the first time ever in a WWF title defense. All of it, though, paled in comparison to the highlight moment of the year: the return of Ric Flair.

Flair's segment opened with Arn Anderson coming out to cut a great promo detailing the history of his and the Horseman's careers. He called out Steve McMichael and Chris Benoit, then he introduced Dean Malenko as the newest member of the group. At that point, he teased that the segment was over, and boy, were the fans ever unhappy to hear it.

"Oh, what a goof," Arn suddenly blurted. "What a goof. You know, I get accused of getting racked in the head a few times, and have a little touch of Alzheimer's. My God, I almost forgot the fourth Horseman. RIC FLAIR, GET DOWN HERE!" It was the perfect setup. When Flair came out, he got an ovation that rivaled, and probably exceeded, any other ovation in the history of wrestling—an ovation that nobody watching will ever forget. After finally composing himself, Flair cut a promo talking about his appreciation for the fans, his life in the past few months, and finally, Eric Bischoff. Eric showed up just in time to hear the following emotional outburst:

"You're an overbearing asshole! You're obnoxious, overbearing—abuse of power! You . . . abuse of power! Cut me off! Abuse of power! You suck!

I hate your guts! You are a liar, you're a cheat, you're a scam! You are a no-good son-of-a-bitch! Fire me! I'm already fired! Fire me! I'm already fired!" And then they cut to a commercial, right in the middle of the speech that the majority of wrestling fans wish they could have personally cut on Eric.

During Flair's absence from WCW broadcasts, fans on the Internet were outraged. They did everything they could to support their hero, including voting for him in *People Magazine*'s online "50 Most Beautiful People in the World" poll. Flair came in second only to Hank the Angry Drunken Dwarf from Howard Stern with 17,145 votes, a feat made even more impressive since Hank was actually among the available choices, while Flair was a write-in candidate. WCW's website actually took advantage of all this free publicity by posting the following ad in late May: "Ric Flair merchandise now on sale in the Pro Shop!! GET IT BEFORE IT RUNS OUT! The WCW Pro Shop now features selected Ric Flair merchandise at a reduced price!! Internet fans, don't read anything into this!"

Thankfully, Flair's promo was so great that it took the minds of many fans off the previous night's *Fall Brawl* pay-per-view, yet another horrible show that the company actually charged fans money to view. There was one good match on the show, Saturn over Raven, and the main event was so atrocious that if you made a list of the very worst major main events in the entire history of this business, it would probably rank in the top five or ten. Dallas Page beat Hogan, Bret, Stevie Ray, Warrior, Piper, Sting, Luger, and Kevin Nash in a double-cage War Games match. It seems unlikely that with so much impressive talent in the ring a match could be this bad, but it was. Technically, there were two teams working against each other, but you wouldn't have known this to see it. Hogan came out with a device known as a slapjack (which looked for all the world like an old

JEFF COHEN

For years a cornerstone of WCW, Arn Anderson's legacy was mocked by Kevin Nash and his crew in an effort to further bury Anderson's friend Ric Flair's career.

dirty sock) and knocked out everyone except Stevie. Neither man bothered to pin anyone, however—they just stood there looking at all the corpses. Warrior then appeared in his magical cloud of smoke. Hogan tore his jacket off, but then the smoke rose again, and when it cleared Warrior was gone, and Hogan was left just holding the jacket. Warrior then ran out from the dressing room. Yes, they went to the trouble of hiring a fake Warrior (the artist formerly known as Renegade) just to do this cartoonish spot. Hogan, with help from Ed Leslie, escaped from the cage and locked Warrior in. Despite magically appearing and disappearing just moments earlier in his magical cloud of smoke, Warrior was now unable to get out of the cage. So he got angry, growled, and finally kicked his way out of the cage. They began to brawl in the aisle, and during this short melee, Warrior, despite having displayed no athletic ability whatsoever in this brawl, somehow managed to both twist his ankle and tear his biceps. Once everyone in the ring emerged from the smoke-induced coma, Page pinned Stevie with the diamond cutter. The crowd's reaction to this whole match took the form of intense and deep-seated hatred.

"WHAT AN EVENT!" Tony Schiavone screamed as the show concluded.

Not only was the action in the ring becoming atrocious, so was the television production. In particular, the *Thunder* prior to this show featured one of the most unintentionally hilarious screw-ups ever. Chris Jericho had been spoofing Goldberg by going to the ring for his matches accompanied by fat security guards (one of whom was a real-life ring crew worker who would go on to minor fame as "Ralphus"). The story line this particular evening was that Jericho got lost trying to find his way to the ring and ended up locked outside the building. Unfortunately, the door didn't really lock, so when he pulled on the handle, it opened right up. He quickly closed it and pretended it was locked, pounding on the door and screaming to be let inside. Apparently, someone inside thought he was really locked out, because a door about ten feet away opened, and this dude stuck his head out. Jericho had to pretend like he didn't see him. It gets better. His opponent, Wrath, got sick of waiting in the ring and ran backstage to find Jericho. They did a chase scene outside the building. Finally, they figured the camera was shut off, so Jericho stopped, and Wrath ran past him. Then they both turned and nonchalantly started walking back towards the camera. Problem was, the camera wasn't off, and this whole fiasco was broadcast to millions.

The string of horrible programming continued the next week on *Nitro*, with an angle in which Warrior, using his magical cloud of smoke, not only kidnapped E. Harrison Leslie, but instantly teleported him from the ring to the rafters. To accomplish this feat, they had Warrior in the rafters hugging a blow-up doll dressed like Leslie—one of the more surreal visuals fans would ever see. It was never explained how any of this was intended to sell tickets. Later, to further hype the Hogan versus Warrior match planned for *Halloween Havoc* the following month, Hogan was brutally attacked—by E. Harrison Leslie. The rest of the show featured only slightly more logical yet ultimately inexplicable booking.

Scott Hall was arrested again the following week for allegedly causing $2,000 in damage by keying a limo outside the Diamond Mine strip club in Orlando during a drunken fit. This led his ex-wife Dana to post a message on an nWo fan site, basically taking WCW to task for still employing him when he obviously had some serious issues to deal with. WCW was so outraged by Hall's behavior that they continued to portray him as a drunk on TV.

As nonsensical as all the previous Warrior segments were, however, nothing could compare to the October 5 *Nitro*, which showcased quite possibly the most absurd angle in wrestling history. The idea was that Hogan

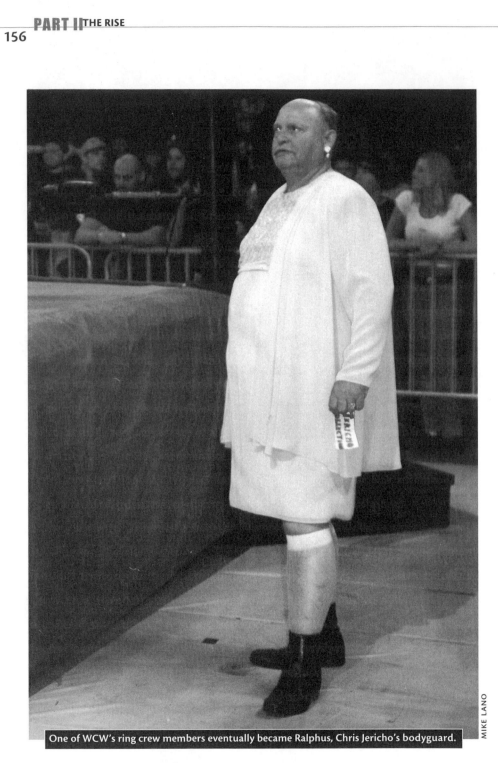

One of WCW's ring crew members eventually became Ralphus, Chris Jericho's bodyguard.

MIKE LANO

couldn't find Leslie, so he was searching for him throughout the building. He ended up in Leslie's dressing room, and in the mirror he imagined that he saw the Warrior. As he was screaming at this vision, Bischoff walked in. He could not see Warrior, however, and thought Hogan was going crazy. This is all fine and dandy, except for the fact that *viewers at home could see Warrior in the mirror*. Of course, this would mean that Hogan was not, in fact, crazy, but that Bischoff was. Or Bischoff was right, and the fans were crazy too. But then, to confuse matters, the Warrior in the mirror disappeared, but Hogan could still see him, which basically meant that everyone involved, from Hogan to Bischoff to the fans, was crazy. In the end, it didn't matter if they were crazy or not, because fans in the arena were booing like crazy.

And this was becoming a very bad trend. Instead of the "good heat" that the nWo had generated a year earlier, this was "bad heat," the kind of heat that results in fans feeling ripped off, angry, and annoyed. Some crowds even began to chant "*NITRO* SUCKS!"

WCW did themselves no favors with *Halloween Havoc*; it almost felt as if the company was trying to see how bad a show they could put on that people would still pay to see. The Hogan versus Warrior rematch was so far beyond atrocious that it actually made their War Games match look like a Ric Flair versus Ricky Steamboat classic. The bout went on for nearly fifteen minutes, and it's no exaggeration that these two forty-plus-year-old men could realistically only go about fifteen seconds. Without question, the highlight of the match was a truly ridiculous spot that looked as though two kindergartners were on the playground. Remember when you were in preschool and you learned how to do the log roll? The one where you lie on your back and just roll over and over sideways? Well, Hogan tried to drop an elbow on Warrior, but Warrior log-rolled out of the way. Hogan decided to try again, and again, Warrior log-rolled out of the way. Suddenly—and I can only imagine the time and effort that went into plotting this spot backstage—Warrior reversed direction and began to *roll towards Hogan*. You'd think that Hogan would have several options at this point: step to the left; step to the right; or, perhaps, jump. Instead, he seemed stricken with fear, because he just stood there as Warrior rolled right into his legs, making him fall down.

If that wasn't bad enough, a spot was planned for later in which Hogan was supposed to throw fire at Warrior. In wrestling, fire is created by lighting a piece of flash paper. In the corner, Hogan poured his fire-making para-phernalia out of a Zip-Loc baggie. Warrior came at him. The audience, surely on the edges of their seats, then witnessed Hogan throw a piece of flash paper at Warrior. You read that right: he forgot to light it on fire. The fans, who had been chanting "WARRIOR SUCKS!" and cheering Hogan earlier, booed loudly. Hogan tried again. This time, the paper lit on fire, but it ignited in his hand and burned out. Hogan looked terrified. Warrior was terrified too, and didn't know what to do.

Finally, Hogan's real-life wrestler nephew Horace ran in and hit Warrior with an incredibly weak chairshot, which Warrior sold like he'd been shot with a handgun. Hogan dove in to get the pin. Afterwards, he told Horace that he'd "passed the test," which begs the question: how bad could the match have been if he'd failed?

Before he'd agreed to do the job to Hogan at *Havoc*, Warrior had also demanded that a new contract pick up where his first one left off. WCW used him on TV less than a handful of times afterwards, so they basically paid him $1 million to agree to lose to Hogan and kill this feud off.

Much more damaging than the Warrior-Hogan fiasco, however, was the fact that WCW had decided—just a few days before the show—that they were going to go three and a half hours instead of the usual three. Fans at home were not alerted to this fact and grew concerned at about the two-hour and forty-five-minute mark, as Hogan and Warrior were still in the ring, and it didn't appear that Goldberg versus Page for the WCW title was going to happen anytime soon. To make matters *significantly* worse, nobody bothered to tell *the cable companies*, because at 11:00 P.M. EST, 25 percent of the folks who had purchased the show suddenly found themselves looking at a blank screen. Local outlets were flooded with angry phone calls and had to struggle to come up with some sort of offer to placate the fans, most of which demanded full refunds. When all was said and done, it's estimated that WCW lost almost $1.5 million in pay-per-view revenue because of this simple miscommunication.

In a dilemma about what to do, WCW decided to air the Page versus Goldberg match for free on *Nitro* the following evening. The cable industry was not cool with this because a replay of the show was scheduled to air Tuesday night, and they figured airing it sooner would kill Tuesday's buy rate. WCW agreed not to air the Warrior versus Hogan match for free— possibly the smartest thing they'd done in ten years of business. Despite having aired the *Bash at the Beach* main event three months earlier on *Nitro*, announcer Tony Schiavone, who was losing credibility with the fans on a weekly basis, claimed that this would be the first time in history that a PPV match was ever shown on free TV.

Goldberg versus Page went shockingly well, not only in the ring, but also in the ratings. Its quarter-hour on *Nitro* set yet another new cable viewership record, a 7.18, beating out the Hogan versus Goldberg match from the Georgia Dome in July. The rating helped win the night, as *Nitro* did a 5.06 to *Raw*'s 4.48, which, despite the loss of $1.5 million the night before, no doubt made Eric Bischoff very happy.

With Warrior now defeated, Hogan was left looking for something to do. And that something came to him in early November, when former wrestler and commentator Jesse Ventura was elected Governor of Minnesota. Hogan and Ventura had been professional rivals for years, and now, Jesse had finally accomplished something that Hogan could only dream about. Hogan, however, was undeterred. He announced on *Nitro* that he was running for President of the United States. The show ended up being crushed by *Raw* with the WWF's biggest-winning margin in history: a 5.03 to a 4.06. Worse, Hogan's segment was beaten 4.3 to 4.1 by *Raw*'s battle between lifetime mid-carders Val Venis and Steve Blackman. This was a super big blow for Hogan, because he didn't attend the prior week's show, and it was beaten in the ratings, and he wanted to convince people that his absence had been the reason for the decline.

Even though the ratings were slowly beginning to decline, the company was still doing incredibly well in terms of ticket sales. In particular, the November 30 *Nitro* at the Astrodome in Houston drew a whopping 32,076 fans. Between the gate and the merchandise, this made them almost $1 million. And what did WCW give those 32,076 fans? You guessed it— a horrible show. There were two main events, Steiner versus Hall and Goldberg versus Bam Bam Bigelow, and neither took place. Fans were outraged and pelted the ring with garbage after the show.

The fans also did this following the December 14 *Nitro*, the lowlight of which was when Ric Flair suffered a fake heart attack, which the company tried to pass off as real. It started with an interview that set up the match he was going to have at *Starrcade* with Bischoff, playing off the real-life lawsuit that the vast majority of fans really didn't know a thing about.

Whoooo! "Nature Boy" Ric Flair was the man most fans viewed as the very embodiment of WCW. Due to petty jealousies of those in charge, however, his career was continually undermined, causing irreparable damage to the promotion.

JOHN LAWSON

Seeing him as nothing more than a mid-carder, Eric Bischoff released Steve Austin, who then moved to the World Wrestling Federation and became the biggest grossing wrestler of all time. Oops.

JEFF COHEN

Despite claims of Tony Schiavone and Eric Bischoff, Mick Foley (shown here in his Cactus Jack persona) most definitely put asses in seats; unfortunately, he did so for WCW's competition. After being fired by Bischoff, Foley went to the WWF and became one of their biggest stars as Mankind.

JEFF COHEN

Awesome on the microphone and in the ring, Chris Jericho was proclaimed "too small" to main-event. When he left for the WWF, he almost immediately became one of their biggest stars. You might be noticing a trend.

JOHN LAWSON

JOHN LAWSON

WCW spent around $3 million per year to obtain the services of Bret "The Hitman" Hart, the hottest free agent in wrestling at one time. They then proceeded to do absolutely nothing with him.

One of WCW's very few homegrown talents, Bill Goldberg was the promotion's best chance for a bright future. Those in charge, however, made sure to undermine his popularity, until eventually he was just another guy fans wouldn't pay to see.

JOHN LAWSON

JOHN LAWSON

Dubbed a "vanilla midget" by booker Kevin Nash, Chris Benoit was shunted to the background of the WCW hierarchy despite being one of the greatest technical wrestlers of all time.

JOHN LAWSON

Lex Luger's jump to WCW on the inaugural *Nitro* telecast was one of those shocking events that record numbers of fans tuned in for.

MIKE LANO

A major star for WCW during its waning years, Diamond Dallas Page couldn't wait to be part of WCW's invasion of the WWF. His joy would be short-lived, thanks to some of the most horrific booking the wrestling business had ever seen.

MIKE LANO

JOHN LAWSON

The *Nitro* girls would open telecasts dancing and energizing the fans. That was fine. Later, bookers would decide that certain girls needed to wrestle and have storyline miscarriages. That was not fine.

Look at this man. Would you say something that might piss him off? Neither would anyone in WCW, which ironically led to the biggest push of Scott Steiner's career.

JOHN LAWSON

Scott Hall led the nWo invasion of WCW, and was a hell of a charismatic wrestler to boot. Eventually, though, his "personal demons" caught up with him. WCW, in their infinite wisdom, decided to book him as a drunk—a part that Hall played to perfection.

JOHN LAWSON

Sting was arguably the company's top draw, and led WCW to their largest buy rate ever at *Starrcade 97*. Thanks largely to Hulk Hogan, that match turned out to be the beginning of the end for both Sting's career and WCW as a whole.

JOHN LAWSON

Rey Mysterio Jr., shown left in his traditional, colorful luchador outfit, was dubbed "unmarketable" by Eric Bischoff, who made him take his mask off. Strangely, Bischoff did little to market the newly unmasked Rey Mysterio Jr. (who looked to be around 12 years old), either.

INSET MIKE LANO   JOHN LAWSON

Formerly a *Nitro* girl, the lovely Stacy Keibler (with her 42" legs) was one of the few reasons fans tuned in during WCW's dying days.

JOHN LAWSON

Bischoff came out, and Flair chased him away from ringside. Flair, who had actually been running really fast, came back looking none the worse for wear or even out of breath, but then began to clutch his chest. Nobody believed it was real, so the company went further out of their way than usual to convince folks that it was, to the point of telling Flair's friends backstage that he really was having an honest-to-God heart attack. Some had actually even started to cry, thinking Flair was going to die. The point of all this was never made clear, unless it was meant to suggest that Bischoff would have the advantage in their match.

Flair, despite suffering that horrible heart attack, was back on *Nitro* the next week at the TWA Dome. This *Nitro* drew nearly 30,000 fans, and it broke the company gate record with $914,389 in ticket sales. Flair returned to an enormous pop and cut one of his great promos, literally crying while hyping up his match with Bischoff at *Starrcade* one last time. On commentary, Tony Schiavone said it was clear he'd never had a heart attack. The original plan, as stupid as this sounds, was to claim that Eric had poisoned him the week before.

Shortly after the Ric Flair heart attack angle, someone in the company really did die. Referee and former wrestler Brady Boone, who began working for Crockett in the mid-'80s, was killed in a car accident. Gene Okerlund made mention of his death on the WCW Hotline. His comment was that nobody had ever said a bad word about Brady Boone because nobody had ever heard of him.

Amazingly, the bogus Ric Flair heart attack/poisoning did little to give *Nitro* a ratings advantage, and the show had settled into a pattern of finishing a point or so behind *Raw* every week. As you can imagine, Bischoff was not pleased, and decided that changes needed to be made, and fast.

Unfortunately, these changes had nothing to do with fixing the atrocious shows the company was presenting. No, a completely different plan was in the works: the "time was right," he believed, to beat Goldberg.

Actually, that had been the plan for a long time: Hogan would drop the strap to Goldberg at the Georgia Dome; then he'd win it back at *Starrcade*. But somewhere along the way, there was a change in plans.

Perhaps you're thinking that the change in plans was for Hogan not to beat Goldberg after all. Perhaps you're thinking that Goldberg was such a good ratings draw, house show draw, and merchandise seller that it would have been foolish to take the belt from him and put it back on Hogan, whose drawing power had waned over the past several months.

You would be wrong.

The change of plans was to have Goldberg drop the title not to horrible wrestler Hogan, but to horrible wrestler Kevin Nash. Nash had just been named new head booker for the promotion, and once this happened everything backstage went into disarray. It went into disarray for fake reasons, however—not real reasons. Confused?

Basically, Nash, Hogan, and Bischoff came up with a scenario to work all the boys. No, not to work the fans in an effort to make money, but to work the boys in, well, an effort to make them not so miserable. You see, pretty much everyone on the undercard hated Hogan. They saw him as a guy who was past his prime and needed to step aside to make room for new stars. Nash, however, was such a great politician that everyone liked him. In fact, no matter what he did, you'd be hard-pressed to find a person backstage who didn't think he was a really cool guy. So the plan was to give Nash the booking position, and Hogan, "outraged with his loss of power," would pretend to quit. He'd disappear for a while, Nash would make everyone happy, and morale would improve. Of course, the longer-term plan was to eventually bring Hogan back and put the belt on him again.

Also, Hogan needed time off to film *Muppets in Space*.

Yes, of course we're serious.

So Nash got the book, and, as most bookers do, he began to write story lines designed to make himself the center of attention. His main idea was to set up his own big win over Goldberg for the belt at *Starrcade*. Step one was to put himself over in the three-ring number-one-contender battle royal at *World War III*, a show that ended up better than expected seeing as it was expected to be the worst ever. Step two was to book himself as a man who ended win streaks. Coincidentally, there was a man on *Nitro* who had been on a win streak lately and was starting to get over. His name was Wrath. He fell to Nash in 4:45 the next night. That was the end of him getting over. Step three was to build Goldberg up as a monster. After all, there's nothing cool about beating a nobody; if you're going to beat someone, you might as well beat a monster. That was accomplished by a 1:34 victory over Giant on *Nitro* the next evening (which was also done because everyone figured Giant would jump to the WWF when his contract expired in February). Step four was to start to write wacky story lines for many of the mid-carders, stories that might not always play out, but that would at least make the guys feel like they were being utilized.

With Nash doing his part, Hogan's job was to go on the *Tonight Show* and simultaneously announce that he was running for President and retiring from wrestling forever. It would only be the third time he had retired forever from wrestling (which isn't too bad when you consider guys like the legendary Terry Funk, who retired and unretired so many times that they eventually lost count). Hogan was asked a few hardball political questions, like whether he was a Democrat or a Republican, and all the time and research he'd devoted to his campaign came through in his answer: "Right now, I'm right in the middle."

"What kind of a lame answer is that?" Leno asked.

Most saw Hogan's "retirement" for what it really was: a carefully orchestrated political maneuver that would benefit exactly one person in the long run: himself. Say what you will about Hogan, but few in the history of wrestling have proven so many times over how adept they are at playing the game. Hogan had taken himself off TV at many times when it was pretty clear the ratings were about to drop (for example, earlier in the year when *Nitro* was being preempted for the NBA playoffs). Obviously, he'd later state that the reason things tanked was that he was gone, thereby increasing his perceived value.

Starrcade was considered a far better show than anyone expected going in. The opener, Kidman versus Rey Mysterio Jr. versus Juvie in a three-way for the Cruiserweight belt, was one of the best matches of the year. Flair versus Bischoff was decent only because Flair, at forty-nine, was still one of the best workers in the world when he had to be. Of course, even as great as he was, Flair still lost the match after Curt Hennig ran in and gave Bischoff a pair of brass knux to KO Flair behind the ref's back.

And then there was the main event. Goldberg destroyed Nash for a long time until both Disco Inferno and Bam Bam Bigelow ran in. Both were slaughtered. Then, as both Goldberg and the referee were distracted, Scott Hall snuck in and zapped Goldberg with a cattle prod. You read that right, a *cattle prod*. Nash delivered a formerly banned powerbomb and got the pin.

The streak was over—in more ways than one.

When Kevin Nash beat Bill Goldberg to end the legendary win streak, there were basically two schools of thought. The vast minority, consisting of Kevin Nash, his close friends, and immediate family, thought that it was a great idea. To the majority, however, it was really stupid. At the time, however, nobody grasped it for what it really was: the beginning of the end of WCW.

"When they ended Goldberg's streak, it was the biggest mistake that company ever made," recounted WCW announcer Bobby Heenan in an interview years later. "The fans weren't tired of him—they were buying tickets to see him, buying his shirts, chanting his name. But some people didn't care about that."

The beginning of the end for WCW was like the beginning of the end for King Kong. Planes were swarming everywhere. He was teetering there on the edge of the Empire State Building, and he'd just put the girl down. Though his immediate future was not looking good, at the moment, everything was fine. Then he got hit with the first bullet. Then he was bombarded with multiple bullets in a very short period of time . . . and that was all she wrote.

Goldberg losing the belt was that first bullet.

And another barrage of bullets was about to hit the company in a very short period of time.

PART III

The Fall

"The biggest mistake was that they had leadership where all the generals were guys who had never been in a battle. They never had anybody who knew what they were doing. There's nobody who ever understood wrestling or the minds of wrestling fans. They never understood the nature of the business."

—Bret Hart, WCW Wrestler 1997-2000

CHAPTER 5

1999: Gambling on a Savior

On the surface, 1998 had been a hugely successful year. Although WCW made every stupid mistake that could possibly be made, attendance was up 47 percent over 1997, ratings were up 56 percent, buy rates were up 18 percent, a whopping 49 percent of house shows had sold out, and the average house show gross was up 90 percent. It's not difficult to see why those on the inside thought there was nothing to worry about.

But the sins of 1998 began to take their toll in 1999. Even worse, 1999 was the year that WCW made some of their most horrendous decisions yet, decisions that, instead of turning things around as hoped, actually sped up the company's decline. Consider this: just two years earlier, WCW was the number-one wrestling company in the entire world. In the 365 days of this year, they managed to lose no less than $15 million—more money than any promotion had ever lost in the history of the business.

In a way, it was shockingly similar to the way Jim Crockett Promotions had booked itself into oblivion exactly ten years earlier. They hired a booker (Dusty Rhodes in the mid-'80s, Nash in 1998) who put himself and his friends over at the expense of all the other talent; they booked screw-job after screw-job, run-in after run-in, show after show, until it drew the infamous "wrong kind of heat," the kind that drives fans away; they put all the old, stale talent on top and pushed them hard despite the fact that the ratings made it clear that fans wanted new blood; and all that exciting, young international talent that Bischoff had scoured the globe for in 1996 had been booked so far into oblivion that they were pretty much unsalvageable. At least with JCP, the wrestlers worked hard and did their best even as the ship sank. But in WCW, things were so bad by mid-year that virtually everyone—from talent to the office personnel—had mentally given up.

Bischoff, however, was anything but ready to surrender. He opened the year with another crew meeting, in which he dropped a major bombshell: WCW had struck a deal with NBC, a deal that would give them six prime-time specials over the course of the year. Not only that, those specials would compete directly against WWF pay-per-views like *Wrestlemania* and *Summerslam*. It would be like the old days of the *Clash of the Champions* specials, giving WCW a huge advantage over the WWF. He claimed that WCW got it because the network wanted nothing to do with the WWF due to the raunchy nature of their programming. He said that while all the swearing and insanity might benefit the WWF at the moment, in the long run, it would work against them. Bischoff was right in the end, but unfortunately for him and many others it worked not only against the WWF, but also against the wrestling industry as a whole. The first special was to air on February 14.

Seemingly rejuvenated by the news of the deal, Bischoff came up with a master plan to restore WCW to its former glory. He would revolutionize wrestling just like he'd done in 1996 by—yep, you guessed it— doing everything he'd done in 1996 all over again.

The scene was the Georgia Dome in Atlanta (or, as it appeared on WCW business cards that year, "Altanta"), home of the now-legendary Hogan versus Goldberg bout. The date was January 4, 1999. And, as Bischoff had hoped, WCW truly revolutionized the wrestling business on this date. Unfortunately, it wasn't a positive revolution, but a new example of just how quickly a formerly successful wrestling promotion could fall.

In hindsight, this show was probably the single most destructive *Nitro* in the history of the company. Yes, other shows were far worse, but this was the one that, more than any other, started the ball rolling towards the company's inevitable doom. It's a cliché, but this program was a disaster of epic proportions.

Nothing much happened in the first hour. Then, just as *Raw* was about to start, some cops showed up and announced that they had a warrant for Goldberg's arrest on an unspecified charge. Goldberg didn't even ask what the charge was. Off he went. So all the fans at home suddenly saw half of the main event they'd so eagerly anticipated (Goldberg versus Nash in Goldberg's first shot at regaining the WCW title he'd lost at *Starrcade*) being escorted to jail just as *Raw* was about to begin. As it turns out, he was accused of the "aggravated stalking" of the now-heel Miss Elizabeth (originally, she was to accuse him of raping her, but Goldberg put the ixnay on that one immediately). Nash, still trying to be a good guy, came out and told Ric Flair, who had become story line president of the company, that Hulk Hogan must be behind this, and that he therefore wanted a "warm-up" match with him prior to the main event. Hogan, who hadn't been on TV in some time, just happened to be in the building that evening. He came out and said that he'd planned to announce his retirement as well as his running mate that evening (yes, he was still on the President kick), but now he was appalled at what that "sexual deviant" Goldberg had done, and he wanted to beat up that "spoon" Kevin Nash for accusing him of being behind it. Yes, those were his actual words.

Back at the police station, Liz changed her story multiple times, and finally, after being threatened with perjury, she admitted to having made everything up. So the race was on: could Goldberg make it back to the Georgia Dome in time for his main event? The unintentional comedy here was that, earlier in the show, it had been revealed that the police station was across the street from the arena.

Goldberg was somehow unable to get back in time, even though he had thirty minutes to walk several dozen feet. Perhaps the crosswalk light was broken. Regardless, Nash and Hogan came out for their epic encounter. About one minute into the match, Hogan touched Nash in the chest with one finger, and Nash took this enormous bump like he'd been hit with a cannonball. On the bright side, it was probably the biggest bump Nash would take all year. Hogan covered him and won the belt. Afterwards, Hogan and Nash hugged, revealing that it had been a setup all along. Goldberg finally arrived and laid waste to everyone in the ring until being attacked by his newest foe—the old, immobile, washed-up Lex Luger.

Fans had paid a record $930,735 to see this show. To say they were outraged by what transpired would be a strong understatement.

If everything that happened in the ring wasn't bad enough, Bischoff also made a huge miscalculation in commentary. As you'll recall, early in the war Bischoff had done something unheard of—he gave away results of taped *Raw*s on live *Nitro*s. The reasoning (aside from this being an attempt to be cutting-edge and cool) was that this would convince fans that there was no reason to watch the opposition. Since this was Bischoff's 1996 revisited, he went back to that strategy by having Tony Schiavone reveal to the fans that in the *Raw* main event, Mick Foley was going to beat Rock to win the WWF title. Worse, he had Schiavone bury him, saying a man like that holding a world title was a complete joke.

The problems here were twofold. First, Foley was greatly respected by hardcore fans, so many of them switched channels to *Raw* not only to see him win the belt, but also to stick one to WCW. Among casual fans, Foley was a big babyface hero, and they really wanted to see him finally win what they felt he'd deserved for a long time. They switched channels as well. Final tally: *Raw* did a 5.76, a brand-new ratings record, to *Nitro*'s 4.96. The biggest gap, not surprisingly, immediately followed Schiavone's announcement that Foley The Joke would win the belt, as *Raw* hit a 6.2 opposite *Nitro*'s 4.1. In total, Schiavone's announcement, designed to keep fans from jumping to *Raw*, effectively led almost half a million of them to immediately do just that.

In other bad news, Eddy Guerrero was involved in a serious car accident that week that almost killed him, both at the time and later down the road. He fell asleep at the wheel on New Year's Eve and crashed in a scene so horrific that EMTs on the scene couldn't believe he'd survived. He did recover, but rushed back to the ring way too early and ended up in tremendous pain. This pain led to an addiction to painkillers that resulted in him later being fired from the WWF. He finally checked himself into rehab, cleaned himself up, and was hired back. Unlike many others, he became one of wrestling's great success stories, and since beating the disease, he's frequently stated that the company saved his life.

The first PPV of the year was *Souled Out* on January 17 in Charleston, West Viginia. Recall the lesson: when wrestling is hot, a promotion can seemingly do no wrong. As horrible as things had been the previous year, this event was a sellout, with 10,255 fans in attendance. Unlike at the Georgia Dome, at least these fans got a good show. The Kidman versus Rey Mysterio Jr. versus Psicosis versus Juventud Guerrera match for the

Cruiserweight title was exceptional. They even had a rare good main event that saw Goldberg—who was underrated as a performer even back then—beat Scott Hall in a ladder match where the idea was to climb up and grab a taser hanging from the ceiling. In commentary, it was teased that Goldberg wouldn't be able to make it as they'd shot a video before the show of him screaming in his locker room and holding his knee. Tony Schiavone theorized that he'd been attacked by someone.

"Or maybe he just fell down," Schiavone added.

At this point, Bischoff was willing to do anything to unseat *Raw* in the ratings, so he continued the very dangerous practice of giving away matches that fans likely would have paid to see for free. Case in point: the following evening's *Nitro* had Ric Flair challenge Bischoff to a match in which the loser would get his head shaved bald. Flair versus Bischoff had been done numerous times, but with the proper build, a hair match between the two would theoretically have drawn some money on PPV, or at least popped a rating on TV. After all, in his entire career, Flair, famous for his bleached-blonde hair, had never shaved his head, and most people really hated Eric and would have loved to see him humiliated. WCW, however, had different plans. Instead of properly building the bout, Ric's oldest son, David, came out and demanded the match; then he got the win a few minutes later, and the Horseman shaved Eric bald.

David Flair was nineteen, and despite being the son of arguably the greatest wrestler to ever lace up a pair of boots, he never had much interest in stepping into the ring. He actually wanted to become a state trooper, but shortly after being convinced to do the *Nitro* show, he decided that wrestling wasn't so bad after all. The large paychecks probably helped. He decided to start training with WCW at the Power Plant, unaware of the curse of being the son of a legendary wrestler (nine times out of ten, the father's boots are way too big to fill). WCW, in their infinite wisdom, decided not to bother waiting until he'd trained for a while. They just kept putting him in the ring.

Even with giving away huge matches, WCW saw the ratings gap widen. Therefore, Bischoff decided to change directions. The latest idea to turn everything around instantly was to emulate the WWF as closely as possible. Prior to the February 1 *Nitro*, booker Nash called a meeting and announced that there would be some programming changes, most notably a move towards a more *Raw*-like program with lots of taped backstage vignettes. Therefore, everyone was going to have to show up on time so they could film their segments. On the very same night the speech about the pre-tapes was given, an angle was shot in which Flair sentenced Bischoff to sit over a dunk tank as his enemies threw baseballs at him. During the course of the two-hour broadcast, virtually none of the ball-throwers managed to even hit the target.

Other changes were made to give the shows a more "entertainment" feel. For instance, Stevie Ray had suddenly and mysteriously become a major part of *Nitro* (despite the fact that he wasn't a great worker by any stretch of the imagination). Not only was he given inordinate amounts of time in the ring, but he was also given tons of interview time. His promos were, well, interesting. He once identified Barbarian and Meng as "two fish-eating chumps from Gilligan's Island." Later, he would call Scott Steiner both "synthetic" (seemingly an accusation of steroid use) and also a "sad, sack-ass fruit booty" (seemingly an accusation of . . . well, we have no idea).

The pre-tapes were in full effect on the February 8 *Nitro*. However, there was an additional change: for whatever reason, it was decided that only fans at home would "see" the pre-tapes. The announcers, who had monitors sitting right there in front of them, were commanded to act as though they didn't see any of the stuff going on backstage. The fans were already conditioned to think that WCW announcers were morons, and this didn't help matters. The show was once again atrocious, but because *Raw* was preempted by the Westminster Dog Show, it did a 5.67 rating—almost a new record. Of course, the bad news was that this meant over eight million fans witnessed yet another horrible show. Instead of easing into the taped segments, it was total overkill to the point that, when it was over, it seemed like there had been more vignettes than wrestling matches.

Perhaps, though, the vignettes were better than what happened that night in the ring: Bret Hart lost the U.S. title to Roddy Piper in a terrible match after interference from Will Sasso. No doubt many of you are asking just who the hell Will Sasso is. He was a fat guy from a program called *Mad TV*, a show on which Bret had done a comedy skit a few weeks earlier. During said skit, Bret "went crazy for real" and "attacked" Sasso, using such "real life" fight moves as a sharpshooter leglock. So Sasso's "revenge" was to come to *Nitro*, somehow end up ringside, and cost Bret the match. Piper, who could barely move due to two bad hips (one of which had already been replaced), had to work almost thirteen minutes in great pain. It was terribly sad to watch.

Almost as sad as the look on the talents' faces when February 14 arrived. As you will recall, this was the date Bischoff was trumpeting as WCW's prime-time debut on NBC. Despite Bischoff's countless references to the date, it came and went—with n o special on NBC whatsoever. Bischoff claimed that they were merely "postponed," which was quickly—and correctly—translated by his wrestlers to mean "canceled and never mentioned again."

In the Wasteful Spending Department, the *WCW Latino* show was canceled, a show that most fans had zero clue even existed. It was a program the company had in development to air on the Spanish-language Telemundo station. It would feature many of EMLL (Empresa Mexicana de Lucha Libre)'s top wrestling stars. Bischoff spent $300,000 to create a fancy new set and began negotiations for wrestlers with EMLL promoter Paco Alonso. Shortly before the first taping, Alonso signed a deal with the WWF (which, coincidentally, was for a Super Astros lucha libre show that also ended up going bust) and pulled out all of his talent. The first taping was a disaster, so Bischoff scrapped the entire project. Telemundo was furious and threatened a lawsuit. To avoid any bad press, Turner came up with an idea: they'd air hour-long edited editions of *Nitro* with Spanish voice-overs for the sixteen weeks they'd promised programming. This would have been a fantastic plan if not for the fact that all the Mexican guys on *Nitro* worked their asses off week after week, and ultimately lost to the white guys week after week. In fact, even when the show was later renewed, showing that the Hispanic population had an interest in WCW programming, the burial of top lucha stars continued.

It was probably just as well, as *Nitro* was getting comically bad by this point; it seemed that every week, a new contender for worst-ever pro-wrestling show aired on television. The February 15 show reached a new low. The main angle was an intensely appalling and hideously long skit in which Hogan and the nWo, wearing ski masks, beat up Ric Flair in a field. If you're wondering what this had to do with wrestling, join the club. Fans at home were able to see this because it was all filmed by numerous cameramen, including one in a helicopter. Do not even ask how much money was spent on this. After the beating, the nWo unmasked—which begs the question why they wore ski masks in the first place—and ran off into the night. Flair was left in the field for one hour. We knew this because there was a cameraman with him, filming his body. The cameraman, however, did not offer any aid or call 911. Neither did the three unidentified friends who had been traveling with Ric in his limo prior to the attack, all of whom were apparently abducted by a UFO because they were never seen again. Finally, a redneck in a turnip truck (don't ask us, it was WCW's angle) picked Flair up and brought him back to *Nitro*. When he finally arrived, stumbling around and wielding an axe handle, Bobby Heenan—who, like all the other announcers, wasn't allowed to see the taped segments—wanted to know if he was drunk. Instead of making a babyface comeback, Flair and all the rest of the Horsemen were treated to another beating.

When the show was over, most involved thought it had been a huge success. But the ratings told a different story. *Raw* did a record 5.90 to *Nitro*'s 3.90—the biggest gap in the history of the war. There was no denying that wacky, skit-laden shows were not what the public wanted to see, and so the very next week, things were back to "normal" (meaning only a few crappy skits and the usual amount of crappy matches). The ratings were also back to "normal," which by this point meant that *Raw* only beat *Nitro* by a million viewers or so.

Still, those in power felt there were other reasons for the 3.90 rating, pointing to guys like Flair, Bret, Benoit, Malenko, Jericho, and Raven who, not surprisingly, also happened to be among the best workers on the roster. Those six, in addition to Kanyon, Bam Bam Bigelow, and Roddy Piper, were singled out in a mid-February booking meeting as guys who needed to be cut off at the legs (not literally, although if Nash could have literally done so, he might have).

Of course, as WCW kept getting trounced in the ratings, the last thing they really needed to do was continue to push the old stale guys while killing off the younger rising stars. Word spread, and the locker room morale sank lower than ever. Benoit and Malenko were outraged when word got around that Nash had referred to them as the "vanilla midgets" (a slang term for small, boring guys), and it seemed more certain than ever that Jericho, their close friend, would get the hell out of Dodge when his deal came due.

Most of the undercard guys were beginning to despise Nash, feeling he was only there to push his close friends (true) and bury the talented workers (also true). Nash, of course, denied this and blamed Hogan. Hogan, he said, had control over all his own story lines, and there was nothing anyone could do about that. It was ruining the shows, he lamented. There was also concern because Bischoff, seemingly having given up all hope himself, was spending less and less time at *Nitro* and more and more time in Hollywood. Everyone figured he knew the ship was going down and was working hard to make sure he'd have a lifeboat to fall back on when it was fully submerged.

One man who managed to get out of WCW before it all hit the fan was Paul Wight, a.k.a. the Giant, who made his WWF debut at the *St. Valentine's Day Massacre* PPV from Memphis on February 14. He came from under the ring, interfering in a Vince McMahon versus Steve Austin cage match and accidentally assisting Austin's win. The WWF, having had so much success with Andre the Giant, had always had an eye on Wight. McMahon repeatedly ridiculed Wight's WCW run, saying the idiots there had no idea how to book a man as a giant. He then proceeded to spend several years booking Wight (who took on the ring name Big Show) a million times worse than WCW had done on their most inept day. In fact, just weeks after his debut, he was presented as just another big doofus doing a clean pinfall job to Austin.

WCW's burial of their talented workers continued on February 21 at the *Superbrawl* PPV. Benoit and Malenko beat WCW Tag champions Barry Windham and Hennig in a nontitle match to win a title shot against them. The title match took place thirty seconds after the first match, and was over in the blink of an eye, as Windham hit Malenko with a belt and pinned him. Both Benoit and Malenko ended up looking like goofs. Months earlier, the plan had been for them to win a tournament for the vacant belts. Plans changed. Nash and Hall beat Rey Mysterio and Konnan to win Rey's mask. Rey, unmasked, looked about fourteen years old, but apparently Bischoff felt he was more marketable that way than as a superhero-like luchador whose mask would sell en masse at the merchandise stand. Hall won the U.S. title from an immobile Piper in an atrocious match. And, in the main event, Hogan beat Flair to retain the World title when David Flair zapped his dad with a taser and joined the nWo. This was also the pay-per-view debut of one Torrie Wilson, a former fitness model who would go on to become one of the biggest female stars in wrestling history, and eventually appear in one of *Playboy*'s biggest issues ever. In the grossest sight imaginable, she made out with David afterwards.

Despite all the damage they had done with their string of horrific shows, *Superbrawl* was a huge success: its 1.1 buy rate nearly beat out the WWF's *St. Valentine's Day Massacre* that had featured the Austin versus McMahon cage match. The office was jubilant.

What they did not know, however, was that this would be the last great buy rate the company would ever draw.

Following *Superbrawl*, Bischoff attempted his latest publicity ploy. Shockingly, however, it had nothing to do with *Nitro*. Instead, Goldberg appeared on *The Tonight Show* and challenged Steve Austin to a fight. Goldberg had never wanted to issue the challenge, rightly feeling that it made him look like a lesser star, but Nash and Bischoff made it clear that he had to. So he did, but with such a lack of enthusiasm that it came off as lame. Then, to make matters worse, after Tony Schiavone hyped it up like crazy on *Nitro*, WCW never showed footage of the challenge or even bothered to mention who had been challenged. The majority of fans at home hadn't watched Leno, and ended up with no earthly idea what was going on. The WWF, obviously, never acknowledged it.

One could argue that it was good that WCW never showed footage of the incident because it would have made them look like clowns. That is probably true. The bad news, however, is that WCW had a bad habit of never showing mainstream footage of *anything*—even stuff that would have made them look cool or hip. Whenever the WWF received free outside publicity, they milked it for all it was worth. WCW's unwritten policy was apparently to just ignore it.

JOHN LAWSON

The WCW announce crew of Tony Schiavone (left) and Bobby Heenan (right). Suffice to say, these two did not care for each other, and Heenan came to hate working for the company. Said Heenan years later: "I just gave up, because they (WCW management) didn't care, and they didn't know what they were doing."

"I remember one time Goldberg met Mark McGuire, who was on the verge of breaking the home run record and was in the news literally every day," recalls Bobby Heenan. "McGuire was a huge mark for wrestling. He and

Goldberg met up before a game, did some batting practice. Had this happened in the WWF, they'd have filmed everything, probably had Goldberg and McGuire going to Louisville to pick out bats. But we never showed anything. We weren't allowed to make mention of it, because it wasn't WCW's idea."

Around this time, Nash realized just how much heat he was getting backstage and attempted to do something about it. The February 22 *Nitro* saw him put over Rey Mysterio. The idea here was twofold: first, it was a "reward" for Mysterio, as he'd agreed to lose his mask and become "marketable," and second, it was a way for Nash to show the crew that he was willing to do a job for anyone, even someone (almost literally) half his size. Nash went for a powerbomb, but Rey punched him repeatedly in the head, and Nash fell onto his back for a fluke pin. In reality, it meant nothing, but Nash used it for pretty much the rest of his career to point out what a "great company guy" he was.

It should be noted, however, that losing his mask caused Rey all kinds of problems in his native Mexico. For instance, the following week, Mysterio and Psicosis had a very controversial match in Tijuana. The original plan was to bill it as mask versus mask and put Psicosis over clean, since Rey was already going to lose it five days earlier at *Superbrawl*. Mexican wrestling tradition, however, bars wrestlers from wearing masks after they've lost them (not that this doesn't happen regularly). Rival promoter Antonio Pena of AAA went to the newspapers and ratted out Mysterio, and the Box y Lucha (boxing and wrestling) Commission—a legit commission despite the fact that it oversees a fake sport (don't ask)—refused to let the match take place as planned. So it was decided instead to have Rey put his hair on the line against Psicosis' hair. For unknown reasons, the Commission put the kibosh on that one as well. Finally, it was decided to just do a straight match for Psicosis' WWA title, which Rey won. The fans in attendance, all aware of what had happened in WCW, booed Mysterio—formerly a huge babyface—nearly out of the building.

Although the *Nitro* featuring the Nash-Rey fiasco was better than the usual crapfest the show had become, WCW got destroyed in the ratings: 4.32 to *Raw*'s 6.32. At the time, the WWF had hit on their own winning formula: big stars (Steve Austin, Vince McMahon, Rock, and Mick Foley) combined with over-the-top raunchiness (half-naked women, transvestites, simulated sex, and more). In fact, things were getting so wild that the mainstream media were starting to take notice, and some of the WWF's own allies were pleading with them to tone it down. One, TSN in Canada, was so outraged that they began to heavily edit the shows (axing both language and entire segments) to the point that some of them in no way resembled the original broadcast.

Bischoff, in a pre-show *Nitro* meeting on March 1, again claimed that the WWF's strategy would backfire because sponsors would pull out within a year (his theory would eventually prove to be correct; it just took longer than he thought). Therefore, the company was going to change its course *again*. He went over a laundry list of things that would now be banned, including crotch-grabbing, talking about hoochies, and lewd dances. He said WCW was going to go in the opposite direction of the WWF, because even if their ratings went down, if they had sponsors and WWF didn't, they'd win. It was a good theory.

More real-life tragedy struck on February 22, when Richard Wilson, a.k.a. the Renegade and many-time "stunt double" for Warrior during his disastrous 1998 run, shot and killed himself after an argument with his girlfriend. He'd been released from his WCW contract weeks earlier and was said to be very despondent about it. In case you haven't noticed by now, the real-life casualties of this so-called wrestling war were beginning to pile up. By the time the Monday Night Wars ended, Rick Rude and Bobby Duncam Jr. would also be dead, and Bret Hart and Sid Vicious would both have suffered career-ending injuries.

Whether or not Bischoff even believed they had a chance to turn things around is debatable, as his trips to Hollywood were on the rise (his longtime pal Jason Hervey of *The Wonder Years* was shopping him around as—get ready—"The Golden Boy Who Saved Wrestling"), and in early March he took his daughter to France on vacation. This was not a several-day excursion in between major TV tapings; he simply left and didn't come back for weeks. This left Kevin Nash completely in charge of the company.

There's an old belief in wrestling that bookers shouldn't be on-screen talent themselves: it's almost impossible for them to do what's right for business, since what's right for business is usually not them. Virtually everyone in the company believed that Nash was slowly turning *Nitro* into a vehicle to get himself over, and since he was smart enough to understand that Hogan, no matter what, was always going to be around, he buddied up with Hulk and built the show around him as well.

Nash's first move was to present a *Nitro* that featured no wrestling in the first hour. None. Not a single solitary match. You might recall that *Nitro* was a wrestling show. Apparently, Nash thought that wrestling on this wrestling show was unnecessary, and he booked the show like this to prove that they'd draw the same rating if they had zero matches in the first hour as they would if there were ten. In lieu of actual, you know, wrestling, the infamous hour featured a video of some kids jumping around at a *Nitro* party; one of the *Nitro* girls talking about life while sitting on the grass with her dog; a Konnan music video; a video of Hogan making fun of Flair; a skit in which Buff Bagwell and Scott Steiner got arrested and were told by the cops that they could get off the hook if they became cops themselves (Fatty Arbuckle and Buster Keaton did this same story line, only they did it about seventy-five years earlier, and it was much more entertaining); a skit in which Hogan and Nash watched the video of Hogan making fun of Flair that had aired earlier; a skit in which Hogan, Nash, and Torrie went to a firing range; and a skit in which Torrie, Nash, and Hogan went to dinner. And then, at 9:00, the first thing to air was a skit in which Flair challenged Goldberg and began to do the one thing he didn't need to do: turn heel.

Raw obliterated the show by almost 2.5 points.

The Flair heel turn, though, would prove to be even more damaging in the long term than the lack of wrestling. Make no mistake about it: Ric Flair was one of the all-time great heel wrestlers; he knew exactly how to beg off and bump around to make his babyface opponent look a hell of a lot better than they sometimes really were. He worked this style for years, and fans grew to love him because he really was the very best, night-in and night-out, year after year. In 1999, however, Flair was fifty years old—a true living legend or elder statesman—and no matter how much he wanted to be the Ric Flair of old (and make no mistake, he was still damn good at it), fans had no interest in paying to boo him. Worse yet, he so badly wanted to work heel again that he convinced Hulk Hogan to turn babyface. Hogan was stale on top, and it was probably time to do something about it, but in the list of somethings that might be done to turn WCW around, this double-turn certainly wasn't near the top.

The turn took place at the *Uncensored* PPV on March 14' before a sellout 15,930 fans at Freedom Hall in Louisville, Kentucky. The good news was that it was a fun show with an insanely excited crowd—almost to the point you'd think you were watching a different promotion. The booking, as always, was ridiculous. As usual, the idea of *Uncensored* was that none of the matches were sanctioned because WCW executives were afraid things were going to get wild, and they wanted to wash their hands of the whole deal (in other words, just like real life). Of course, how three titles could change hands at an unsanctioned event was never explained. The main event was scheduled to be Hogan versus Flair in a First Blood match for the WCW title with a big stipulation: if Flair lost, he had to retire, and if he won, he got control of WCW forever. Yes, forever. For non–wrestling fans, in a First Blood match, two men wrestle, and the first guy to bleed loses. The irony of this was that Turner had clamped down on usage of the word "blood" on TV, so in the weeks leading up to the match, the announcers were unable to utter the "Blood" part of "First Blood." This is true. So during the match, which took place inside a cage, Flair got gashed in the head with some razor wire and began to bleed. The announcers, con-fused, couldn't figure out why the match was continuing. They would have been comforted to know that fans watching at home couldn't figure it out either. Then Hogan bled. Then a bunch of people ran out, including David Flair (whose helpful advice to Hogan was "HULK UP!") and Arn Anderson. Finally, Anderson threw a tire iron into Flair, which Flair used to knock out Hogan, get the pin (in a First Blood match, mind you), and win the belt. Sure enough, Flair—who'd been telling people backstage that he was *sure* he could pull off this double turn—was roundly booed.

The only exciting thing about the Spring Breakout *Nitro* from Panama City, Florida, on March 22 was that after Rey Mysterio Jr. beat Flair in a title match via DQ, he tossed him into the swimming pool that the ring was floating on. Some observers strongly believe that if a wrestler was thrown into a swimming pool on every single edition of *Nitro*, the company would still be alive today.

The Flair-Hogan double turn didn't help to slow the ratings plunge—it added to it. At this point, *Raw* was really beginning to pull away in the ratings battle, setting a brand-new ratings record: 6.51 to *Nitro*'s 3.51. If that wasn't embarrassing enough, the HHH versus X-Pac (Sean Waltman) *Raw* main event did a 6.47 to *Nitro*'s 2.85, one of the biggest gaps of all time. And what was *Nitro*'s main event? Dallas Page versus the newly turned–babyface Hulk Hogan. Hogan, of course, placed the blame on Page, no doubt saying that the rating proved he wasn't a main event–quality star.

Part of the reason for the ratings decimation—besides the obvious fact that *Nitro* had grown so hideous that more and more fans were giving up entirely on the product—was that WCW was foolishly throwing away the perfect opportunity to attract fans. As you'll recall, *Nitro* was three hours to *Raw*'s two. The final two hours were head-to-head, but WCW's first hour was completely and totally unopposed. Instead of using that first hour to, say, build up the rest of the show or present blow-away matches or angles that would compel fans to keep watching, they turned that free hour into a kind of pre-show, a sixty-minute period so forgettable that there wasn't any reason to even tune in. In fact, on the March 28 show, the announcers were instructed not to even talk about that day's events until the second hour began. Keep in mind, they had a full unopposed hour to go all-out promoting the Bret Hart versus Goldberg confrontation set to take place in Bret's native Canada with interviews and history packages. Instead, they aired horrible matches and lame Hogan skits.

After all the banter back and forth, the online accusations, and the radio show interviews, Dana Hall got back together with Scott. Mean Gene was so happy for the couple that he immediately requested fans drop $1.49 per minute to hear the details on the WCW Hotline.

The Bret–Goldberg angle was one of those things that could have led to monster business if anyone in the company had even the slightest clue. The backstory, obviously, was that WCW had dropped the ball on Bret literally since the day he'd signed his contract. You've surely noticed that since Montreal, very little has been written about Bret in this book, and that's because very little of importance happened. Despite being paid almost $3 million a year, he had been booked into oblivion. In the months leading up to this show, Nash had made it clear that he didn't think Bret was a draw and that his contract was completely unjustified.

Of course, that's the catch-22: if you don't believe someone justifies their paycheck and you utilize them accordingly, there's no way they'll ever possibly justify said paycheck. Bret had spoken with Bischoff about an idea he had for an angle that would lead to him actually becoming a main-event player in the company. Nash, upon hearing it, tried to kill it off (when Bret confronted him about this, he claimed he wasn't *really* trying to kill it, he was just working an angle since everyone assumed they had heat). Although Nash was booker, Bischoff still got final say, so in the end the angle went pretty much exactly as Bret had formulated it.

For one day, at least.

Bret, who was a heel at the time, came out for his interview. Since this *Nitro* was in Toronto, he got one of the biggest babyface reactions of the entire year from the crowd. He didn't even bother trying to remain a bad guy; instead, he recited the Canadian national anthem to deafening cheers; then he started to run down various guys, including Goldberg. Fans booed Goldberg's name in a thunderous manner, but since WCW wanted to keep him a good guy, Eric demanded they pipe in the fake "GOLDBERG!" chants louder than ever. Bret, in a line that got him some heat, said it was ridiculous for Goldberg to challenge Steve Austin, seeing as how he (Bret) had beaten Austin every time they had wrestled. Goldberg finally came out and speared him. The crowd did not like that one bit, but you wouldn't be able to tell this from watching on TV due to all the piped-in chants. After the spear, however, both guys just lay there dead. Finally, Bret recovered, turned Goldberg over, and counted his own pin. The crowd went crazy and counted along with him. Afterwards, Bret removed his shirt to reveal that he'd been wearing a steel plate.

"Hey, Bischoff," he growled into the house mic. "I quit!" Then he stormed off.

Regardless of the ridiculous notion that Bret would come to *Nitro* with a steel plate under his jersey so he could knock out Goldberg, some people in the company actually thought this was real. Part of that had to do with a loud argument between Bret and Eric backstage right after the segment, with no cameras present. Most everyone in the company, however, knew it for what it really was: another lame attempt to work the boys. Bret disappeared from TV for a while, in part because he had to undergo groin surgery that would keep him on the shelf for several months. Ultimately, nothing became of the angle, but for once, Bret's absence wasn't WCW's fault, and this time, the reasons behind it were devastatingly tragic.

On May 23, 1999, Bret Hart's brother Owen died. While any wrestling death is tragic, this one was different. Owen didn't die due to a heart problem likely brought on by excessive steroid abuse; he didn't overdose on the popular combination of alcohol and pain pills; he didn't die by any fault of his own. Owen James Hart died because he was a company man, a pawn in a ratings battle that had already been over for a long time.

The scene was the WWF's *Over the Edge* pay-per-view at Kemper Arena in Kansas City. The time was approximately 7:40 P.M. CST. Owen stood high in the rafters above the ring dressed up in a ridiculous blue superhero costume and hooked up to a harness. Early in his career he'd wrestled as the Blue Blazer, a masked, high-flying good guy. This was 1999, however, and masked high-flying good guys were not cool. Instead, they were comedy material. Owen, back in character, told children to drink their milk, and because guys who told children to drink their milk weren't cool anymore, he was a bad guy. He was, essentially, a spoof on the babyface Hulk Hogan, and his descent from the rafters was a spoof on the babyface Sting. The plan was for him to descend to the ring for his entrance, but then get "stuck" about ten feet above the canvas and do a pratfall once released. For days, Hart had been nervous about the stunt, but, as a model employee, the closest he ever came to refusing was when he told them he wouldn't do a second practice run-through on the day of the show.

Obviously, a pratfall from above the ring would require a quick-release mechanism. Those who watched Sting's previous descents will probably recall how long it took him to get his harness off once he reached the ground. He had to unhook the main harness, then the safety backup. Neither had a quick-release mechanism.

Tragically, the harness Owen was attached to on this evening was not designed to hold the weight of a 220-pound man; it was actually used on sailboats. As a video of him cutting a promo aired on the TitanTron, the harness released prematurely, and he fell seventy-one feet into the ring. The physicians on hand attended to him; then he was rushed to the hospital, where he was pronounced dead on arrival.

Moments after his body was taken through the curtain, in a moment still debated to this day, Vince McMahon made the decision to continue the show. Nobody involved, from the wrestlers to the announcers to the employees backstage to the fans, can likely remember very clearly much of what happened in the next two hours.

The next day's *Raw* was a strange show, seen as an example of damage control by some and as a beautiful tribute by others. They presented several straight-up wrestling matches with clean finishes, and in between, interviews with the wrestlers. Many of the wrestlers openly broke down and wept when talking about Owen. *Nitro* opened with a graphic and a three-bell salute; then Tony Schiavone offered his condolences to the family.

Hours after the accident occurred, Bischoff met Bret at the airport and chartered him a flight back to Calgary. He told him that he didn't expect him to come to *Nitro* at any point in the future and that he could take as much time off as needed to get through this. Bret strongly considered retirement, feeling he'd never get his passion for the business back, and it would be virtually impossible to ever feign anger toward someone during the course of a wrestling story line again. Obviously, all plans to do a Bret versus Goldberg program were shelved indefinitely.

///

Owen's death wasn't the only tragedy to hit the Hart family around this time. On April 5, Bret's brother-in-law Davey Boy Smith lay in the ICU at Calgary's Rockyview Hospital, being fed through an IV. It had been a rough few years for him. First, he suffered multiple knee injuries at the end of his WWF run in 1997. Then, he was so upset with what happened in Montreal that he requested his release from the company. Vince McMahon, generous soul that he is, said sure—but it would cost Smith $150,000 to get out of his contract. Smith paid up after he negotiated this down to $100,000. Things didn't end up any better in WCW, as he took a bodyslam during a match with Alex Wright at *Fall Brawl* and landed right on the trap door that was used to help Warrior magically appear and disappear. He crushed the C-9 and C-10 vertebrae in his back, and fractured four other vertebrae. To mask the pain, he was taking a laundry-list of pain medication, including morphine, and when he finally checked into rehab after his wife Diana tried to scare him straight by overdosing on 100 Xanax (not the ideal way to try to scare someone straight), he took three weeks to detox instead of the usual five days. On top of all that, he was suffering from a staph infection and was confined to a full-body cast. At the time, many speculated that his career was over, and he was in bad enough shape that there was some fear he might not survive. WCW, obviously deeply concerned, cited the ninety-day injury clause in his contract and immediately fired him via their usual delivery method, FedEx. This caused such an uproar that Bischoff immediately went on the defensive, saying he had no idea what rough shape Smith was in when he made his decision, and for a period of time at least, Davey Boy's checks kept coming.

Although Goldberg was a top draw, things were starting to collapse for him. In addition to the loss of the feud with Hart, each week it seemed that events, either planned or unplanned, were watering him down. Goldberg's descent continued at the *Spring Stampede* pay-per-view, where he wasn't even booked in the main event that saw Dallas Page pin Ric Flair in a four-way also featuring Sting and Hulk Hogan to win the WCW World title for the first time in his career. Page was in his mid-forties but he looked older thanks to years and years of "hanging and banging" at the beach. From an athletic standpoint, it was no big deal to put the belt on him because he was a hard worker, and he usually had very good matches. The problem was that WCW, over the last two years, had gained a reputation of being an old man's company, and taking the belt off a fifty-year-old and putting it on a guy who looked fifty did nothing to counter that stereotype.

It didn't help that the match was such a mess that most fans didn't even know what happened at the finish. As a result, the crowd reaction to the title change—which would have been disappointing in any case, given that Page was the least popular of all the guys in the ring—was even less extraordinary. Perhaps the biggest news coming out of the match was Hogan's fake knee injury (well, his knee really was hurt, and he did have it scoped a few weeks later, but he didn't get hurt in this match, and they overplayed the severity of the injury). Hogan sold it to the point that he even used help to get into the hotel that night during a period where there weren't any fans around to see it. Most knew what was going on here: he realized he was getting stale on top, plus he saw WCW falling apart at the seams and didn't want to be seen as the guy on top during that period.

Following the airing of an ESPN *Outside the Lines* special that touched on steroid and human growth hormone use in pro wrestling, WCW scheduled a "surprise drug test" before the April 15 *Thunder*. Strangely, Scott Steiner no-showed the event, claiming he had suffered a back injury, and was therefore not tested. Not only had Steiner become so muscular he could barely move, he had also developed a short temper, seemingly flying into an uncontrollable rage at the slightest provocation, to the point that he had been arrested several times. In a match the following week on *Nitro* (his back seemingly miraculously healed in less than a week), he carried the near-400-pound Scott Norton all the way across the ring before giving him an atomic drop. The crowd, oddly, chanted "STEROIDS!" during the match. Bobby Heenan responded by shouting, "I've never heard a crowd so pumped up before!"

While *Nitro*'s ratings had unquestionably begun a downturn, other WCW shows were in a flat-out freefall. Longtime WCW fans are probably wondering why little mention has been made so far of the company's other television programs, *Thunder* and *WCW Saturday Night*. The main reason is that we decided to give the shows as much attention as WCW gave them, which, as you can see, was essentially zero. *Thunder* was considered an A-show for a week or two, and from that point on, it was just two hours of mostly filler. *WCW Saturday Night* made *Thunder* look like *Raw* at its peak. When you have a wrestling show and you treat it as filler, fans quickly stop tuning in. By this point in the war, *Thunder*, which had been drawing ratings in the 4s just a few months earlier, was down to a 2.0, and *Saturday Night* was down to a 1.7. The *Thunder* rating was especially bad since advertisers had been sold on the show doing a 3.5. Since the show was promised to do a 3.5 and it did a 2.0, WCW had to recoup advertisers with "make-good" ads. This costs money. *Thunder* was consistently so horrible (most weeks, the only entertainment the show provided was unintentional comedy and two hours' worth of bickering between announcers Mike Tenay and Tony Schiavone, who hated each other) that it almost seemed as if WCW didn't *want* the show to get to the 3.5 range, so they were willingly losing money *and* providing horrible programming week after week. This is not a formula for profit.

And now *Nitro* had begun its ratings collapse as well. The April 19 *Nitro* illustrated just how bad things had become. Quality-wise, *Nitro* kicked *Raw*'s ass, but it didn't matter because, as they say in the stock market, *Nitro* was on a downward trend. They did finally put some effort back into the unopposed hour, including an awesome Cruiserweight match and a great interview in which Flair appeared to go insane, but it didn't matter. The damage of all those horrible shows, specifically in the first hour, was done. Overall, *Raw* did a 6.11 to *Nitro*'s 4.08 that night.

The tragically bad shows weren't about to stop, either, as confusing, convoluted story lines were now becoming the order of the day. The "Crazy Flair" interview, in which he stripped down to his boxers, featured the man who was once WCW's top draw ranting and raving about how he was not only President of WCW but also President of the entire United States and World Heavyweight champion as well. This led to Roddy Piper managing to convince a mental institution to lock Flair up as a madman upon his son David's request. It should also be noted that three days later on *Thunder*, it was announced that Flair had been released and was President of WCW again. Then, four days after that on *Nitro*, the show opened with footage of

Flair "still locked up." (On the bright side, nobody ever watched *Thunder*, so that story line snafu could be ignored.)

While Flair quite literally danced around the hospital in his underwear with other insane inmates, J.J. Dillon announced that since he was Vice President of the company (which was news to viewers), Charles Robinson would be the new acting President until Flair returned. For those who don't know the name "Charles Robinson," he was a referee whose sole claim to power in WCW was apparently that he was a big Ric Flair fan who had bleached his hair blonde like the Nature Boy. Piper then did an interview saying that since Flair was gone, he was in charge. Although the story line was not likely designed this way on purpose, it drew close parallels with the real-life WCW in that nobody really had any clue who was in charge, and if someone said they were in power for the day, everyone just sort of went along with it because they'd given up long ago.

Piper and Robinson then had an in-ring confrontation that ended in Piper being arrested. This ultimately led to Flair versus Piper being signed for the PPV, the stipulation being that if Piper won, he would become WCW President. Perhaps you'll recall that when Flair won the presidency in the match with Bischoff, the stipulation was that he'd be President "for life." There is no such thing as "for life" in wrestling. Flair then ran into Scott Hall, who, as you might recall, had been off TV for some time. It was never explained why Hall was in the mental hospital, and his appearance was never acknowledged by the announcers. Apparently, someone just thought it would be funny to put him in there for a cameo, not understanding that when wrestling fans see something happening on TV, they automatically (and often foolishly, especially in WCW's case) assume that there is a reason behind its occurrence. It wasn't until the following week, in Charlotte, North Carolina, that Flair returned to TV. He explained that Arn Anderson had bailed him out. Bet you never knew that when you're confined to a mental institution, you can leave simply by posting bail. His first order of business was to put a bounty on Kevin Nash's head. Over the course of just this one show, the dollar figure changed from $100,000 to $50,000 to $1,000,000, depending upon who was telling the story. His second order of business, since it was Charlotte, was to get knocked out by DDP in the main event.

If you thought the last three paragraphs were confusing, imagine watching it play out in all its glory on your television set. And this was just your average convoluted *Nitro* story line from 1998-1999. This is not to say that the WWF was writing great TV; many times, a *Raw* show would draw a tremendous number, and folks would sit there wondering how this was even possible. The WWF writing was full of plot holes and angles that made no sense, angles that often insulted the intelligence of the average human being. But the big difference was simply that WWF's writing *was better than WCW's.* World Championship Wrestling set a standard for bad television in the late '90s that will never be equaled. There have been countless other bad wrestling TV shows, but they were all bad for other reasons; perhaps they had no real talent (GLOW), or bad production (your typical independent promotion), or the people writing it did so just to get a family member over as a star (NWA-TNA, though to be honest, most every promotion has been guilty of this).

WCW was different from all the others; they had a deeper talent pool than any other promotion in the history of this business, and Turner owned them, so they certainly had the capacity for tremendous production. The greatest difference of all, though, was what they did with their talent. While some companies tried way too hard to get a family member over as a star, they were at least trying to get *someone* over as a star. WCW killed all their talent. They killed the undercard guys by making them out to be bit players, they killed the mid-carders by making it very clear that they were mid-carders for life, and they killed anyone even close to the top of the pack by booking them as goofs or losers and having them turn heel and babyface with such rapidity that fans had no idea whether to boo or cheer them. As it turned out, nobody was a star, and worse, when it appeared a wrestler was starting to get some fan support, he was immediately booked into oblivion.

If it wasn't apparent to everyone by this point that the company was in severe trouble, the Charlotte show offered proof positive. The fact that the show was massacred by *Raw* in the ratings battle by over three points was one thing. More damning, however, might have been the fact that despite always drawing big crowds in the Carolinas, they had to give out thousands of free tickets just to get a respectable crowd into the building for TV.

WCW had no one but themselves to blame for that. Over the years, they had booked Flair, a "hometown hero" in the region, so badly that it had become a running joke that whenever they were about to run a show there something stupid was inevitably going to happen with him. Obviously, having Flair go crazy in a mental institution in a period when heels were supposed to be young and cool was stupid. As entertaining as Flair was, even in roles as idiotic as this, his drawing power was killed in a matter of weeks. This was especially distressing since he and Goldberg were the only two guys in the entire company that had been able to affect the ratings in any way. Well, in any positive way, at least.

///

Thanks, in the story line, to Roddy Piper, Randy Savage finally returned to the promotion, and, like Scott Steiner, he came back so muscular it looked as though he'd been pumped full of air at a service station. He brought with him a new girlfriend, Stephanie Bellars, a young blonde stripper who had been dubbed Gorgeous George. The backstory there is that Rob Kellum, an undercard worker known as the Maestro, had purchased the rights to the name from the family of George Wagner, who had used it during his run as the biggest star of the early days of televised wrestling. WCW signed Savage's brother, Lanny Poffo (formerly the Genius in the WWF), who was planning on going as Gorgeous George. It would turn out, however, that Poffo would never once appear on WCW TV, so they gave the moniker to Bellars instead.

It should be noted that despite never wrestling a single match for the company, WCW saw fit to pay Lanny Poffo $150,000 per year.

At this point, the company decided that perhaps they could slow the ratings slide by playing "hot potato" with their belts. The April 26 *Nitro* featured no less than three title changes. First, Sting beat Page in an awesome match to win the WCW title, and then, an hour later, Page won it back in a four-way also featuring Nash and Goldberg after hitting Nash with an international (called as such because Turner officials wouldn't allow the word "foreign") object. The latter was, um, not as good as the former. Also, Mysterio beat Psicosis to regain the Cruiserweight belt that he'd lost a week earlier. This was the beginning of the desperation booking of the belts (frequent changes) that led to the belts meaning nothing, which led to fans not caring about them, which led to them being useless as far as drawing ratings or PPV buy rates. Like the Flair story line, however, it would only get worse as time went on. Coming up short in poorly promoted World title matches week after week was also killing Goldberg's drawing power (and he was the last guy with any left after they'd killed Flair in the mental hospital). The saddest part of this whole scenario was that this hotshotting didn't do a rat's ass worth of good: the show only did a 3.89 rating to *Raw*'s 5.99.

///

After having put all their banter back and forth, all the online accusations, and all the radio show interviews behind them in order to get back together, Dana and Scott Hall separated again.

\\

It didn't appear that things could get any worse for the company, but starting in early May, it happened. The show began a several-week period of preemptions for the NBA playoffs. Normally, whenever one of the two shows was preempted, the other show would gain 20 percent of their audience for that night. On May 10, the first night of preemption, *Raw* gained a whopping 50 percent of WCW's audience to draw an 8.09 rating with 9.2 million viewers, making it the most-watched wrestling TV show in the history of the USA Network since the original *Royal Rumble*. The main event overrun, featuring Rock and Austin and Vince versus Undertaker and Triple H and Shane McMahon, did a 9.17 rating and 10.4 million viewers, another record. Although the war had really been over for some time, this put the exclamation point on it.

At this point, it was clear there was no turning around anytime soon. The entire WCW product—from the matches to the look of the TV to the announcers to the guys on top to the entire promotional philosophy—was old and stale. The only hope for a turnaround was to basically scrap everything and start all over again. Doing so, obviously, would lead to a further decline, and realistically, it would take a long period (perhaps a few years) of reprogramming before new wrestlers would start to catch on. Some decline was inevitable if the company hoped to turn around, but it would have been better to start when the show was in the 4s rather than in the 2s.

Sadly, there was a wrestling war going on, and those in charge at WCW had zero patience. Nobody had a two-year plan to turn the ship around;

they wanted to turn the ship around *that week*, by any means necessary. Past history should have made it clear that hotshotting generally does more harm than good, but for whatever reason, nobody internally (at least nobody with the power to do anything about it) could see that, despite the fact that evidence—in the forms of ratings and buy rates—was readily at their disposal.

The bad TV was killing business so fast that the *Slamboree* PPV at the massive TWA Dome, with three title matches and a "winner gets control of the company" stipulation match resulted in just 13,789 fans paying $494,795. It was a respectable crowd that sadly was generated only by giving away almost 7,000 free tickets. Only six months earlier, in the same building, 30,000 fans had paid almost a million dollars to get in. When the momentum shifts downward, it does so very quickly. Part of the problem might have been that the previous week's *Thunder* had ended with the following: "*SLAMBOREE*! TOMORROW, 8 P.M. EST." The problem being, of course, that *Thunder* aired on Wednesday and the PPV aired on Sunday.

Slamboree made no effort to reverse the nonsensical booking trend. Flair beat Piper after hitting him with brass knux to retain his "Presidency" of the company. After the match, Bischoff, who hadn't had any power in story line for almost six months since his loss to Flair (and had in fact last been seen on TV working as a janitor!), came out and reversed the decision. Long story short, six months of story lines were tossed right out the window with Bischoff's magical (and totally incomprehensible) return as babyface company owner. In the main event, Nash beat Page to win the WCW title. Since this was the fourth time the belt had changed hands in four weeks, it would be an understatement to say that nobody cared. The show ended up doing a 0.45 buy rate, putting the company, at mid-year, $12 million behind budget in PPV alone.

Nitro was a comedy of errors the following night. Flair, who had supposedly lost the presidency, was back as President because Bischoff apparently didn't have any power after all. Of course, if that was the case, the Nash title change shouldn't have been allowed to stand either, since Bischoff restarted the match after Page had won via DQ. Later, however, Gene Okerlund identified Bischoff as a "powerful executive" in WCW, though exactly what kind of power he possessed was never specified. Then Piper gave an interview saying *he* was President, but later in the speech he revealed that he was the Commissioner. By the time the show was over, nobody had any idea what in the hell was going on, and that included both fans at home and the people writing the story lines.

As the ratings spiral continued, the company decided that fresh blood was in order. Unfortunately, they decided that this fresh blood should be in the form of Tank Abbott, and they signed him to a huge three-year deal. Abbott, a big fat barroom brawler from Huntington Beach, California, had made his name in the Ultimate Fighting Championships by knocking out a few guys in devastating fashion and going on to garner the worst record of any professional fighter in the history of that organization (8-10-0). He was charismatic, however, and his occasional knockouts were so vicious that he remained a draw and had some people convinced that he was one of the baddest men on the planet. Keep this in mind throughout the rest of this book as you see his name pop up here and there.

In addition to signing Abbott, they re-signed Dennis Rodman. The same Dennis Rodman who no-showed the final *Nitro* before his last PPV appearance, showed up at the big show in no condition to perform, did nothing in the match, then sued the company for $550,000. WCW's ingenious plan to settle that suit? Offer him a new contract for five more dates. Coincidentally, Rodman's first day was supposed to be the Georgia Dome *Nitro* on July 5th. And, of course, he no-showed.

Deciding that they hadn't thrown quite enough money out the window that week, they also signed rapper Master P. Why they decided to sign a rapper, who had no interest in getting in the ring and working, is anyone's guess. Despite this, he was given $200,000 per appearance. Yes, *per appearance*. So over the course of a month, WCW paid Master P around $1 million . . . to not wrestle.

All the signings made no difference. On June 7, *Raw* beat *Nitro* by over 3.5 points, which was complete and utter destruction. The main angle on the show saw a mysterious white Humvee crash into a limo containing Kevin Nash, seemingly killing him. This was a brilliant idea, considering that he was supposed to headline a PPV six days later. Worse, $50,000 was spent to shoot this, and it drew a pitiful 2.7 rating. On commentary, Bischoff hinted that the driver was the WWF's Sable (Rena Mero), who had just filed a $140 million sexual harassment lawsuit against McMahon (years later, she'd go back to work for him and play the role of his mistress—welcome to wrestling). Though she did show up a week later, she only did so by sitting in the front row, saying nothing. She never came back. Another angle hinted that it was several different people, including Carmen Electra (yes, *that* Carmen Electra). In the end, the real driver was never revealed.

As if *Nitro*'s ratings freefall wasn't bad enough, *WCW Saturday Night* had plummeted to a 1.3 rating, its lowest ever. "Ever" meaning "in three decades." So WCW came up with a solution: put old-timer Dusty Rhodes on commentary. In reality, this might not have been the worst idea, because the viewing audience for *Saturday Night* skewed quite a bit older than for *Nitro* and particularly for *Raw* (whose median viewing age was about twenty-four). The problem was that Dusty was far more interested in putting himself over than the product, plus it didn't make any sense for a show viewed by so many middle-aged and older people to be used to debut new talent. The exact opposite held true for *Nitro*; the average viewer of that show was in their early thirties, yet WCW continually built the show around wrestlers in their forties and fifties.

The following Sunday, WCW presented *Great American Bash 1999*, an event that so clearly illustrated everything that was killing the company that it could be considered a textbook example for future promoters of what not to do. The show opened with Tony Schiavone, Mike Tenay, and Bobby Heenan running down the card. You might wonder why they would run down the card on the PPV broadcast that *fans had already paid for*. The reason, of course, was that they had failed to promote any matches in the weeks leading up to the event.

Compare this to, say, McDonald's. You'd never go to the restaurant and wonder what your order is going to consist of. Their commercials run a million times during the day, and in the restaurant itself, you're bombarded with information in the form of giant menus which not only describe in detail what is in each meal, but also feature full-color pictures of the meal in question. If McDonald's only served one item—the McMystery Meal—and you never knew whether you were going to get a hamburger, chicken nuggets, a fish sandwich, or whatever, few would dare to purchase it.

WCW pay-per-views were like McMystery Meals: you never knew what you were going to get. WCW never bothered to run down their cards on TV, fearing that fans would switch over to *Raw* while they were doing this. Ironically, they'd then complain that nobody was buying their PPVs.

Then the wrestling started, and man, was it ever bad. Hammer versus Mikey Whipwreck: horrible. Ernest Miller versus Horace Hogan: atrocious. Ric Flair versus Roddy Piper: abysmal. Rick Steiner versus Sting: miserable—and worse, nobody could figure out who won since it just ended when Sting got attacked by three dogs. Yes, as in actual canines. Finally, Nash (not dead after all following the *Nitro* Humvee attack) beat Randy Savage via DQ in a horrific match when Sid Vicious ran in. Sid, you might recall, had left WCW about ten years prior on horrible terms after nearly stabbing Arn Anderson to death for real in a hotel room brawl in England. If only it was possible to make stuff like this up. The show, taking place during the middle of the biggest boom period in American wrestling history, ended up doing a 0.43 buy rate, the fifth lowest up to that point in their history.

Nitro the following Monday was at the SuperDome in New Orleans before a paying crowd of 15,593. Master P had bragged to the company that his presence would make the building sell out. Considering that the building could hold over 55,000, Master P was wrong. The show was built around him and his crew, the No Limit Soldiers, who repeatedly chanted "HOOTIE HOO!" to progressively louder boos. The idea was that Master P and his crew were supposed to be good guys, taking on the bad guy group of Curt Hennig and his posse (Barry and Kendall Windham and Bobby Duncum Jr.), who would become known as the West Texas Rednecks. The problem here was twofold. First, there were ten or so Soldiers and four Rednecks, which meant the Rednecks got cheered for valiantly holding their own against tremendous odds. Second, Hennig and his crew wrote a hilarious country song called "Rap Is Crap," and since WCW had its roots in the South, this also got them over as big heroes. "Rap Is Crap" became so popular at one point that several country stations around the nation played it in rotation. WCW, of course, responded as they always did when lucking into something like this: they killed the angle dead. Also on the show, Eddy Guerrero returned and had a lackluster match with Juventud Guerrera. Despite having nearly died in a car wreck earlier in the year, his return was presented as an afterthought.

Things were collapsing so quickly at this point that wrestlers were actually going out in public and burying the company. Hogan, who had been off TV for months rehabbing his knee, made a bunch of friends when he appeared on the Mancow morning show in Tampa that week and ridiculed WCW and all its wrestlers. He even went as far as to say that he was sick and tired of hearing "Malenko and the rest of the midgets" complain about their roles. He also downplayed Goldberg's popularity, saying anyone could win 20,000 matches in a row. Never mind that when Hogan first made it huge in the WWF, he did so by winning approximately 20,000 matches in a row.

It was obvious that things weren't going to change for the mid-carders, and any of them able to get out of the promotion was doing just that. On June 30, Chris Jericho signed with the WWF. In the six months prior to his contract signing, WCW had made very little effort to retain him. In the last few weeks, they panicked, but to no avail, as his mind had already been made up for some time. WWF saw real potential in him and even went so far as to say he'd be the next Shawn Michaels. Jericho was willing to take a pay cut for an opportunity that he was absolutely not about to get in WCW; specifically, he had lobbied for a showdown against Goldberg, and despite having done several interviews setting up the angle, nothing ever transpired.

Many of the wrestlers in WCW were upset, because Jericho was well liked, and they couldn't believe the company wouldn't offer him a good deal while it was throwing money away on limos, Humvees, fired NBA stars and rappers (one of Master P's henchmen, Swoll, a huge guy with no talent, was signed for $400,000 per year). Instead, Chris Jericho, who had always been told that he was too small, couldn't sell tickets, and wasn't a ratings draw, made his debut later that summer in a confrontation with the Rock and helped *Raw* obliterate *Nitro* in the ratings that evening by over four points.

As if Jericho couldn't wait to get out of the company fast enough, his fiancee went to the store one day and bought a Jericho–Malenko WCW doll set. Strangely, the receipt claimed that she'd purchased a Hogan–Sting package. Of course, that meant that Hogan and Sting got the residual revenue from the purchase, not Jericho.

Nitro on July 5 broadcast once again from the Georgia Dome, home to some of its biggest past successes. Those days were long gone. The show drew 25,338 fans, just over half a house, and $594,745. WCW blamed the low attendance on the holiday weekend. If you haven't already noticed, promoters almost never put the blame for a poor house on themselves. Instead, they blame any outside force they can think of. The crowd is low because it's summer. The crowd is low because it's winter. The crowd is low because it's raining. The crowd is low because it's sunny. By refusing to address the real issue (nobody gives a shit about their show), promoters often delude themselves right out of business.

The show was built around two things: the return of Goldberg, and the return of Bret Hart, who had been away since Owen's death. The company advertised neither of these highlights ahead of time. (They did, however, advertise an Ernest Miller versus Jerry Flynn kickboxing match that nobody outside Flynn's and Miller's immediate families could possibly have cared about.)

Bret's interview began with him saying that WCW had told him to go ahead and talk for as long as he wanted. He basically said that his family had lived for wrestling their whole lives, and now, tragically, they'd also died for it. He said he wasn't sure if he'd ever wrestle again (this was met with a violently negative reaction), and also that if he never got a chance to say it to his fans again, thank you. Getting into the ring was obviously a lot harder than he had thought it was going to be, and it was upsetting to him to hear the few hecklers who obviously didn't understand the gravity of what had happened to his family.

"And that's about it," he concluded. "Thank you very much."

The Goldberg return was also epic. First rock group Megadeth came out to play a tune. WCW would soon learn that concerts on wrestling shows are death in the ratings, as the segment garnered a 2.13, *Nitro*'s lowest number in years. The crowd hated the concert with a passion, but then when it was over, an explosion went off, and Goldberg emerged from the flames. The crowd went haywire.

WCW responded by immediately cutting to a commercial.

It should be noted that just days after the Megadeth rating came in (the lowest in years, don't forget), WCW contacted KISS and asked them to play at the August 23 *Nitro* for $500,000. Then in late July, they contacted Chad Brock, an obscure country singer, and asked if he'd play a song on the August 9 *Nitro*.

Next stop: the *Bash at the Beach* pay-per-view from Fort Lauderdale— another truly wretched show in a seemingly unending series. The incident with the most far-reaching consequences was a Junkyard Battle Royal featuring Public Enemy, Jerry Flynn, Steve Regal, Horace Hogan, David Taylor, Brian Knobbs, Ciclope, and Mikey Whipwreck. Though they spent $100,000 to put on the match, which took place in a real, honest-to-goodness junkyard, WCW did not see fit to advertise the match on *Nitro*. Therefore, no one bought the show to see it. Furthermore, Damian, Ciclope, and Whipwreck all suffered serious legitimate injuries, as the junkyard was a truly dangerous environment. All three men were out of action for months.

The main event saw Savage and Sid Vicious beat Sting and Nash in a tag match, so Savage won the WCW title. Yes, the belt was on the line in a tag match. It was quite ironic that Savage was given the belt, considering that he'd been involved in a woman-beating story line the week before that had the brass at Turner outraged. It also had the wrestlers outraged since, in a completely unscripted moment during one of his skits, he had slapped Torrie Wilson across the face. She was so shocked by this that she actually began to laugh on live television. Savage's valet, Gorgeous George, who showed up on TV sporting two black eyes, sat in Nash's corner during the PPV match, but then turned on him at the end to help Savage get the win.

Nitro the next night, despite being built around Hulk Hogan's return and subsequent title win over Savage, was shockingly good. Of course, that's "shockingly good" in comparison to the usual WCW fare. Hogan, because he'd been gone for so long, got a big babyface reaction coming out, and the fact that the main event ended with a babyface winning the belt instead of a hundred guys running in for a DQ made the people very happy. Afterwards, Nash came out and challenged Hogan to a title match at their annual *Road Wild* PPV debacle.

A few days after his title win, Hogan was on WCW's Internet radio show, *WCW Live*. Now that he was back and champion again, he did a complete 180 from his Mancow interview the previous month, this time putting over guys left and right (Goldberg, for example, was now "a big star and a dynamic personality"). He also claimed you'd never see him in the red and yellow outfit again.

Leading up to *Road Wild*, Dennis Rodman finally began to make appearances on WCW telecasts. On the bright side, he showed up every week. The bad news was that his mainstream appeal had vanished; his appearances meant nothing for the ratings, nothing for publicity, and nothing for the matches and angles he was involved in. On top of this, he made claims in public that for the five dates, he was making $1 million, which was probably legitimate, as Master P was being paid this amount, and he had nowhere near the name recognition as Dennis Rodman.

And so *Road Wild* came, and as you can probably guess, it was atrocious. But little did anyone watching know just how unraveled things had become behind the scenes in the days prior to the event. The event was preceded by the annual motorcycle ride to Sturgis, which saw Jason Hervey and Dustin Runnels crash their bikes, and Goldberg and Rick Steiner get so lost that there was concern they'd been killed in an accident. As if that weren't bad enough, Buff Bagwell and Ernest Miller got into a real fight backstage after Buff complained about the planned finish of their match.

The biggest blow-up, however, came between Hogan and Savage. The two had always had an intense love/hate relationship; when they could make money together, they were in love, and when they couldn't, they weren't. Savage, a well-known paranoid who often carried a gun in his gear bag, went insane, screaming at Hogan that he was holding him down, giving the top spot to Sid, and furthermore, he'd killed off the Humvee angle. While he was at it, he should have yelled about being booked to work a match at *Road Wild* with Rodman that involved being thrown into a porta-potty. Following the show, Savage walked out and no-showed the next several events.

Master P henchman Swoll was arrested for speeding, and was held when they found he was late on his child support payments. This despite the fact that WCW was paying him $400,000 per year.

With tensions mounting behind the scenes, it was certainly no shock when Bischoff finally snapped and blew a gasket in front of everyone backstage. He yelled at Raven for making disparaging remarks about the company in public, at Konnan for saying the word "pussy" on TV, at Rey Mysterio Jr. for making gay references on TV, and at Public Enemy and Bagwell for crying about having to lose matches. He told Raven that if he didn't like things, he could leave right now. Amazingly, Raven got up and left. Bischoff, figuring nobody else would have the balls to do the same, made the same offer to the rest of the crew. That night, Konnan and Kidman approached him privately and said they wanted out. Mysterio was planning on doing the same if Bischoff agreed to let them out. All three were upset that Eric had singled them out in front of everyone but hadn't said a word to guys like Sting, who had made disparaging remarks about the company in a *USA Today* article, and Savage, who had just disappeared. Eric ended up reneging on the offer to everyone except Raven, who decided that working for a small outfit like ECW was better than staying in the hellhole that WCW had become.

Whereas in the old days Bischoff could comfort himself with the Tuesday-morning ratings report, they no longer gave him any relief. *Nitro* had drawn its lowest number in years, a 2.92. The KISS concert, as expected, bombed, doing a 2.25 rating. Nothing like spending half a million dollars to get a number like that. Despite the horrific rating, only weeks later, a plan was put into motion to create a New Year's Eve PPV that would feature a three-hour wrestling show followed by a full-length KISS concert at the 70,000-seat Fiesta Bowl in Tempe, Arizona. This would seem to indicate that Eric, under the severe amount of stress, did, in fact, go totally insane.

That would be the only explanation for the next main event feud, which was to feature Sid versus Goldberg. In order to promote the eventual encounter, Sid came out on *Nitro* one week and claimed that he was 55-0. Never mind that he hadn't had fifty-five matches on WCW TV since coming back. Or, while we're at it, the fact that he'd lost several times on

TV over the past few weeks alone. By midway through the show, he was at 59-0 despite not having won any matches. Bobby Heenan explained this by saying he'd already beaten up nine men. Nobody was sure how 55 plus 9 equaled 59. The next week, despite losing at every house show the company ran, he was suddenly up to 68-0. Then he pinned Juventud Guerrera, Lenny Lane, and Lodi. This made him 70-0. Again, do not ask how 68 plus 3 equals 70. Three days later, on *Thunder*, Sid said he couldn't wait to get to six more wins so he could break Goldberg's 176-0 streak. And, ummm . . . yeah. Once he did this, Sid inexplicably added, he was going to "shake all over." By September, Sid at 76-0, lost to Saturn via DQ when Rick Steiner ran in. On *Nitro* the following Monday, however, he was billed as being 77-0. So yes, losses were now counting as wins in this streak.

Shockingly, the Sid winning streak didn't stop the downward spiral. The following week, *Raw* was moved to 11:00 P.M. due to the U.S. Open Tennis Tournament, which meant *Nitro* had all three hours unopposed. They responded by putting on a horrendous show that actually seemed designed to fail. Final tally: *Nitro*, unopposed, did a 4.00 rating, *losing* to the 11:00 P.M. *Raw*, which did a 4.16. It got even worse, as that Thursday, the WWF debuted their *Smackdown* show opposite *Thunder* and destroyed WCW once again in the ratings, 4.16 to 1.94.

Finally . . . *finally* . . . it was too much for Turner brass to take.

And so Eric Bischoff, the man who led WCW to its most profitable two-year period ever, was "reassigned" on September 9. (Bischoff would later claim that this basically meant he was sent home to Colorado, where he hunted and fished for many months while still collecting huge paychecks.) There really was no other decision the Turner brass could have made, as under Bischoff's watch, WCW had not only grown to never-before-seen heights, but was also now tanking at mind-boggling speed. Turner was so upset with Bischoff that he was banned from all WCW events as well as from the office. On top of this, Turner demanded that no references to Bischoff be made and that no footage of him be used in any future video packages. To the company, the man who once turned it all around had just suddenly ceased to exist.

A strange little man by the name of Bill Busch, who started at Turner almost a decade earlier as an accountant, was put in charge as Executive Vice President. Because he knew virtually nothing about wrestling, TV producer Craig Leathers was put in charge of creative. And who was working under him, doing all the real grunt work in putting the shows together? None other than the three men who had helped get them into this mess in the first place: Dusty Rhodes, Kevin Nash, and Kevin Sullivan.

Busch, along with Dr. Harvey Schiller, the Turner representative in charge of overseeing WCW, met with the wrestlers and announced that some things were going to change. The New Year's Eve pay-per-view idea with KISS was canned; a ridiculous contest to give away $1 million (to a lucky fan rather than, say, an inebriated Dennis Rodman) was canceled; the annual *Road Wild* PPV from Sturgis, now an annual money-loser at a time when money could not afford to be lost, was canceled; and a proposed *Nitro* cartoon (seriously, and by a "cartoon" we mean an animated children's program, not just another episode of the show) was scrapped.

Further tragedy struck on September 8, when referee Brian Curtis Hildebrand passed away following a long battle with stomach cancer. Only thirty-seven, he was such a courageous and loveable person that condolences were sent out on Monday night not only on *Nitro*, but on *Raw* as well (where he'd never worked). Like Owen Hart's death, this was particularly tragic as he left his friends and family behind through no fault of his own.

The first post-Bischoff PPV was *Fall Brawl*. If anyone needs evidence of how screwed up WCW was at this point, consider the fact that they'd done such a poor job of planning that there wasn't any card at all a week before the show aired. Even the cable companies finally lost it, and the following ad appeared in newspapers nationwide: "We're the advertising agency and they won't even tell us who's going to be there! For God's sake don't miss it!" Below that, it read: "Sunday, September 12. Insert time here." When the buy rate numbers came out, WCW's incompetence was illustrated quite painfully: the show did a 0.30, lower than any number the WWF or WCW had ever done.

And then, on October 3, it happened: the beginning of the end.

Well, the latest beginning of the end.

That was the day Vince Russo, after a lengthy meeting with Bill Busch, signed his WCW contract.

Russo was a longtime wrestling fan and video-store owner who broke into the business in the early '90s by sponsoring a wrestling radio show in New York. Eventually, the WWF hired him, more to shut him up than anything else. He was put to work as an editor for the *WWF Magazine*, and after he wrote a few fantasy story lines that the company liked, they put him in charge of the division. Eventually, he worked his way up to being a television writer, and he had significant input into the late-'90s product that laid waste to *Nitro* week after week.

Russo was good. Not at writing wrestling TV, mind you, but at spinning folks into believing that he and his buddy Ed Ferrara, who'd also jumped with him, were the sole reason behind the WWF's success.

In hindsight, it's clear that Russo was a very creative man. However— and many in the WWF expressed this belief long before he ever even started work for WCW—his creativity had to be harnessed by an editor, and in the WWF, that editor was the same guy who'd had final say since day one: Vince McMahon. In WCW, he had no editor, and the results spoke for themselves. Despite anything he might ever say to the contrary, the history of his regime follows in hard numbers, and will hopefully settle a few arguments once and for all.

The October 4 *Nitro* was broadcast from the Kemper Arena in Kansas City, where Owen Hart had passed away several months earlier. The story lines were no better than usual, but this can be blamed on the old regime, as Russo's first day was scheduled to be *Halloween Havoc* later that month. Kevin Nash, who had retired forever months earlier, returned on this show along with Scott Hall, who took his stint in rehab so seriously that he acted drunk during his promo. Hall actually said that Nash was working a fake retirement, and that when wrestling got fun again, he'd return. When Gene Okerlund tried to say it was fun, Hall said Okerlund must not have been in the dressing room lately.

There was one very bright spot on the show. Several months earlier, Bret had asked if he could do an Owen Hart tribute match with Benoit on the show. The company agreed, although they nixed his request to let Benoit win, feeling it would dampen the spirits of the crowd. The match was excellent, and went 27:33, making it by far the longest in-ring TV encounter of the year. Although fans had been groomed to only accept short, crash TV–style matches, they responded very well to this and gave both guys a standing ovation afterwards.

Prior to his first *Nitro*, Russo appeared on the *Wrestling Observer Live* radio show to promote himself. He said that, years back, when WCW started *Thunder*, everyone in the WWF had rejoiced because they knew it would lead the company to sink at a rapid rate due to overexposure. However, they clearly didn't learn a lesson from that because they had just recently started their own second two-hour show, *Smackdown*. He said he had been working ungodly hours and was rapidly burning out, so he went to McMahon and asked for a raise, a fifteen-month contract to give him a little job security, and the freedom to move out of Stamford, Connecticut. He'd always hated Stamford, but because the WWF offices were located there, he was stuck. McMahon shot him down. Russo said this was ridiculous, because in the real TV business, if you were writing one show and were suddenly asked to write another, you wouldn't be asked to do it for free. He was especially irate when, after saying he never had time to see his three children, Vince told him that he made enough money to hire a nanny.

Almost nothing of value happened on *Nitro* over the next few weeks since they were all lame-duck shows written by a regime that was simply holding down the fort until Russo took over. The most notable thing was that Hogan was absent, supposedly teasing another retirement after getting word that Russo thought he needed to be phased out. In reality, he was in cahoots with Russo for another story line. A strong Goldberg push also began. Management had decreed several weeks earlier that Goldberg should be the top guy in the company, and Russo believed that he could be the biggest thing in wrestling, but he'd just never been pushed properly.

Although Russo wanted to push Goldberg, he made it clear that there were others he wasn't interested in doing anything with. In an online interview with Ben Miller of the website WrestleLine.com, he made the following statement, which he'd live to regret:

I'm going to tell you something right now that you will absolutely not agree with, but I've been a wrestling fan my whole life and I will live and die by this. It's hard enough, believe me, I write this shit, it is hard enough to get somebody over. You will never, ever, ever, ever, ever see the Japanese wrestlers or the Mexican wrestlers over in American mainstream wrestling. And the simple reason for that is, even myself, I'm an American and I don't want to sound like a big bigot or a racist or anything like that, but I'm an American. If I'm watching wrestling here in America, I don't give a shit about a Japanese guy. I don't give a shit about a Mexican guy. I'm from America, and that's what I want to see.

Russo and Ferrara ended up starting early, on October 18 in Philadelphia. It was quite the *Nitro:* a three-hour car crash that featured two or three things happening in each of the sixteen quarters scripted. To say that this was overkill would be putting it lightly, as by the end of the third hour, the live crowd was completely burned out, sitting in their chairs like zombies staring at the ring. Russo had a plan to take care of that, however. No, it was not to book less "stuff," but to eliminate the third hour of *Nitro* at the beginning of 2000.

It was a completely different show. Backstage, everyone was handed very detailed scripts, yet as detailed as they were, some still couldn't figure out whether they were supposed to be good guys or bad guys. The majority of this was tied to the fact that Russo didn't believe in the traditional good guys versus bad guys thing; he felt that every character should be a mix of both, a shade of gray, so to speak.

He also apparently believed that every fan scoured the Internet for insider wrestling news twenty-four hours a day, seven days a week. Because he'd praised Bagwell in one radio interview, he booked a segment in which Bagwell came out saying that "everyone knew" he was the chosen one according to the new writers. Of course, not everybody knew that. Worse, he then had a "fake match" with La Parka (yes, a fake fake match) and "took a dive." Afterwards, he jumped up like nothing had happened, grabbed the mic, and proclaimed: "Hey, Russo, did I do a good 'job' for you?" Of course, "doing a job" means "losing a match" in wrestling.

The point of these angles was never explained. After all, 95 percent of the fans weren't online looking for wrestling news all day, so they had no idea what Bagwell was talking about. And the 5 percent who were aware didn't buy it anyway, so there was no logical reason for it. The longest match on the program went nine minutes, actually a lot longer than many people expected. Also, for historical purposes, it should be noted that the first match of the Russo era went to a no-contest when a third man just sauntered into the ring. The match was Juventud Guerrera versus Evan Karagias, and the third man was Bret Hart. The best part of this was that nobody bothered to clue Juvie and Evan in, so they had no idea on Earth about what was happening and just stood there looking totally confused.

On the bright side, the show did a much better rating than the week before, jumping 0.7 to a 3.30. Of course, it still lost to *Raw*'s 5.39, but things were much closer for once. Many fans and wrestlers felt this was proof that Russo's formula was the way to go. Others noted, correctly, that the 2.61 rating from the week before had been for a lame-duck Nash presentation that had seemed to stretch about six minutes' worth of thought into a three-hour broadcast. A review of the monthly averages proved there hadn't been a major jump (which media reports at the time pegged anywhere between 25 and 32 percent). July averaged a 3.37; August averaged a 3.27; September averaged a 3.38; and Russo and Ferrara's first three shows averaged a 3.33. Despite the hype, not much had changed.

One of Russo's first orders of business was to raid Jeff Jarrett, the WWF's Intercontinental champion, from the competition. Jarrett had been a colorless heel for much of his WWF tenure and had just started to get over doing an angle in which he beat up women. Everything was building towards a

PPV match where he would defend his belt against the top women's wrestler in the company: Chyna, a huge female bodybuilder with an alleged 350-pound bench press. But, for once, it was the WWF who had the problem. The PPV was on a Sunday, and Jarrett's $350,000 contract expired the night before. Vince McMahon was in a quandary. His Intercontinental champion suddenly didn't have any contractual obligation to return, and could show up on *Nitro* the day after the PPV. Because the ball was in Jarrett's court, the WWF ended up paying him $150,000 to come back and wrestle the one match, losing his belt to Chyna clean in the middle of the ring. Jarrett was especially pleased because earlier in the year, despite the booming business, he'd been forced to take a $100,000 pay cut.

The October 14 *Thunder* was one for the ages. Since it was the last under the Nash era, he basically turned it into one giant inside joke. He sat in on commentary and did nothing but make shoot comments all night, the vast majority of which were not only too inside for 99 percent of the audience, but also not funny at all. His very first statement was that everyone had accused him of being a horrible booker, but he had outsmarted them all by booking himself in the greatest angle ever: his own retirement. If only that were true.

Halloween Havoc, Russo and Ferrara's first WCW PPV, took place on October 24 at the MGM Grand Garden Arena in Las Vegas before 8,464 fans. It definitely illustrated a new direction, although it was too early to determine whether or not it would pay off. It was an angle-laden show, and the wrestling itself was largely bad. Some of it just made no sense whatsoever. For example, Goldberg won the WCW U.S. title from Sid on a blood stoppage, but then, in the very next match, Flair bled a total gusher, and the match wasn't stopped. Bret Hart, who was being groomed for the WCW title, lost to Lex Luger.

And then there was Hogan versus Sting, which never took place. The idea Russo wanted to get across was that he told Hogan to lose the match and Hogan didn't want to. So Hogan went out in street clothes, whispered something to Sting, then lay down so Sting could pin him and win the WCW title. Nobody watching had any idea what in the hell was going on, the cameras quickly cut away, and the announcers never bothered to try to explain it. They attempted to explain what was happening in the main event, saying Goldberg versus new WCW champion Sting was non-title. A few minutes later, Goldberg pinned him and was handed the WCW title. The show ended with everyone in a state of utter confusion.

The show was also the last decent buy rate the company would ever do. Regardless of what anyone might say about the quality of the show or the style of Russo's writing, the fact is that this PPV did a 0.52 buy rate. Whether it was because they toned down the in-ring product in order to present significantly more angles or ran angles targeted towards a great minority of viewers, the fact is that fans were turned off by the idea of paying to see World Championship Wrestling on pay-per-view. Within eight months, things would get so bad that the company would loudly celebrate buy rates in the 0.19 range.

Going into the October 25 *Nitro*, Goldberg was the WCW World and U.S. champion. However, J.J. Dillon explained that Sting versus Goldberg from the night before was not a sanctioned match, and therefore, the belt had been held up. A thirty-two-man tournament was set up, with the final two men squaring off at the next PPV to determine a new WCW champion. The first tourney match took place in the *Nitro* main event. Bret, on a losing streak, beat Goldberg not only to advance, but also to win his U.S. title. Also on the show, Nash, who had retired forever in August, finally returned to the ring. What was the big angle to bring him back, you ask? He was told he had a match. That's it.

Prior to the show there was another major shakeup, as Busch went crazy about how upset Turner Standards and Practices had been lately. It was said in no uncertain terms that there would be no more swearing, no more bleeding, no more ref bumps, and no more hitting women without 100 percent authorization. Busch even went so far as to say that if things didn't change, Turner would consider shutting down the company outright.

Russo's insanity took center stage on the October 28 *Thunder*. They did a skit backstage in which Kidman came across Scotty Riggs and Buff Bagwell having a conversation. Here, printed verbatim, is their conversation:

Bagwell: "You're pinning me? One, two, three?"

Riggs: "That's the finish they gave me!"

Yes, *they were in the midst of planning out their fake wrestling match.* It gets better. During the match, Bagwell rolled him up with a small package and "refused to let him go." The ref counted two, paused, then grudgingly counted three. Bagwell ran off laughing, having supposedly put one over on those evil writers from up North. Again, insider fans considered it a stupid fake angle, and casual fans had no idea what was happening, so there was ultimately no reason for doing it. But Russo trudged on.

What was also strange was that the November 1 *Nitro*—now operating under the new decrees to the point that they were bleeping out the word "screw"—was widely regarded both internally and by fans at home as a really good show. Of course, "really good show" meant a really good show for *Nitro*, not necessarily a really good show by any other standards. There were production snafus galore, including cameramen giving post-angle cues before they'd cut away, wrestlers blatantly breaking character because they thought the cameras were off, and just plain downright horrible acting. They also continued the World title tournament, which was a booking disaster. Most of the matches lasted about a minute, death in any tournament that you're trying to make seem important. Plus, weird things were happening, like guys advancing to the second round despite never actually having won a match in the first round.

Nitro also introduced a new character, one that would soon be the spotlight of every show: Russo's voice. That's right; he was sitting behind a wall, so all you could see was an arm, and he'd talk to guys like Dr. Claw from the old *Inspector Gadget* cartoons. On *WCW Live* later that week, he vowed that his face would never been seen on television.

"NEVER!" he reiterated.

In a strange turn of events, Dr. Harvey Schiller, the man who made the move to can Bischoff, suddenly left Turner to take a job with George Steinbrenner. He was replaced by Brad Siegel, whose name you'll hear quite a bit more in the coming pages.

The November 8 *Nitro* was the exact opposite of the show the week before: this program was horrible on countless levels. Instead of three things happening in each of the sixteen quarters, about ten things happened in each, and none of it made any sense at all. Sid opened the show with a weird promo in which he informed everyone that he was not as stupid as he looked. Madusa, a woman booked into a tournament for the men's Heavyweight championship who had already been eliminated, was reinserted into the brackets . . . and then eliminated again. Probably the highlight of the booking insanity was Brian Knobbs beating Bam Bam Bigelow via countout in a Falls Count Anywhere match. Yes, the falls could count *anywhere*, even, presumably, in another universe, but somehow, Bam Bam Bigelow got counted out. He was fighting with Knobbs backstage, then ran off to help Kimberly. The referee apparently decided that if Bigelow wasn't there, he wasn't anywhere, so he counted to ten, and when Bigelow didn't return, he called for the bell.

The sad thing is that show actually made more sense than the one the following week, which was notable for a skit in which Ferrara went out in front of the live audience and mocked WWF announcer Jim Ross, who had been suffering from Bell's palsy for years. He then introduced his new sidekick, Steve Williams, a longtime friend of the real-life Ross. Williams' task was to run in during a Piñata on a Pole match with the Mexican wrestlers and beat them all up. He beat them up all right, and put El Dandy, Juventud Guerrera, and Psicosis in the hospital for real. Sid, whose interviews were quickly becoming a weekly highlight of the show, said he was twice the man Kevin Nash was, then added: "I have half the brain you have!" Main event was Sid versus Nash in a no-DQ match that ended in a DQ. All of this is true. The show did a 3.07, well below average. Russo, still eyeing that lone 2.61 the Nash show had drawn, continued to insist that things were turning around thanks to him.

It should be noted that *Raw* did a 6.20. Why is this important? Well, besides claiming that he turned WCW's numbers around, Russo also claimed for years that when he left the WWF, things started to rapidly go downhill. In reality, everything across the board—from ratings to buy rates to merchandise figures—increased, in some cases dramatically, and this was during a time when three of the company's biggest stars (Undertaker, Austin, and McMahon) had been off television for months.

And so Russo continued with his wacky skits and matches. Wrestlers retired forever . . . and then unretired days later. Matches ended when wrestlers who weren't in the original match pinned other wrestlers who also weren't in the match. Sid's promos somehow began to make even less sense. And then, in perhaps his finest hour, Russo unveiled his newest color commentator: Juventud Guerrera, who spoke almost zero English.

Russo would later tell the *New York Times*: "There is one word that we start and end every conversation with: logic. Once you lose the logic of the situation, then you lose the realism and you lose the audience."

Indeed.

The WCW *Mayhem* PPV, which replaced the annual debacle known as *World War III*, drew 12,119 paid ($313,847 U.S. at the gate) for the finals of the disaster known as the WCW World title tournament. Because Russo's emphasis was on wacky angles instead of in-ring work, four of the matches (Evan Karagias versus Disco Inferno, Meng versus Lex Luger, Vampiro versus Berlyn, and David Flair versus Kimberly—yes, Kimberly) were in the infamous negative-star range, and three (Bagwell versus Hennig, Scott Hall versus Booker T and Goldberg versus Sid) were only slightly better. The crowd in Toronto turned on the show big-time, and some of the seemingly most popular babyfaces, including Goldberg, were booed vociferously (although it made sense with Goldberg since the last time he was in the area, he did the steel-plate-under-the-jersey angle with the super-popular Hart). The fans left happy, at least, as Hart beat Benoit in a good match to win the tournament and the title. Unfortunately, because the tournament had been booked so poorly, and because the title had been devalued so greatly over the past year, he actually won a belt nobody cared about.

And speaking of titles, Psicosis was suddenly the Cruiserweight champion. Thankfully, WCW.com explained what happened: "Psicosis was awarded the belt after the West Hollywood Blondes angle was dropped."

But fear not! Russo had a plan.

For weeks there had been talk that he was gearing up for his big angle, the story line that was going to turn the company around once again. It was originally set to peak at *Mayhem*, but then was pushed back to their biggest show of the year, *Starrcade*. Fans and wrestlers wondered what it could be. Did a major name jump ship from *Raw*? Had Russo, the "insane genius," come up with an idea that nobody in wrestling had ever thought of before? What was it?

It was Montreal.

Yes, again.

Bret Hart beat Goldberg to retain the WCW title after Roddy Piper, playing the role of Earl Hebner, came out and rang the fucking bell when Goldberg was locked in the sharpshooter. It was quite something to see Bret playing the role of Shawn Michaels. Fans had no idea how to react to this, except with hatred. It was a hell of a way to cap off a show featuring thirteen mostly bad matches.

Amazingly, things were about to get worse.

Nitro the next night featured Goldberg damn near ending his career as the result of a stunt gone wrong. The beginning of his match against Hart was to see Hall and Nash tease hitting Bret with a baseball bat, but then hitting Goldberg instead to lead to the pin. Roddy Piper would then run down and cover Goldberg's body to save him from further damage. Piper missed his cue, so he covered Goldberg immediately after Hall and Nash hit him with the bat. This caused a problem seeing as how Bret hadn't pinned him yet. So Bret tried to pull Piper off, but since Piper had been instructed to stay on top *at all costs*, he refused to move. So finally, the ref just counted three with Roddy on top, then announced that Bret, somehow, was the winner. Afterwards, Bret, Hall, and Nash reformed the nWo for the eighty-seventh time.

As the show was about to end, Goldberg stormed to the back, vowing to kill every member of the new nWo. He broke many things. One of the things he decided to break was the window of a white limo that supposedly contained the evil scriptwriter, Vince Russo. Russo, of course, was responsible for him not beating Bret at *Starrcade*, and also for causing him to lose to Roddy Piper moments earlier. The original idea was for Goldberg to break the window with a sledgehammer. It was decided that this would not look cool enough. Instead, he was going to break through the window with his bare fist, aided by a concealed piece of pipe. Unfortunately, he dropped the pipe, and since he wasn't done breaking things, he tried to bust through a window with his bare elbow. A shard of broken glass ripped through his flesh, and he began to bleed profusely. The cameras quickly cut away, and guys rushed in with towels, several of which were soon completely drenched with blood. Goldberg was rushed to the hospital to undergo plastic surgery. Later, he was told that he'd lost 31.5 liters of blood (!) and that he'd come within one centimeter of losing his arm.

This dangerous stunt meant zero for ratings, though, as the show ended up doing a 3.20 to *Raw*'s 5.83.

Russo, irate at the negative Internet response to the two shows, went ballistic on *WCW Live*, saying none of this was his fault, and the reason ratings hadn't turned around was because Standards and Practices had banned, among other things, angles like Roddy Piper calling Rhonda Singh "fat" and Ed Ferrera mocking Ross' Bell's palsy. Nobody was sure how a fat Rhonda Singh or a poor Jim Ross impersonation was going to turn the company around, but Russo was indignant. He said Turner could either have a squeaky-clean show or ratings, not both. Again, nobody was able to explain why not. As revenge, he said, he was going to repackage Lenny and Lodi as a dork tag team called Standards and Practices. That would show them. It sure would.

The last *Nitro* of 1999 was quite fitting, as the man who told the *New York Times* that he began and ended every conversation with the word "logic" wrote an angle in which Sid was locked in a car, then Bret ran it over with a monster truck. Not only did Sid survive, he was back the following week. The show did a miserable 2.86 to *Raw*'s 5.85. Russo insisted that everyone relax; the turnaround, he said, would take at least six months.

Little did Russo know that he himself didn't have six months left.

"They always say, 'you can't kill this business, you can only bruise it.' But what happened with WCW is living proof that you can kill this business when the people running it know nothing about it."

—*Bobby Heenan, WCW announcer from 1994 to 2000*

CHAPTER 6

2000: Everything Falls Apart

WCW entered 2000 in poor shape. The promotion wasn't dead yet, but it was certainly very ill. As mentioned in the previous chapter, when all the numbers came in for 1999 the company was found to have lost $15 million. The reasons for that were many, although some simplistically tried to pin the blame on "guaranteed contracts." Many wrestlers were guaranteed huge money, they argued, and this created a tendency to not work as hard. As a result, the product suffered.

It's time to debunk that theory once and for all.

The real reason WCW lost so much money had nothing to do with guaranteed deals; in 1996 and 1997, wrestlers with guaranteed deals were making tons of money, and because the company itself was making bank, these wrestlers were actually underpaid. There were a few complaints about guys being lazy, but those who were would have been lazy no matter what kind of contract they had. The problem wasn't the guaranteed contracts—it was that the people in charge failed to elevate or create new main-eventers when they had the perfect opportunities to do so. And when business started to fail, all of a sudden those same guys who were underpaid in 1997 were now overpaid.

Things got worse in 1999 because so much money was spent on stupid things like destroying Humvees and paying rock bands hundreds of thousands of dollars to do 2.13 quarters. In the past, this could easily have been covered, but because the buy rates were tanking, there wasn't enough revenue to make up for those expenses. The good news seemed to be that, under the soon-to-be AOL–Time Warner corporate umbrella, $15 million was merely a drop in the hat. Plus, it wasn't like there was no hope whatsoever for the company; even in early 2000, it appeared that one good idea could potentially turn everything around. Sadly, the mistakes from 1999 were not only repeated in 2000, but even dumber errors were made. As buy rates continued to sink, the company found itself buried deeper and deeper in debt. By early 2001, 1999 looked like the cheery days of yesteryear.

Going into 2000, however, Vince Russo was confident. The company was rolling into the new century primed for some major ratings changes. Interestingly, the changes had nothing to do with his booking savvy or lack thereof.

In early January, *Nitro* moved from three hours to two. There were a couple of reasons for this. The first was that three hours was just too damn long to run a wrestling show, both for the writers and for the fans (especially shows that had become as ponderous as *Nitro* had). The second was that by cutting out the opposed third hour, the composite two-hour rating would pretty much automatically magically jump by several tenths of a point.

Perhaps equally important was the fact that football season was about to come to an end. Historically, wrestling ratings always took a major hit in September, when the season started, and then in January, when *Monday Night Football* ended, they would return to normal. Often, wrestling bookers would try to swerve people by claiming that they were "turning business around" in early January, when in reality, what they wrote had nothing to do with drawing in new viewers. The rating jumped simply because the viewers who had left in September to watch the NFL were returning from their annual hiatus.

Long story short, Russo was about to find himself looking like the company savior.

But all was not so peachy. Taking away an entire hour of *Nitro* meant that the company was also taking away an entire hour of advertising revenue. In order not to lose money, this change meant that *Nitro* had to add one-third of its rating to the other two hours. Since the show was averaging a 3.2 at this point, this meant that the move to two hours and the elimination of football competition would have to bump *Nitro* all the way up to a 4.5 or 4.7. Even those who knew the game doubted that things could change so dramatically.

Ratings aside, business was hardly exploding under Russo. By the end of December 1999, *Nitro* was averaging a miserable 5,000 paid. Worse, the December 14 *Thunder* from Mobile, Alabama, drew only 1,797. Despite what anyone claimed, clearly none of the wrestlers was over with the fans, because merchandise sales, which had been as strong as $10 per head at the company's peak, were now in the $4 range. The buy rate for *Starrcade*, the biggest show of the year, came in at a dismal 0.3, which was especially pathetic since they'd had over a month to build up the quest of their biggest star, Goldberg, towards the WCW title. Russo, again, insisted that a turnaround was going to take time.

The first *Nitro* of the year looked pretty much like almost every *Nitro* of 1999: that is, it was horrid and illogical on every level. The big angle on the program was the introduction of Terry Funk as the new WCW Commissioner. The fans were so excited to see Funk that they immediately began chanting "WE WANT FLAIR!" In real life, Flair and the company were again at odds, and in the story line, he had been buried in the desert. And no, that's not a joke.

The show was built around a tournament for the World Tag Team titles, and for some perverse reason, Russo booked it in such a manner as to make the WCW title tournament look stellar in comparison. The matches themselves were abysmal, and the worst team on the roster, David Flair and Crowbar, beat Nash and Scott Steiner in the finals. The finish saw Arn Anderson, now Funk's enforcer, hit Nash with a crowbar (the physical object, not the wrestler of the same name), leading to the pin. Afterwards, David attacked Arn, no doubt as a way to thank him for helping them to win the tag belts. And then Nash and Steiner beat up Funk as well.

If you're wondering why Funk was beaten up on his first day in, the answer is that the show was in the Carolinas. You see, Flair was supposed to be the Commissioner, and was therefore scheduled to take the beating, to once again be humiliated in front of his hometown crowd. Since he refused, Funk took his place in the pummeling.

This *Nitro* was the first to be cut to two hours, so everyone eagerly awaited the ratings to see if the show would jump up to the 4.5 or 4.7 range needed to make it worthwhile. Finally, it came in.

3.29.

Yes, the exact same number that they'd been doing at three hours. To say people were appalled and terrified would be quite the understatement.

The ratings weren't the only thing taking a pummeling. On January 4, during a hardcore match with Terry Funk on *Thunder*, Bret Hart took several blows to the head with various objects, including trash cans. Bret had been taking quite the beating over the past few weeks, as his *Starrcade* encounter with Goldberg saw him take a brutal kick to the head that had caused a concussion. Figuring it was really no big deal, he continued to wrestle over the course of the next few weeks, and because his brain had swollen, he suffered another minor concussion every time he took a major hit to the head. Shortly after the Funk match, he penned a column for the *Calgary Sun* newspaper. He'd been writing the columns for some time, but had taken several weeks off without explanation.

"A couple of weeks ago, I ended my column by saying that I'd have some explaining to do," he began. "I haven't written since then because I had a lot on my mind and I wasn't sure how to say it."

In detail, Bret described how much wrestling had changed, and how he felt the sport had passed him by. He wrote about the superkick from Goldberg at *Starrcade*, and how, in the following few weeks, he'd had a very physical match with Chris Benoit, a match with Jerry Flynn in which he got kicked full force in the ribs, and finally, the hardcore match with Funk.

"I signed an autograph for a guy who asked me the ever-present 'Is it fake?' question and I was stunned to realize that I'm not even sure I know the answer anymore. Is what fake? The lump on my head is sure real enough."

He was also outraged about having been asked to drive the monster truck that ran over Sid's car, and about another angle that required him to screech out of the arena in a get-away car.

"I'm flooring it, tearing out of backstage, with no time in the scene to even put on a seat belt, and it turns out an icy rain had coated the ramp. There I am, careening out of control, toward a huge trailer truck filled with television equipment. In the last moment, I was somehow able to swerve to safety."

He said this was made worse by the fact that, on the same night, Goldberg had cut his arm all to shreds on the limo window. In the old days, nothing like this would have ever happened in wrestling.

"I'm a wrestler, not a stunt man," he wrote. "And even a stunt man has time to strap himself in. I'm a professional wrestler and I get paid to wrestle in a ring. What am I doing fighting in the back taking falls on concrete and doing stunts in speeding cars?" He said he was especially appalled to think that he was doing the same sort of thing that had resulted in his brother Owen's death.

"So what's the point of all this?" he concluded. "I'm not sure I know. I just know I've emptied my head and my heart and this is as real as it gets. Maybe the whole wrestling business is pathetic . . . including me."

A week after the *Thunder* match with Funk, Bret went to the doctor. He was diagnosed with a concussion so severe that his doctor banned him from doing pretty much everything, including lifting weights and flying in airplanes. Wrestling was absolutely out of the question. Sadly, it would turn out that after an illustrious twenty-four-year run, Bret Hart's final official match was a lame no-contest with Kevin Nash on the January 10 *Nitro*.

Bret immediately called the office and told them the news. Since he was WCW champion and obviously wouldn't be able to defend the belt against Sid (whom he'd had the temerity to accuse of being a "big stupid dummy") at Sunday's *Souled Out* pay-per-view, the decision was made to strip him of the title. The next day, Jeff Jarrett called up and said that he had a concussion as well, suffered when he took a splash from the fifty-six-year-old Jimmy Snuka off the top of a cage four nights earlier on *Nitro*. Right there, the company was out four matches, because Jarrett and Chris Benoit were scheduled for a best-of-three series. The PPV was dead.

Russo, the "insane genius," came up with a plan, and it truly was insane. There would be a battle royal to crown a new champion at the PPV, and the eventual winner would be someone nobody would have predicted going in—Tank Abbott. The real reason nobody would have predicted this is that nobody was quite stupid enough to think that WCW would make Tank Abbott, the shoot fighter WCW had hired last year, who hadn't connected with the fans at all, the World Heavyweight champion.

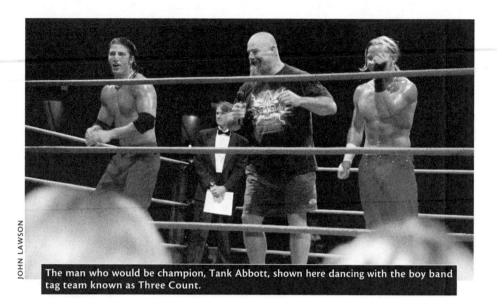

JOHN LAWSON

The man who would be champion, Tank Abbott, shown here dancing with the boy band tag team known as Three Count.

Even Bill Busch, who knew nothing about wrestling, knew it was a stupid idea. This, combined with the fact that guys had been in his ear for months telling him that Vinny Ru was an idiot, led him to remove Russo from his position as head writer. In a move that was probably designed to get him to quit, Busch told him that he could stay on as part of a booking committee with Kevin Sullivan, J.J. Dillon, and Terry Taylor—similar to the committees he worked under in WWF when he actually did help turn the place around. Russo quit, or—more precisely, since he was under a long-term deal—he just went home and continued to collect his checks.

To finally settle any dispute about what Vince Russo accomplished in WCW, let's look at his run from a pure numbers standpoint. The final tally from day one to his departure in January 2000 looked like this:

- *Nitro* ratings went from a 3.08 average to a 3.10, though it was realistically a 2.9 since the 3.10 was for the new two-hour show. Don't forget, this also resulted in the loss of tons of ad revenue money, since they deleted the third hour.

- Attendance fell from 4,628 per show to 3,593, due largely to the fact that the company had failed to create any new stars and had made their previous draws, such as Ric Flair and Goldberg, look like total idiots.
- Buy rates, the company's main revenue source, plummeted from 0.52 to 0.26. That's not a typo—buy rates actually dropped in half.

The numbers do not lie.

With Russo gone, everything fell into complete chaos. The company scrambled to come up with new ideas for the PPV, and some of them, quite frankly, were almost as stupid as the Tank Abbott deal. For example, one idea was for Nash to beat Funk and become Commissioner, and then, in his very first act, say that Scott Hall was the number-one contender and would face Sid for the belt. Hall, however, would be in Florida drinking (in the story line—or maybe not, to be honest), and so Nash would announce that the number-two contender was getting the shot. That, of course, would be Nash himself, and he'd win the title. Nash, knowing how unpopular he already was in the locker room, turned it down.

Finally, they decided to give the shot to Benoit. Sadly, there was a flaw in this plan. Benoit hated Sullivan, who was more or less the head of the booking committee. In fact, Benoit and at least fourteen others hated him so much that they all got together the Saturday night before the PPV and decided to ask for their releases. Their main gripe was that when Sullivan was briefly in charge of booking the year prior, he'd done everything in his power to keep the mid-carders down, and there was no reason to believe that he'd do any differently this time around. By Sunday afternoon, half of the wrestlers had changed their minds, probably for fear of losing their guaranteed deals without any other concrete offers on the table. The WWF likely would have taken some, but not all of them, and most were unwilling to gamble their financial security on it. So Benoit, Dean Malenko,

Eddy Guerrero, Perry Saturn, Konnan, Billy Kidman, and Shane Douglas all went to Busch as a group and said they wanted out. Busch, totally unprepared for this, told them to please wait a week, and he'd try to handle the situation.

Even though Benoit had asked for his release, they still went with the original plan and had him win the belt from Sid with his crossface submission at *Souled Out,* in Sid's best match since 1996 (which really isn't saying much). Sid's foot was underneath the bottom rope while he was locked in the submission, which, in traditional wrestling rules, should have meant that the hold had to be broken, and the match should have continued. What should have been a ploy to set up future matches between the two ended up being used as an excuse to explain why, eighteen hours later, Benoit was no longer champion.

Before *Nitro,* Busch tried to reason with everyone. He said that if they stayed, he'd take Sullivan off *Nitro* and *Thunder* and put him in charge of only *WCW Saturday Night,* which none of them would ever have to work on. That seemed to be cool with everyone. Then, a few hours later, Busch called everyone except Benoit back into his office and said they were being sent home. When Benoit found out, he said if they were being sent home, he was going as well. Busch, obviously trying to play to Benoit's ego, said the plan was for him to beat three men on *Nitro* en route to retaining his WCW championship. Benoit, wisely seeing the belt as a prop in Busch's plan and nothing more, repeated his statement: if everyone else was going home, so was he. He would, however, drop the belt to whomever they chose on TV before doing so. In their seemingly never-ending quest to destroy the credibility of their World title, they told Benoit to just go home. He left the belt with referee Nick Patrick on his way out.

That night on *Nitro,* the announcers basically told the truth: the title was being held up because Sid's foot had been under the ropes, and because they truly didn't know what its status was, fans would have to tune in to *Thunder* to find out.

One week later, in what came as a shock to many, Busch actually lived up to his word and sent Benoit, Malenko, Guerrero, Saturn, Douglas, and Konnan unconditional releases. Konnan and Douglas did not sign due to the fact that both had bad blood with the WWF from years back (when Konnan was the original Max Moon and Douglas was a supposed dean), and they were therefore unlikely to get jobs there. But the other four did and found themselves the focal points of the January 31 edition of *Raw*.

Eddy Guerrero was yet another talent that grew tired of being looked over and passed up for main-event chances. He, along with Dean Malenko, Chris Benoit, and Perry Saturn, would eventually leave WCW and deprive the company of four of its best workers.

JOHN LAWSON

Most would look at this story as typical WCW ineptitude. But in reality, this was much more significant; the departure of the four was a huge nail in the coffin of WCW. While they weren't the biggest stars or the most charismatic guys on the roster, they were the heart of the company—four young guys who should have been given a chance to run with the ball in 1997 and 1998 when it was time to create a new generation. All of them, Benoit in particular (considered by many to be the best technical wrestler in the world), were workhorses who went out there every night and did the absolute best they could under what was usually the worst of circumstances. In early 2000, WCW didn't have a lot left. Really, the only thing they could brag about in comparison to the WWF was a strong roster of workers. When they lost these four, they lost those bragging rights and were left with virtually nothing.

Those backstage in WCW downplayed it, saying the four would get lost in the shuffle due to their size and their lack of interview skills. They were just the "Vanilla Midgets." They also had what they thought was an ingenious back-up plan: the reintroduction, or digging-up in story line, of Ric Flair. Where did it take place, you ask? On a huge, heavily hyped *Nitro* event, perhaps a show unopposed by *Raw*? On the *Superbrawl* pay-per-view?

Of course not. It took place with no hype on the January 25 edition of *Thunder* from Las Vegas (which was, in fact, where Flair had been buried in the story line, so for once WCW had some level of continuity). His big role on the show was to go out and say "good job" to Sid for having regained the WCW title from Kevin Nash. The whole process of Sid's losing and winning the belt was so convoluted that we won't explain it here for fear of causing serious brain damage to readers.

OK, we will—but be forewarned that it is so baffling, it almost makes the previous year's Flair-Piper insane asylum story line seem logical in comparison.

After Benoit left, Terry Taylor announced on *Thunder* that there was going to be an nWo versus WCW match on the January 24 *Nitro* for the vacant title. Sid, he announced, was the WCW representative, and the nWo was going to be able to choose whomever they pleased. Nash, the Commissioner, chose Jarrett. But, he said, if Sid beat Jarrett, he wouldn't get the belt. Instead, he'd get a match with Nash for the belt. If Jarrett won, Nash would presumably just get the belt via forfeit.

Nitro came, and it was announced that Jeff Jarrett couldn't wrestle yet because of his Snuka-induced concussion. So Nash said that Sid had to beat Don Harris instead in order to win the shot against him for the title later. Confused yet? It gets even more ridiculous. During the Sid versus Don match, Don switched places with his twin brother Ron. Sid pinned Ron. During the commercial break, however—and keep in mind, this was therefore not seen by fans at home—it was announced that Sid had beaten the wrong guy and had to return to beat the right one. He didn't return, so he was counted out. Logically, this should have meant that Don Harris was the new WCW champion. Or Nash was. Who knows. Anyway, since this happened during the break, on TV they pretended that it had never happened. So in the main event, Sid got his title shot against Nash anyway in the most horrendous match since, well, the last time they had a horrendous match, which was at *Starrcade* the month prior. This particular technical classic was highlighted by them screwing up the very first move they tried, which was a bodyslam. Jarrett ran out and accidentally hit Nash with a guitar, allowing Sid to get the pin and become the new WCW World champion.

A mess, to be sure, but at least WCW had an undisputed champion.

Well, actually, they didn't. After all this went down, it was announced on *Thunder* that Sid had, in fact, pinned the wrong Harris twin. So, Nash ruled, he (meaning Nash) was the champion. He then signed a new main event, himself and the Harris Twin that Sid Did Not Beat (that would be Don . . . well, we think) versus Sid in a cage match for the title. He made sure to note that the only way Sid could win the belt was to pin both himself (meaning Nash, though by this point we wouldn't have put it past WCW bookers to have Sid actually pin himself) and Ron. Sid managed to beat both Nash and Harris, thankfully putting an end to perhaps the most nonsensical and convoluted story line in the history of pro wrestling.

Or at least in WCW that particular week.

Flair made his return to *Nitro* on January 31, head-to-head with the debuting Radicals (the new team name given to Benoit, Malenko, Guerrero, and Saturn) on *Raw*. Despite the fact that the ex-WCW guys had been portrayed as mid-carders for years and told in no uncertain terms that they could never draw as main-eventers, *Raw* did a 6.59 rating to *Nitro*'s 2.79. Those who argued that *Raw* was just hot and the number had nothing to do with the arrival of Benoit and company were about to be in for a big surprise.

Even with Russo gone, the string of stupid story lines continued. One angle featured Big T, who had several years earlier been the WWF's Ahmed Johnson, filing a lawsuit against Booker T claiming that he owned the rights to the letter T. Big T would eventually win the bout (and the letter) in a match that would have been a main event on any episode of *Sesame Street* worldwide.

The February 7 ratings war, if you can even call it that, was something else. *Nitro*, which should have seen its ratings increase automatically after having eliminated a full hour, instead drew an abysmal 2.66. The only number even remotely in that neighborhood was the final show of the Nash era, which drew a 2.61. However, that show was three hours long, so realistically, this was the lowest number in years. *Raw*, on the other hand, did a 6.49 rating, peaking at an 8.11 for—that's right—the former Vanilla Midgets and DX versus Rock, Cactus Jack, Rikishi, and Too Cool. Not only that, but 25 percent of *Nitro*'s audience switched to *Raw* when the show went off the air. Suddenly, Bill Busch was looking like a bigger fool than ever.

Poor Busch. Besides having to deal with criticism over how he handled the Benoit situation, he also had to deal with the money pit that WCW had become. Hearing that the company had lost more money in one year than in all three years of Jim Herd's reign of terror put together, he decided to cut costs. But fear not, he had a plan. Get this: they'd only fly in the guys who were going to work on a given show. Yes, it sounds incredible, but it's true. Believe it or not, up until this point they were literally buying airline tickets to each event for the entire roster of 160 or so performers, but using only twenty to thirty of them during a show. Now they would only fly in the folks they were going to actually use. Very clever, and truly a revolutionary concept for WCW.

At this point, the company had no clue what to do, so they turned to the man who claimed to have always been their savior: Hulk Hogan. Having been absent since *Halloween Havoc*, Hogan made his big return on *Thunder* for no explicable reason. Even less explicable was the fact that when he returned, he made no mention of *Halloween Havoc*, no mention of why he'd walked out on the match with Sting, and no mention of where he'd been, though he did manage, in the span of two minutes, to say the word "brother" five times, "dude" four times, and "Jack" twice. In this epic speech he also talked about how the "young guys" like Lex Luger (a spry forty-one at the time) needed to go because they thought they were stars. He attacked both Luger and Liz when they came out, giving the latter the single worst atomic drop in the history of wrestling—she sold it by gently patting her own ass.

Amazingly, that wasn't even the worst bump on the show. The company had been building up a new wrestler named The Machine, who was scheduled to debut later in the night against Dallas Page. They had your typical 1980s prelim bout, with Machine climbing to the top rope to do some sort of wacky high-flying stunt. Page, however, bonked into the ropes just before he took flight, so Machine was supposed to crotch the top turnbuckle. Instead of immediately doing so, Machine did the following.

First, he stood up from his crouched position. Then he uttered a scream of terror. Finally, he jumped literally about six feet from the top turnbuckle and crotched himself on the ropes. It is unlikely that anyone who ever saw this could possibly forget it, and Page was said to still be laughing about it months later. And in his big debut that they'd been hyping up all night, Machine got pinned, and was never seen again.

In an effort to give the younger guys something to do, Evan Karagias, Shane Helms, and Shannon Moore were dubbed Three Count, and given a boy band gimmick. They would come out and sing and dance to the delight of, well, no one in particular. The highlight of their run came when Karagias said that Three Count's first album, which was not available anywhere, had somehow gone platinum, and that their next album, which would be even bigger, was going to go gold.

There was no such comedy the following Monday, as the performers, watching the company die around them, began to openly lash out at both the company and each other. Scott Steiner cut an unscripted promo on *Nitro* that totally buried Ric Flair (though not literally this time). Steiner went on a rampage, calling Flair, among other things, a "jealous old ass-kissing, butt-sucking bastard." He said last week when Flair came out on TV, everyone watching at home turned to *Raw* to watch Steve Austin, because WCW sucked. He ranted for so long that the format for the show went right out the window, and several pre-taped segments had to be axed. His punishment was to be suspended from *Thunder* . . . with pay, of course.

Steiner wasn't the only one on the warpath that week, as Hogan did an appearance on the *Bubba the Love Sponge* radio show later and once again ripped WCW apart. He went after Billy Kidman, saying he wouldn't be able to headline a wrestling show at a flea market. A few weeks later, in another interview, he ripped apart most of the roster, saying nobody under the age of forty could draw.

It seemed that even WCW.com was against Kidman. The website would commonly post "best match" polls every night after *Nitro*. The polls, however, were strange in that if fans voted for, say, Booker versus Kidman, credit would go to Sid versus Abbott instead. Sometimes, the polls were so weird that if you voted for Kidman, a main-eventer would get the votes, and the poor guy would actually lose votes.

This interview made clear two of the problems in the organization at the time. First, nobody under forty could draw (and it should be mentioned that Goldberg was under forty and had been quite the draw for a long time before his legs were cut off) because nobody over the age of forty had made any effort to turn them into superstars back when things were hot. Second, nobody over the age of forty was drawing anymore either, because the lack of new stars had led fans to tune out in droves. The worst part about all of this was that when Hogan had signed with WCW, they'd given him a creative control clause that pretty much allowed him to book his own story lines, so the company was resigned to catering to his whims until at least 2001, when the contract expired.

To be fair, it should be noted that too much emphasis was placed (and still is at times) on the chronological age of the wrestlers. The real problem was not their actual age, but their "TV age," or how many times they'd been in a prominent spot on television over the course of a year. For example, in early 2000, with only a few exceptions, all the top stars in the WWF were under thirty-five. Just three years later, though, the newly dubbed WWE was experiencing the same problems WCW had in 1999: the top stars had become stale. It wasn't as if the top stars went from age twenty-nine to forty-nine in the span of three years, though. They were only three years older, but because WWE was putting on four hours of television every single week, the main-eventers had appeared in approximately 300 main events, and in "TV years" they had become just as old and stale as the forty-five-year-olds who were killing WCW's business in 1999. Not only that, but in 1997, WCW's top stars were in their forties, and the company was killing the WWF business-wise. If it was all about age, that shouldn't have happened since the main WWF stars were years, and sometimes decades, younger. Instead of arguing about "old guys versus young guys," or the need to "elevate young wrestlers," the argument should be about "fresh versus stale" and the need to elevate new faces—regardless of their actual age—to the top of the cards.

Never was this more evident than at the *Superbrawl* PPV on February 20, as Hogan (against Luger) and Flair (against Funk) were both featured in main-event matches. A year earlier, the two of them facing off against each other drew a $550,000 house and a 1.1 buy rate. Just 365 days later, they helped draw a $177,324 house and 0.15 buy rate. If ever there was proof that running with a pat hand for too long was death, this was it.

//

The *Superbrawl* main event saw Sid beat Scott Hall and Jeff Jarrett in a three-way to retain the WCW title. In a strange coincidence, Hall took a guitar shot from Jarrett and a powerbomb from Sid, and was injured for real. The reason this was so weird was because everyone was sure that as soon as both guys walked through the curtain after the match, Hall was going to be fired. Earlier in the week, on a flight to Germany for a tour, he'd gotten so messed up that he wasn't even allowed to board a plane back to the U.S. (they just happened to get the same flight crew going back as they had going over, and they said there was no way they'd spend another sixteen hours with this man). Consequently, he missed the *Nitro* that aired six days before his scheduled PPV main event.

Tony Schiavone often said such ludicrous things on air that most fans believed he was either (a) trying to help kill the company or (b) really, really stupid.

MIKE LANO

On top of that, prior to the *Thunder* tapings the next night, he claimed he was going to hit Terry Taylor with a guitar during an angle, and because Terry took this as a serious threat, Hall was pulled off the show. Because of this, the program started late, and to kill time, ring announcer Dave Penzer entertained the crowd with horrible jokes for forty minutes. Everyone thought this was it for sure, but because Hall claimed the spinal injury and scheduled an MRI for February 22, he was not fired. It should be noted that, spinal injury or not, Hall thought there was no chance of him ever being fired. He told friends that he was just in "time out," and that the company couldn't afford to lose him because he was too valuable a witness in the WWF versus WCW trademark infringement lawsuit.

The show also made it apparent that the crutch of using celebrities didn't help matters, either. The third match on the show featured the Wall versus the KISS Demon in what was billed as a "Special Main Event." The Demon was a wrestler Eric Bischoff debuted in 1999 as part of the deal with Gene Simmons in which the band was paid $500,000 for a 2.13 quarter-hour. As part of the agreement, WCW was required to use the Demon in a certain number of main-event matches. In reality, they gave up on the KISS Demon (Dale Torborg) within, oh, one week, leaving him as nothing but a jobber with a fancy ring entrance doing third-match-on-the-card main events.

A much less costly, but perhaps even more idiotic celeb miscue happened later in the show. For months, WCW wrestler Ernest "The Cat" Miller had proclaimed himself the Godfather of WCW, dancing to the ring to a tune reminiscent of many James Brown hits. He claimed that he knew James Brown, and that he'd bring him out to the ring one day. He did this on a weekly basis, to the point that no one believed that Brown would ever show up. Brown did in fact show up at *Superbrawl*, but since WCW never promoted this, fans at home didn't find out about it until the following night on *Nitro*. Inexplicably, the company kept Brown's appearance a secret, so he was ultimately paid $25,000 to show up, dance, and bring no additional viewers with him.

The only other "highlight" of the show was a match between Tank Abbott and a guy named "Big Al" that no one had ever heard of before (or since, come to think of it). At the end of their leather jacket on a pole match, Tank pulled a knife on Al, and screamed, "I could fucking kill you!" He then placed the knife squarely on Al's throat as the cameras quickly cut away. Tony Schiavone, thinking on his feet, came up with a remarkable explanation: Tank, he said, was just trying to shave Al's beard.

Unfortunately for Tony, Al had no beard.

Nitro and *Thunder* were just boring shows for the next few weeks. It's hard to determine whether they were better or worse than Russo's horrible shows, because at least the latter were comically horrible. Fans used to spend those two hours debating whether to laugh or to cry, but now the two hours began to just drag on and on and on.

Actually, there is a business answer to that question. These boring shows were worse. *Far* worse. The February 28 *Nitro* did a 2.57 rating, its lowest in years, versus *Raw*'s 6.50. Yes, *Raw* nearly *tripled* their number. At one point in the evening, it was 6.70 to 1.89 in *Raw*'s favor. Then, on March 6, they drew 2,236 paid to the Chapel Hill, North Carolina, *Nitro*. Keep in mind that, a year earlier, they had sold out all 16,000 seats in this building the very first day tickets went on sale.

Bret Hart, who had been severely injured in the line of duty, was sent a letter informing him that he'd been on the shelf for so long that they were cutting his pay in half. Not only that, but as of April 15, they could fire him. He wasn't fired, but the pay cut stipulation ended up being a huge source of controversy. The deal, which was written into most of the contracts, was that if you got hurt and were going to be out for a long time, your pay was cut in half until you were able to return. Actual sports stars out in the real world could not believe their ears when they heard this. WCW's argument was that these guys were making huge money, and if they didn't want to work, they could just claim an injury and sit at home, still making a ton of money. WCW did not realize two things. The first is that, as bad as WCW was, the vast, vast majority of the wrestlers, even those who hated the environment, still loved to perform and weren't going to stay off television any longer than absolutely necessary. And second, the threat of pay cuts did far more harm than good, since it led many guys to return to action way before they were healthy enough to do so, which in turn led to more injuries, more pain pill addictions, and, in a few cases, tragedy.

With business in the toilet domestically, WCW turned to Europe for help. The week of March 13 was actually a spectacular one for the company, because fans across the pond were starved for wrestling. In England, as a result, they drew the biggest houses since their U.S. peak: 11,812 in Birmingham; 10,450 in London; and 16,318 in Manchester. After these tremendous successes, they came back home and made absolutely zero mention of them on either *Nitro* or *Thunder*.

Europe was where the good news ended. The March 13 *Nitro*, the latest in a string of boring, nothing-happening shows, set a new record low: a 2.53 against *Raw*'s 6.28. And then came *Uncensored*, which in years past had garnered the reputation of being one of the worst PPV events of the year. This was no exception. The show was miserable, exposing once again all that was wrong with the company. You'd think that by now, every glaring mistake would have been obvious and the bookers would have made a strong effort to turn things around. You'd be wrong. The first day tickets were made available, WCW grossed about $90,000 in sales. They then did weeks and weeks of horrid television building up the show and adding wacky stipulations to many of the matches. When show time finally rolled around, they'd sold $97,925 worth of tickets.

Amazingly, all that TV—all those angles, everything—resulted only in approximately *200 additional tickets* being sold. This was the epitome of television writing that sold—almost literally—no tickets. It was one horrible match after another. If you take star ratings seriously, exactly one of the first ten matches broke the two-star mark. Then Hogan beat Flair in the main event in a strap match. The rules of this match were that in order to win, you had to drag your opponent around the ring and touch all four ringposts in succession. The announcers calmly explained this to all the confused fans at home. So what happened at the finish? Hogan hit Flair with the Legdrop of Doom and pinned him. Then he won a second time by touching all four corners.

One year and one month earlier, the exact same Hogan versus Flair match (minus the strap stipulation) had drawn a 1.1 buy rate.

At *Uncensored 2000*, it did a 0.13, nearly a *90 percent* drop-off in business in just over one year!

Following this latest debacle, the tables turned again. Brad Siegel, who oversaw the wrestling division, decided to shake up the power structure by bringing Russo and Bischoff back together to head creative. Bill Busch, outraged, said that if Bischoff came back, he'd quit. Siegel didn't believe him. So Busch quit. This was not good news. Siegel, having seen the $15 million WCW lost in 1999 under Bischoff, made it very clear that Eric would only be involved in the creative side of the company, and that he'd have nothing to do with the business. Busch was supposed to handle the business, but once he quit, Siegel ended up having to work twice as many hours to deal with that situation as well. Kevin Sullivan was also sent home.

The return of Bischoff and Russo was pushed as the pairing of the man who'd turned WCW around and the man who had turned the WWF around. (To be fair, Bischoff had actually turned the company around twice, once for the better and once for the worse.) Most in the company figured it was only a matter of time before the two self-destructed; their personalities were such that it didn't seem possible for them to work together for any length of time.

Despite this, the two had allegedly been talking for a while. A month or so earlier, Siegel had asked Sullivan and his crew to come up with a booking plan for the rest of the year, or at least an overview of what they were going to do. Russo and Bischoff, at the same time, decided to submit a plan of their own. Their plan was basically to create a group of young guys headed by Russo to feud with a group of old guys headed by Bischoff. On the surface, this looked like a fine plan; at least it would get the young guys mixed up with the old guys and hopefully, in a perfect world, create some new stars. You all know the dilemma; WCW was absolutely not a perfect world.

On *WCW Live* that week, Russo did what he did best: he talked about himself and why it was everyone else's fault that things had tanked in late 1999. He also spun the numbers something fierce, claiming he took *Nitro* from a 2.5 to a 3.5 in twelve weeks. This, of course, would have made Bill Busch look like a major idiot if true. He said he'd wanted to bring Bischoff back for a long time, but during his first run, nobody went for it. Now, he said, Eric would be back leading the nWo, which would help turn things around. That, plus more emphasis on the Cruiserweight division, would improve the situation. Keep in mind that in Russo's first run, the Cruiser weight division was built around an Oklahoma versus Madusa feud—one of these wrestlers was not a Cruiserweight; the other was not, actually, a man. He said he wanted *Thunder* moved head-to-head with *Smackdown* (it had been switched from Thursday to Wednesday nights at the beginning of the year in an attempt to boost ratings), and *Nitro* head-to-head with *Raw* for both hours. Last, but not least, he said he wanted to bring Warrior back, because "in all honesty, there isn't anybody out there that wouldn't love to see a Goldberg versus Warrior match." Shockingly, Brad Siegel did not fire him the second this statement came out of his mouth.

The March 27 *Nitro* was a fun little show, mainly because it was the annual Spring Breakout event in which the ring was set up poolside. This was a lame duck show, one of the last before Russo and Bischoff regained power, highlighted by a Hogan versus Wall feud that built throughout the show. It started with Gene Okerlund interviewing Hogan in mid-ring. As Hogan ranted and raved, a tiny figure in white appeared on top of a building about a mile away. The cameras zoomed all the way in but could barely make out this mysterious figure's identity. Hogan, who wears glasses in real life, immediately identified this person as the Wall. "THE WALL!" he desperately screamed. "IT'S THE WALL, BROTHER!" The tiny figure raised a hand up in the air to signal for a chokeslam. Hogan took this as a challenge and said he'd beat Wall up later. They ended up wrestling in the main event, and the match ended in a no-contest when, after Wall actually kicked out of Hogan's vaunted Legdrop of Doom, Vampiro ran in. Wall got to chokeslam Hogan through a table afterward, but, sadly for him, that was pretty much the end of their program. Also on the show, Sting beat Luger after he backdropped him into the ocean, and the referee counted the pin on the surface of the water.

On April 3, the company ran a taped *Nitro* designed to set up the return of Bischoff and Russo, who had obviously lied months back when he said his face would never be shown on TV. Most mind-boggling was that, in hyping up the event, Tony Schiavone actually said that they were doing it to remind fans of how great *Nitro* used to be. Yes, he outright told viewers that *Nitro* used to be good, but now sucked so bad that they were going to have to start over. Running a "best-of" program was actually an ingenious little ploy, because the taped, nothing-happening show drew a 1.78, which meant they had quite the number to build on. The show was a mix of factual and fictional history (mostly fictional), and in closing, announced that the teaming-up of Russo and Bischoff was, literally, the biggest news of all time in wrestling.

On April 10 they did their first show, and one thing was very clear: no matter what anyone wanted to say about Russo, he could write a hell of a first chapter. The problem, as would be made clear countless times down the road, was his inability to follow up on that first chapter and maintain momentum.

The show was built around three men: Russo, Bischoff, and Hogan. The story line that had Eric heading one group and Vinny Ru another was thrown out in favor of having the two of them team up to lead a group of young guys, the New Blood, against the old dudes, the Millionaires Club. To their credit, they actually got two things to happen that most in wrestling thought were impossible: Flair wrestled his real-life nemesis Shane Douglas, and Hulk Hogan lost to Kidman, the guy who couldn't headline a flea market wrestling show.

While that sounds all fine and dandy on paper, a distinction should be made between "losing" to someone and "putting someone over." To "put someone over" means to make them look credible—like a real, legitimate threat, an equal of sorts. Ric Flair put a lot of guys over in his career, meaning they beat him, and in doing so, became superstars. The best example of this, obviously, is Sting: at the very first *Clash of the Champions*, Flair allowed Sting to beat the crap out of him throughout their forty-five-minute match. It should be noted that Sting didn't even win that match—it was a draw. Despite this, Flair had done such a masterful job of making Sting out to be an equal that fans bought him as being on par with the Nature Boy. In essence, Flair made Sting a star that night.

Just losing to a person doesn't necessarily mean anything, and it was clear from the beginning that Hogan wasn't willing to do for Kidman what Flair had done for Sting. In their first match, Hogan beat the hell out of him the entire time, until Bischoff finally hit Hogan with a chair and Kidman got the pin. Even though Kidman "won," the fans saw it for what it was: Hogan getting screwed and Kidman merely being in the right place at the right time. In other words, Kidman didn't get over at all, and it was a waste of a match. Sadly, this trend was only just beginning.

The lower-card guys were so desperate to get noticed that they would come up with idiotic and dangerous moves. Later in the year, for instance, Johnny the Bull did a springboard legdrop over the top rope and to the arena floor. A legdrop, of course, requires the person doing the move to land on their ass. He was warned repeatedly that this was not a good idea. He did it anyway, and everyone was right. He ended up—literally—breaking his ass. Johnny the Bull did not return to TV for a long, long time.

Also on the show, they announced that all the titles were being vacated. This led to one of the most telling moments of the year for the company, a moment they should have learned from, but didn't. Basically, Eric asked Sid to hand over the World title. Sid said no. So Eric made a crack about how he didn't have scissors. This was, of course, in regard to the U.K. hotel room incident ten years ago in which Sid and Arn got into a real fight and Sid almost killed Arn with a pair of scissors. The announcers went crazy, feigning complete disbelief that Eric would say something like this.

The crowd, however, sat there in complete silence. Eric figured they must not have heard him, so he said it again.

Silence.

The problem, of course, was that 99 percent of wrestling fans did not scour the Internet for wrestling news every day, and probably only 5 percent of them, at most, had ever even heard of that story. Russo, however, who lived and died by the Internet responses to his shows, was so surrounded by the medium that he came to the conclusion that every single fan had heard every single inside story that had ever happened in the business. The simplicity of wrestling booking is that it's fake, so you can make up any story you want, and as long as you push it hard on television and it's even remotely credible, fans are going to go along with it simply because they enjoy suspending their disbelief. The thing is, you have to push it hard on television. This was not the first or the last angle created on the assumption that fans knew way more than they actually did. The *Halloween Havoc* deal with Hogan and Sting, where Hogan laid down for him and then walked out of the building, ended up meaning less than nothing, because in order to get fans to think it was "real," the announcers never mentioned it and never talked about it again. They assumed that every fan knew what had happened and why it had happened, when in reality, virtually nobody did. Instead of being left eagerly anticipating what would happen next, they were instead left utterly confused.

Even more perplexing is this quandary, again in relation to *Havoc*: the finish was booked to fool the insider fans. However, because they're insider fans, they weren't fooled; they knew the entire story by that night or the next morning. Meanwhile, those who weren't insider fans had no idea what had happened, and never found out because the announcers never explained it. The angle accomplished absolutely nothing.

On the bright side, Vince and Eric's first *Nitro* was a big success, doing a 3.06 rating to *Raw*'s 6.17. Better, fans really seemed to enjoy it and were excited to tune in the following week. And best of all, there was a very positive team meeting before the show started at which everyone was told that they had a chance to turn it all around if they just worked together for everyone's benefit. The wrestlers left the meeting feeling more positive about the future than at any point in the last several months.

On the not-so-bright side, opening that weekend was *Ready to Rumble*, a WCW-commissioned movie about two of the dumbest human beings on the planet, both of whom ended up being wrestling fans. Critics showered the movie with praise, calling it everything from "moronic and insulting" (*Entertainment Weekly*) to "dumb and clueless" (*TV Guide*) to "spectacularly inane" (*Screen It*) to "the new worst movie of all time" (*Orlando Sentinel*).

There was also turmoil behind the scenes. In yet another effort to re-create 1996, WCW went after some big stars outside the company. Since everyone in WWE was completely locked up, Bischoff and Russo went to ECW champion Mike Awesome and offered him a huge-money deal to jump ship. Awesome verbally agreed. The problem was that Paul Heyman claimed he had a three-year contract with Awesome's signature on it. Both sides went back and forth. Finally, a concession was made: Awesome could appear on *Nitro* as ECW champion (without the belt), do an angle with Nash, and the announcers would hype up his April 13 ECW match in Indianapolis (where he was scheduled to lose the title). WCW said OK, but then failed to mention Indianapolis directly and to let Awesome cut a promo, both of which reneged on the agreement. For a while, it looked like WCW wasn't going to be able to get him after all.

Finally, though, a resolution was reached. WCW paid a reported six-figure settlement to get Awesome out of his contract, and, per the terms of the deal, he was allowed to go back to ECW for that one date in Indianapolis and lose the belt. Despite having lost the belt, Awesome was now one of the hottest topics in wrestling. Therefore, WCW brought him and gave him virtually nothing to do. He bounced around the mid-card, portraying horrible characters such as "That '70s Guy," in which he wore a leisure suit, and "The Fat Chick Thriller," in which he made . . . ummm . . . fat chicks swoon. Neither got over, and in the end, Awesome's booking made his signing just another colossal waste of money.

ECW owner Paul Heyman came up with a scenario he thought was ideal for Awesome to drop the ECW title: the WWF's Tazz, who'd first made his name in ECW, would return and beat Awesome with help from Tommy Dreamer. Heyman felt it would be great to have a WWF guy beat a WCW guy in an ECW ring. Unfortunately, this whole deal did more harm than good. The match went just 1:13, and then when it was over, Awesome simply got up and walked out of the building as if nothing had happened. Because the bout was so short, it neither hurt Awesome nor helped Tazz, but did major damage to the title itself. In hindsight, what was really worst of all was that Awesome's departure ended up being another one of many nails in the coffin of ECW.

The first major PPV of the Russo–Bischoff era was *Spring Stampede* on April 16 at the United Center in Chicago. It was a success in many ways, drawing 8,377 paid for a $272,930 gate and being pretty well regarded by fans. They put the New Blood over strongly, having members of the group win the Cruiserweight (Chris Candido), Tag Team (Shane Douglas and Buff Bagwell—yes, they were considered young guys), U.S. (Scott Steiner), and World titles (Jeff Jarrett). The downside was that, just like their first *Nitro*, virtually every single match had a run-in or interference of some sort leading to the finish. Despite all that, the match quality was still better than usual, and worlds better than *Uncensored* one month prior.

There was more bad news than good on the April 17 *Nitro*. The show was still built around Hogan, and in one of the main angles, he got revenge on Kidman for "beating him" the week prior when he ran a Humvee into a Dumpster that Kidman was supposedly in, apparently killing him in story line. In one of those only-in-WCW moments of unintentional comedy, the announcers made mention that in the new WCW, there were going to be real winners and losers because the refs weren't going to be calling for DQs. This comment was immediately followed by three DQs in a row.

The rating for the program was dismal: a 2.47 to *Raw*'s 6.75. The final segment, which featured a Hogan–Bischoff confrontation and Bret's return, did a mere 1.73 to *Raw*'s 7.68. Granted, *Raw* had quite the trump card: they announced the return of Steve Austin, who had been out since late 1999 following his spinal surgery.

Thunder the following Wednesday night was a better show, though it did feature the debut of a person no hardcore WCW fan will ever forget: David Arquette, star of *Ready to Rumble*. Keep in mind that a "better show" for WCW still featured such implausibles as Sid beating Harlem Heat 2000 in a no-DQ handicap match via DQ, and clips of the finish of a Sting versus Los Villanos match that, because of an editing problem, aired before the match had actually taken place.

The April 19 *Thunder* also saw Brian Knobbs' last appearance in the world of wrestling, as he was doing an angle with Meng in which Meng hit him with a life-sized cardboard cutout of Goldberg (which Knobbs sold). He was then thrown out a thirty-foot window. He didn't really fall thirty feet, but it was in fact the last time Knobbs ever appeared on a nationally televised pro-wrestling event. If you're going to go, you might as well go in style.

Production woes, however, would soon be the least of the company's problems. *Nitro* in Rochester, New York, on April 24 was headlined by DDP beating Jarrett to win the WCW title in a cage match. It was the only thing resembling a good match on the show, but still, it was a textbook example of how to kill off a heavyweight title. As DDP hit his diamond cutter finisher and was about to win, Mike Awesome ran down and ripped off the cage door—a truly stupid move, because the point of a cage is to convince fans that nobody is going to be able to run in. It was ten times as dumb here, because the main event of the PPV two weeks later was scheduled to be—that's right—a cage match. Kanyon came down and brawled with Awesome, and as he was doing so, Page got the pin. Because so much was happening at once, nobody cared about the title change. Also on the show, Kidman got another "big win" over Hogan. It was a two-on-one match, with Kidman and Awesome teaming up to take out the Hulkster. Hogan beat them both up for what seemed like forever; then Awesome finally powerbombed him through a table, and Kidman got the pin with a legdrop. With each passing week, this angle made Hogan and Kidman progressively less over, the exact opposite of what a young guy versus old guy feud should do. And it wouldn't be complete without something like this: Sting went to a no-contest with Vampiro in a First Blood Match (yes, a no-contest) when blood fell from the ceiling and drenched Vamp.

And then, on *Thunder* two days later, the company made perhaps its biggest mistake ever.

The show was built around Jeff Jarrett being upset with Arquette, claiming he had cost him the title, an odd claim since Arquette hadn't been involved in the *Nitro* match in any way, shape, or form. One can only surmise that perhaps Jarrett had watched *Ready to Rumble* that weekend, and his brain was so fried that he was unable to concentrate on his title bout. Regardless, this led to Arquette and Page versus Bischoff and Jarrett, the stipulation being that whoever got the pin got the belt. Page gave Bischoff the diamond cutter; then Arquette, the movie star, covered Eric and became WCW World Heavyweight champion.

The WCW title, which, in story lines at least, dated back to 1905 and had been the catalyst for huge pay-per-view matches and giant house show gates throughout the company's history, was now dead, buried, and had a headstone resting above it.

The idea, of course, was to get WCW some mainstream publicity and to help rebuild their ever-decreasing audience. To Arquette's credit, he pushed hard not to be given the belt, saying he was undeserving, and, as a life-long wrestling fan himself, he understood that fellow fans would absolutely detest the switch. Unable to change Russo's mind, he went along with the bout, and sent all the money he made during his WCW run to the families of the recently deceased Owen Hart and Brian Pillman, and also to WWF star Darren Drosdov, who had been paralyzed from the neck down in a tragic in-ring accident on *Smackdown*.

Was Russo's idea of putting the belt on Arquette a success? Not in any way, shape, or form, no matter what anyone might argue to the contrary. Although they garnered a fair amount of mainstream press, including an article in *USA Today* and a mention on *Entertainment Weekly*, all it did was make WCW look like complete idiots because they had an actor winning their top belt. *Nitro* confirmed this, doing a 2.46 rating to *Raw*'s 7.40 the following Monday. The quarter-hour ratings made it very clear that casual fans were irate about the handling of the belt and were, in essence, boycotting WCW.

All of this fantastic television led to the *Slamboree* show on May 7. Again, this was a mix of good and bad, both from business and story line standpoints. The bad was that they did a horrible number at the gate: 4,862 paid for $139,202. Keep in mind that, eighteen months earlier, their shows were almost breaking the $1 million mark. Tickets were actually selling pretty well until May 1, when they came to a screeching halt. That was the day, coincidentally, that it was announced that Arquette would defend the title in the main event of the show. The decision to do so also resulted in a buy rate so low that WCW refused to release it publicly (it was rumored to be around a 0.14).

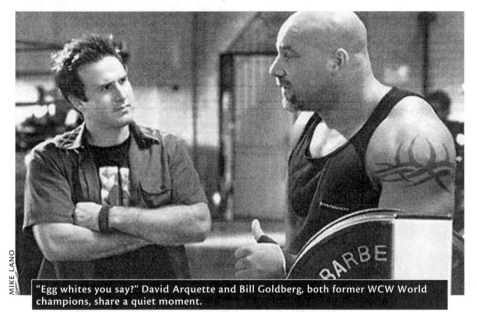

"Egg whites you say?" David Arquette and Bill Goldberg, both former WCW World champions, share a quiet moment.

On the bright side, the wrestling was better top-to-bottom, and the main event, a triple-decker cage match with Arquette defending against Page and Jarrett, could only be described as a modern-day miracle. The triple-decker cage, obviously, came from the *Ready to Rumble* movie. Arquette got bumped early on, allowing Jarrett and Page to do most of the work. The only way to win was to climb up to the third cage (they were all stacked one on top of the other) and grab the belt, which was hanging from the ceiling. Arquette got up there first, but he sold it like he was afraid of heights and just lay on his belly. Finally, Jarrett and Page got up there with him, and in the big swerve, Arquette took a guitar and clonked his best friend DDP in the head with it, allowing Jarrett to regain the championship. Afterwards, they did a brawl with Awesome and Kanyon that saw Awesome throw Kanyon off the second cage onto the ramp. Obviously, the ramp was heavily padded, and Kanyon, who had practiced the stunt three times that afternoon, was fine. Pretty much everyone watching just thought it was a really cool bump. Fans live, however, were appalled, as the show took place at the Kemper Arena in Kansas City—the site of Owen Hart's death. Although this wasn't meant to spoof it, it hit way too close to home for a lot of people in the crowd.

Nitro on May 8 was a real sign of the times, as the TWA Dome, which a year and a half earlier had drawn a legit 29,000 paid, had under 3,500 fans in attendance. At least Tony Schiavone didn't downplay it like in the old days and claim, say, 1,500 in the building. The main event saw Jarrett pin Sting after Sting was sucked down into the ring by a mysterious force that later turned out to be Vampiro. He emerged covered in blood and was quickly pinned. In another Vampiro-related angle on *Nitro* a few weeks earlier, a big pool of blood had fallen from the ceiling and drenched him. For whatever reason, Sting showed up on *Thunder* a few days later still covered in blood, indicating that he did not, in fact, shower regularly.

There was trouble behind the scenes again, as the May 9 *Thunder* taping saw Buff Bagwell get arrested after an altercation with crewmember Darryl Miller backstage. According to Miller, he was trying to get a roll of carpet through a door that Bagwell, Luger, and Liz were standing in front of. A local news report added that the carpet was "taken from the wrestling arena following a match that involved much spilling of a bloodlike substance." Miller asked the wrestlers to move. Bagwell said they were busy. Words were exchanged, and Miller claimed Bagwell—and this is a direct quote from the police report—"punched him upside the neck." He punched him so hard, in fact, that he was left with a "fist-print." Luger and Liz were questioned and claimed they hadn't seen or heard a thing, "because wrestler Goldberg's monster truck was crushing a Buick outside the convention center at the time." Buff was taken to jail and released after posting $500 bail; then Brad Siegel suspended him for thirty days.

The show itself was another comedy of story line errors. It opened with a brand-new video package, and for whatever reason, there was no footage whatsoever of Ric Flair. This was especially funny given what happened on *Nitro* the following week, when David Flair, Daphne, and Crowbar did an angle walking around New York City. They went into a strip club, and David acted as though he'd never seen a naked woman in his life. Then he asked Daphne, his story line girlfriend, to marry him. That's all well and good if you want to suspend disbelief and accept that Ric Flair's son had never seen a naked woman before. However, fifteen minutes later, David, standing beside his story line girlfriend to whom he'd just proposed, cut a promo about his long-legged blonde girlfriend. Daphne, it should be noted, was neither long-legged nor blonde. It seems he was talking about Stacy Kiebler, who had zero relationship to David in story line, but was his real-life fiancée. The idea was to get across that his father neglected him as a child, but that he'd done very well for himself, regardless of that. Clearly, nobody in the crowd had any earthly idea what was happening.

More hilarity occurred later in the program, when Kevin Nash was the target of the dreaded red blood. However, something went awry as the blood was dropped from the ceiling, and it missed him by a mile. In fact, the only people it drenched were the folks who had spent decent money to get front-row seats. Unlike all the wrestlers, the fans did not sell the blood as being poisonous. They showed a shot of Nash looking utterly confused, then cut to a shot of a horrified Vince Russo standing there with his jaw hanging open. Konnan and Juvie, standing behind him, totally broke character and burst out laughing.

Nitro on May 15 began to build towards the next big PPV, *Great American Bash*, with the following lineup (see if you notice a trend): Nash versus Jarrett for the World title; Ric versus David Flair, with the elder Flair having to retire if he lost; Hogan versus Kidman, with Hogan having to retire if he lost; Sting versus Vampiro in an Inferno match (a bout in which the ring is surrounded by fire, a gimmick made popular in Puerto Rico); Dallas Page versus Mike Awesome in an Ambulance match (in which the loser had to leave on a stretcher in an ambulance); Wall versus Shane Douglas in a Tables match; Lex Luger versus Chuck Palumbo in a "Lex Flexer" (one of those weird 1970s muscle-building bendy bars) on a pole match; and Scott Steiner versus Tank Abbott in a fake shootfight. As you can see, Mr. Russo was fond of stipulation matches. It's too bad he had no clue about the point of putting a stipulation on a match; instead, he just added stipulations for the sake of stipulations, and they never meant anything.

The show was better than usual, mostly thanks to Ric Flair, who, in the main event at fifty-one years of age, pinned Jarrett with an inside cradle to win the WCW title. The fans went crazy, viewers watching at home went crazy, and the announcers . . . well, the announcers just sat there because nobody had alerted them about the title change. They just assumed that the referee must have screwed up. The title change popped an unexpectedly great quarter-hour rating (3.29, up almost a full point from the previous segment), so the decision was immediately made to take the belt off him, fast. On *Thunder* two days after he won the belt, Flair fell down in the main event, and WCW sold it like he was having a heart attack.

Yes, again. You'll recall that, a year or so earlier, they had tried the same thing, and it went across horribly, mainly because nobody believed it was real (which was good, because it wasn't). They went to such lengths to convince folks—even Flair's closest friends—that it was real that everyone lost what little trust they still had for management. Flair claimed that an inner-ear imbalance threw off his equilibrium this time, but true or not, nobody believed the story.

On the May 22 *Nitro*, to further put over how fake the heart attack was, Russo did a mock funeral complete with a casket, saying that Flair had died of a brain aneurism, and gave Jarrett the WCW title belt. Of course, there can't be a coffin in wrestling without someone coming out of it. That someone ended up being Nash, with great difficulty. He grabbed the belt and ran off. The main event ended up being Nash versus Jarrett for the apparently vacant title. The encounter was a five-minute disaster, the likes of which hadn't been seen since the Black Plague. The finish saw Russo run out, so Nash grabbed him and tried to powerbomb him in the aisle. The evil red blood fell from the ceiling, and once again, it missed. This time, Nash tried to move into its path and managed to get some of it on him and Russo. For reasons never explained, the substance incapacitated Nash, but not Russo, and Jarrett subsequently got the pin.

Nash would win the title back on the following *Thunder*, but for Russo, two title changes in one week just weren't enough. Therefore, the May 29 *Nitro* saw the WCW title change hands twice inside of two hours! First, Nash came out with the belt and said that since Flair had never lost it in the ring, he was giving it back to him. Jarrett came out and said he wanted a title shot. Flair said no. So they showed footage of Ric's son David holding Reid and Beth Flair hostage. Reid and Beth Flair, as you might have deduced from reading their last names, were Ric's wife and son, and also, strangely, David's mom and brother. If you're wondering why David was holding them hostage, then you'll likely also wonder why, when Ric saw this, his first reaction was to give Jarrett that title shot he'd asked for. Jarrett won the match when David (assigned to be the referee) hit Ric with a guitar so that Russo could run down and count the pin for Jarrett. Fans pelted the ring with garbage in anger.

The show wound up doing a 2.98, thanks in part to the return of Goldberg, who had been out of action following his run-in with the car window earlier in the year. But even his old ratings magic was largely gone—weeks later, he would take on Tank Abbott in a much-hyped match that delivered a mere 2.90 quarter.

Following the Goldberg match, Abbott was made into a groupie for Three Count, WCW's boy band tag team. In all honesty, he'd been booked into such oblivion that it made no difference in his career, and years later, he talked about how much fun he'd had singing and dancing like a total goof. At one point, the company offered to pay for singing lessons. Tank declined, saying that his voice was going to suck no matter what.

More and more, Russo was booking himself to be the star of the show, eventually pitting himself against Flair inside a cage. Flair carried him to what was undoubtedly the best match of Russo's career until finally putting him in the figure four. Russo wouldn't quit, and because of a timing snafu involving more blood falling from the ceiling, he withstood the pain for longer than likely any other wrestler in history. Finally, the blood dropped onto both of them, and for whatever reason (none of this was ever explained), only Flair was incapacitated. David Flair, who wasn't even in the match, then put his dad in the figure four, and Russo covered him for the pin.

//

In his ongoing effort to present matches that had never been seen before, Russo booked Terry Funk against Chris Candido in a match that saw them wind up in a horse stable. Funk was almost legitimately killed when a horse bucked him. This caused Funk to exclaim, "You fucking horse! I'll kick your ass!" Unfortunately, Russo didn't book the natural follow-up bout pitting Funk against the horse.

\\

Around this time, Turner executives began to look at ways to get out of the whole WCW mess. It seemed likely that the original plan was to announce a deal for a promotional group called SFX, which handled many major concerts, to purchase the rights to promote all of WCW's live events. Bischoff did an interview on the May 31 *Thunder* in which he announced that he would soon reveal a landscape-changing event, and he did so in such a way as to indicate that it was not just another wrestling angle. As it turned out, SFX had made an offer to outright buy WCW for an estimated $500 million (keep that number in mind), but Ted Turner himself quickly shot it down.

A huge deal had been made about Bischoff's announcement, and with Turner himself having killed that idea off, a back-up plan was put into place. Russo then went into ultra-hype mode, promising an event at the *Bash* show so colossal that it would change the landscape of the industry forever. Following weeks of hype, Russo's "shocking event" was to turn Goldberg, one of WCW's few remaining draws, heel.

The Goldberg turn was met by a hugely negative reaction, as fans once again pelted the ring with garbage for several minutes after the show went off the air. The company had yet to learn that while this was a positive thing in 1996 when the nWo caught fire, by 2000 it was a sign of what it really was: fans were throwing garbage at the ring out of legitimate anger. The turn was a horrible idea, mostly because Goldberg had just returned following the injuries he had suffered in the limo window incident, and fans were salivating to cheer him killing bad guys.

The *Bash* was also home to a Vampiro versus Sting Inferno match. The gimmick was that you had to light your opponent on fire. The torch to be used, however, was at the top of the giant WCW movie screen near the entrance. Both Sting and Vampiro climbed to the top; then the lights went out, and all sorts of crazy lighting effects started. The lights were a distraction so that the real Sting could be replaced with a stunt double. The double then lit himself on fire, jumped off the screen, and crashed through a hole on the ramp into a foam pit. The announcers then broke down into the same solemn tone of voice that Jerry Lawler and Jim Ross had used (sincerely) when Owen Hart really fell from the ceiling and died. It was a tasteless move, one that inspired even more hatred toward the company—hatred they could ill afford.

Despite the garbage being thrown in the ring, WCW trumpeted the show as a major success. And when the buy rate came in, they were right: it had jumped a whopping 25 percent from the previous show. The bad news, of course, was that even with the increase, the show still did a miserable 0.19.

The biggest match on *Nitro* the following evening was Ric Flair and his son Reid versus his son David and Russo. The stipulations were that if Flair's team lost, he had to retire forever (again), and if Russo's team lost, Russo would be shaved bald. Now you might wonder, why not do this match on PPV and try to make money out of it? Instead, it was thrown out on free TV so that they could draw a 3.01 quarter to *Raw's* 6.67. Ric, after interference from everyone in the world (including his wife Beth and daughters

Ashley and Megan), lost yet again. They shaved Ric bald afterwards, and it actually looked like the beginning of a hot angle. As it turned out, Flair disappeared later that week to get rotator cuff surgery, and by the time he returned, all his hair had grown back. The show, despite all the hype, drew a 3.00 rating to *Raw*'s 6.84.

On June 15, Russo got mad and quit again. This time, he was upset that management wanted to bring back Lex Luger, Kimberly, and Elizabeth—he'd sent them all home earlier and had no plans to ever use them again. The issue was actually quite complicated. In Luger's case, he didn't want to work with Chuck Palumbo, a young Power Plant guy Luger felt wasn't at his level. There was really no good justification for this; he just didn't want to do it. Kimberly walked out because the company wanted her to do a physical angle with Scott Steiner, who terrified everyone in the company with his short fuse and physically aggressive nature. Liz's problem was that she didn't want to be a pro wrestler. Her $156,000-a-year contract, which was disproportionately huge for the amount of work she did, was for her role as a manager; her contract gave her the right to refuse to get into the ring. Russo kept her around early in his tenure and was constantly trying to get her to strip down to her bra and panties on TV, probably since when he was a wrestling fan growing up on Long Island, she was the biggest sex symbol in the WWF.

Russo, apparently feeling that having Liz in the ring and Luger versus Palumbo was going to help turn the entire company around, said that if those two got away with refusing to do angles, the inmates would soon be running the asylum. He went home, though the betting lines were that he'd be back shortly. After all, he had a big mortgage to pay off in Atlanta, and the WWF, despite what he'd forever claim, was doing just fine without him. Internally, it was said that he was taking a few days off to nurse a concussion.

There was another reason that Russo was likely looking to vanish for a while. Internal estimates were suggesting that WCW was on track to lose nearly $80 million for the year, thanks in large part to his inability to get fans to rush out and buy tickets or pay-per-view events. Several employees within the company began to request transfers to other divisions within Time Warner. As it turned out, they had more foresight than pretty much anyone else involved in the wrestling business.

The haplessness continued. Scott Hall, who still had not been fired, cared so much about the company and his job that on the June 13 *Thunder*, when they called his house so he could do a phone interview on live TV with Nash, he wasn't home. This was not grounds for his termination, either. In early July, booker Terry Taylor told Scott Steiner that he was going to have to do a job on *Thunder*. Steiner responded to this by blowing a gasket and threatening to kick Taylor's ass. WCW was so outraged with his behavior that they sent him home over the weekend of July 4 . . . with pay. It eventually became such a joke that it was worked into story lines; a few months later, Commissioner Ernest Miller said that if Nash or Goldberg did anything to screw up his show, he'd send them to jail. "I'm not gonna send you home!" he screamed. "Because someone in the office might pay you!"

June 15 was notable for a $50,000 ad that ran in the international version of *USA Today* plugging *Monday Nitro* that evening on TNT.

Sadly, WCW placed the ad so that it appeared in a paper that came out on Thursday.

As for Russo, he actually ended up staying out for the rest of the month, and neither he nor Bischoff was in attendance at the July 3 *Nitro*. The show was building towards the July 9 *Bash at the Beach* PPV, to be headlined by

Jeff Jarrett defending the WCW title against Hogan. The rumor was that they wanted Hogan to do the job, but he was refusing due to his creative control contract stipulation. If only it were that easy in the end.

The fun and games went right out the window at *Bash at the Beach*, as Russo booked another one of his beloved shoot angles. Before going into what really happened backstage, let's take a look at what fans saw on television.

Russo came out before the match looking sad. Jarrett and Hogan both came down to the ring and looked at each other. Jarrett proceeded to lie down in the ring, and Hogan, feigning confusion, put his foot on Jarrett's chest for the pin. Russo threw the belt into the ring for Hogan. Jarrett walked to the back, looking irate. Hogan told Russo this was all bullshit, then stormed off himself. Fans sat there wondering what in God's name was happening.

Later, Russo came out and just went off on Hogan. Amidst chants of "Russo sucks!" from the crowd, Russo bared his soul to the world:

> From day one, since I've been in WCW, I've done nothing but deal with the bullshit politics behind that curtain. The fact of the matter is I have a wife, I have three kids at home, and I really don't need this shit. But let me tell you the reason why I did come back. I came back for every one of the guys in that locker room that, week in, week out, busts his ass for WCW . . . I came back for the guys behind that curtain that give a shit about this company! And let me tell you who doesn't give a shit about this company—that Goddamned politician Hulk Hogan! Because let me tell you people what happened in this ring here tonight. All day long I'm playing politics with Hulk Hogan because Hulk Hogan tonight wants to play his creative control card. And to Hulk Hogan that meant tonight, even though he knows it's bullshit,

he beats Jeff Jarrett. Well, guess what? Hogan got his wish. Hogan got his belt, and he went the hell home, and I promise everybody or else I'll go in the Goddamned grave you will never see that piece of shit again! And Hogan, you big bald son of a bitch, kiss my ass!

What really happened? Backstage that night, no one seemed to know. Many had heard that the original plan was for Jarrett to win after Scott Steiner interfered for a DQ. Perhaps this is sounding vaguely familiar to those of you who recall what happened to Bret Hart in Montreal. Everyone saw Hogan storm out of the building backstage as if he was really upset. Some thought it was a shoot, believing (rightfully) that Russo would have to have been out of his mind to go to such lengths just to fool the other wrestlers. Among these people was Kevin Nash, which should tell you something, since he was responsible for some really stupid booking ideas in his day. Others figured it had to be a work. After all, if the Jarrett versus Hogan thing wasn't supposed to happen, why were there conveniently two World title belts in the building that day? Why would they have been allowed to go to the ring in the first place if they hadn't agreed on a finish? Plus, many had heard that Booker was going to end up champion at the end of the show, and that couldn't have happened had the "shoot incident" not taken place.

As it turned out, it was a shoot—and a work. Or, more precisely, a work that turned into a shoot. Even more precisely, it was a half-work–half-shoot that turned into a full-fledged shoot. If this sounds confusing, what's even more confusing is the fact that, as complicated as it was, it didn't draw one penny.

Basically, it's believed that only Hogan, Russo, and Bischoff were in on it. Yes, even poor Jeff Jarrett, Russo's best buddy, wasn't filled in. To this day, if you ask him, he'd probably still insist that the whole thing was real. The idea appeared to be an amalgamation of three different angles: Montreal, *Halloween Havoc*, and the deal Nash and Hogan had concocted in 1998, prior to Hogan's "retirement" on Jay Leno. They'd do the *Bash* angle. Hogan would storm out. Russo would say he was gone forever. Everyone in the locker room would cheer. Russo would become a hero. Then, down the road, Hogan would come back with his belt to feud with whoever the WCW champion was at the time, claiming he was the rightful title holder. Russo would then captain the New Blood team with their champion against Bischoff's Millionaire's Club team with Hogan at the helm.

As confusing as that would have been, it likely would have worked, had it not been for one thing: that little speech Russo gave, the one in which he called Hogan a "big bald son of a bitch." Originally, it was supposed to be a much shorter and much less vicious speech. After Russo was done, Hogan legitimately felt he'd been double-crossed, so when he stormed out of the building in anger, he was really storming out, and he really was angry. In fact, he was so angry that he filed a character defamation lawsuit against Russo. Regardless of what some folks might think, real lawsuits are not filed in real courts over fake angles, especially since a lawyer could be disbarred for doing it. And even if someone did go to such lengths, the lawsuit wouldn't still be going through the courts years after the company where the angle started had gone out of business (because the suit was still outstanding in 2004, Hulk Hogan refused to work for Jerry Jarrett's NWA TNA promotion if Russo was involved).

On *Nitro* the next night, to further ensure that no money was made from this, they barely mentioned that anything had happened, and they gave absolutely no details about the Hogan versus Jarrett match. The show was pretty generic, and that was actually a good thing at this point since it meant that it wasn't filled with mind-numbing amounts of pointless angles, and it featured Jarrett pinning new champion Booker T in a four-way to win a title shot at the next PPV. The show did a 2.58, which should put to rest any arguments that these sorts of shoot angles are money in the bank, or even good for a one-night curiosity ratings pop.

As Russo scrambled to come up with something—anything!—to regain the fan base's interest, more non-wrestling employees fled the company, among them a gentleman by the name of Matt Williams. It's a name that no one outside WCW would even recognize, but he probably could have helped to save the company if anyone had bothered to listen to him.

Matt Williams was Director of Research for WCW. He spent a year of his life polling fans about what things they liked and disliked about the company, and what they felt should be changed to make it a more enjoyable product. He polled not only the fans that were still watching, but also fans that had long ago given up on the product. The results were unsurprising: fans wanted more wrestling and less "sports entertainment." When Mr. Williams presented his findings to WCW, Russo had the entire study thrown out. He couldn't fathom the notion that wrestling fans were interested in watching—GASP!—serious wrestling. Williams, outraged, quit for a job in another Time Warner division.

So nothing changed. At the end of July, the internal estimates came back and showed that the company had lost $7 million over the course of the month. For one month! Keep in mind that until 1999, the most WCW had lost in an entire *year* was $6 million.

Changes were immediately made. First, almost two dozen undercard guys were cut. This was in addition to the two dozen or so that had been cut over the past year. Then discussions about cutting some of the higher-priced guys began, names as big as Hogan, Goldberg, Luger, DDP, and Bret.

The belief was that these guys were being paid too much on their guaranteed deals, and it was killing the company.

The stark reality was much different: the company was being killed, and therefore the revenue wasn't coming in to pay off those deals. Realistically, not only were the big stars making just as much money two years earlier, but they also had 260 guys under contract, some of whom, like Kevin Wacholz and Lanny Poffo, never made one single appearance ever for the company. Despite this, the company made a huge profit, because they were still making tons and tons of money from house shows, pay-per-views, merchandising, advertising, and so forth. As it turned out, had every single wrestler in the company worked for free in 2000, the company would still have been on track to lose $40 million.

Internally, there was another big management shakedown, and when the dust settled, Bischoff was relegated to being a consultant, and Brad Siegel had put all his faith behind Russo. This was a very controversial decision, since many in the company, unlike Siegel, actually had backgrounds in wrestling and saw Russo for the flop that he was. In fact, a week earlier, an internal memo had been passed around detailing the "Ten Questions Not Asked of Vince Russo." Among them were "How many 'young and hungry employees' does it take to screw up an entire company?" and "What does the second 'W' in WCW stand for?"

Russo, learning of the memo, went on a rampage on the August 7 *Nitro*, spouting delusional figures about how the company was better off now that he was there, and how WWF was in much worse shape. No one was quite sure where he was getting these numbers, since the WWF went from grossing $251.5 million in 1999 to $379.3 million in 2000, the year after Russo had left. However Russo tried to spin things, hard numbers told a different story. Nobody was sure what the point of doing this interview on

Nitro was, either. And, quite the coincidence, the show did a horrid 2.44 rating, well below what it was averaging when he first started.

The following Sunday, prior to the *New Blood Rising* PPV in Vancouver, B.C., Siegel called a meeting with the boys to announce that further changes were afoot. The first move was to cut back drastically on production (making Russo irate, since one of *his* first moves had been to greatly boost the production values, convinced this would make the show more competitive with *Raw*), getting rid of two of the three big screens, and igniting less pyro at the beginning of the show and for the wrestlers' entrances.

The biggest change planned was that, effective in late October, they were going to cancel the *Thunder* tapings and film the show immediately after *Nitro* on Monday nights. Obviously, the idea was to dramatically cut costs, since the *Thunder* shows weren't drawing fans. The downside was that nobody was going to *Thunder* because they did not like *Thunder*, which meant few were likely to stay after *Nitro* ended to watch the second show. Some fans, who watched WCW only for its perverse comedy value, anxiously awaited these tapings since the plan was to film the entire two-show block in three and a half hours with no commercial breaks. This meant that all the pre-tapes would be done earlier, then inserted into the shows. Seeing as how pre-tapes had often been inserted into *Nitro* in the wrong order, the thought of the production crew trying to get things right with this new taping plan appeared to be a disaster in the making.

New Blood Rising was, of course, a horrible show, not only because the production was drastically cut back, but because the matches were awful and the angles were atrocious. The fans were so clearly sending a message, but nobody was listening. This was another one of those shows where they sold almost 5,000 tickets very early on, and then as soon as they started to announce matches on the television programs, ticket sales stopped dead in their tracks. The message, obviously, was that WCW was booking things fans did not want to see. WCW, instead of learning a lesson from this, went on to attempt to force fans to like what they were presenting, and you can imagine how that worked. As if the message wasn't clear enough, it should be noted that almost 3,000 free tickets were snatched up around the Vancouver area; when the day of the show came, only 1,300 of those folks actually bothered to show up.

Those who attended left wishing they hadn't. The opener, Jung Dragons versus Three Count, was good. The main event, Booker T versus Jeff Jarrett, was good. Everything else set new standards for bad. The coup de grâce, however, saw Nash beat Goldberg and Steiner to win a shot at Booker T at the next show. Nash cut a promo before the match saying that Goldberg was claiming to be hurt due to a motorcycle accident in Sturgis, but was actually faking the injury and wouldn't come out because of it. They played Goldberg's music twice, and sure enough, he didn't come out. The match started, and a few minutes later Goldberg finally appeared. They had a horrible match. Nash went to give Goldberg a powerbomb, but Goldberg dead-weighted him and walked out of the ring. The announcers started screaming about how Goldberg wasn't going up for the move and was screwing up the finish. When Goldberg got to the top of the ramp, Russo came out and yelled at him. Goldberg screamed "Fuck you!" and stormed off. The announcers began to insinuate that Goldberg was being completely unprofessional and wouldn't do the scripted loss. So Nash and Steiner continued their horrible match. Tony Schiavone, in a direct quote, then said, "If, in fact, the jackknife powerbomb was part of this design, what are they going to do now, improvise?" Finally, Nash pinned Steiner with the powerbomb, and the announcers went off about how professional Steiner was for going up for the move. The irony of all this was that it was supposed to be a shoot, yet not even the dumbest hardcore fan could ever believe that Steiner was this much of a professional.

The idea in all of this, which was lost on 99 percent of the people watching at home, was that Goldberg didn't want to lose two straight shows in a row in real life, so they were going to turn it into a story line. Of course, in order to do so, they had to pretty much admit that all wrestling matches were fake. WCW never grasped that even though most fans accept that wrestling is not on the level, they still want to get lost in the action and suspend their disbelief for the few hours that they watch. It's just like going to the movies. Everybody knows that what they see in the movies is not real, but we're still able to let ourselves go for two hours and "believe" what we see up on the screen. Imagine what would happen if, during a key scene in a movie like *Jurassic Park*, there was a technical screw-up, and everyone suddenly saw the animated dinosaurs on a computer screen running after rendered versions of the actors? Or if, during a key dramatic moment in another film, both actors just started laughing and said they needed to start over again? The effect would be ruined. It's the same with wrestling.

Nitro the next night was better, but that's like saying a gunshot wound to the foot is better than one to the head. It opened with another wacky "shoot" segment in which Russo said Goldberg was going to have to face Tank Abbott, and this time, unlike at the PPV, there was going to be NO SCRIPT! This segment's quarter did a 2.0. The show as a whole drew a 2.40 rating, which means at this point it was doing well below what the horrible Kevin Sullivan programs had drawn many months earlier. Also, keep in mind that in order to make up for the ad-revenue loss in the move from three hours to two, the show needed to be averaging in the 4.5 range, nearly double what it was doing. Clearly, that wasn't about to happen anytime soon.

But at least *Nitro* was still on the air. *WCW Saturday Night*, which had been on the air for twenty-seven consecutive years on TBS, and which was the cornerstone upon which Ted Turner built his Superstation, simply vanished altogether. Done. Finished. No graphic, no farewell message, nothing. One week, it simply wasn't there, never to be seen again. After nearly three decades, WTBS quietly axed the program without any forewarning.

The company was now in a full-fledged state of panic, and began cutting costs left and right. More people were also fired that week, including every Mexican in the entire company with the exception of Rey Mysterio Jr. and Juventud Guerrera. This certainly did not help WCW in regard to Sonny Onoo's racial discrimination lawsuit. By the time the bloodletting was over, they were down to less than fifty wrestlers under contract. That's pretty impressive when you consider they went into the year with 234. A freeze was also put on the hiring of any more new talent.

WCW contracts were often used in Russo's story lines, the idea frequently being that if the worker could destroy the contract, they were free to leave the company. Strangely, however, these contracts could seemingly not be destroyed. For example, one day Goldberg got mad and ate Scott Hall's contract on TV. Yes, he ate it like it was, say, a taco. Amazingly, the next week, the contract was back on TV, looking as pristine as ever.

WCW got some rare good news as *Nitro* on August 28 did a 3.52 rating, up quite a bit from the week before. Was the company turning around? Did the improved in-ring action from the week before result in an influx of new viewers? No, *Raw* was preempted by the Westminster Dog Show. WCW, knowing this was their chance to hit a home-run show, threw everything they could muster into an attempt to win fans back. The big angle to end the show had Bret Hart return and meet Goldberg in the desert. Don't ask why they were there, or how Goldberg got all the way to the desert within ten minutes of leaving the *Nitro* building. Bret said he wanted Goldberg to kill Russo as revenge for what had happened in Montreal. Truth be told, Russo had zero to do with Montreal, and in fact, he had no idea what a double-cross was at the time. The swerve, of course, was that Bret was actually mad at Goldberg for ending his career at *Starrcade* in December, with the superkick that nearly knocked his head right off his shoulders, so he beat him up. You might wonder why this was booked if Bret wasn't going to ever be able to wrestle again, and would therefore be unable to have a money match with Goldberg? Or why Goldberg had initially trusted Bret, who was mysteriously right there in the Las Vegas desert after having been in Canada since January? You'd need to ask Vince Russo.

To give an idea of how much of a joke the company became to even their most loyal followers, one *Thunder* taping in 2000 featured a fan holding up a sign that read "I'M AT A WCW EVENT" while wearing a bag over his head. This wasn't the only sign-related comedy. A man named Peter Goldschmidt sued another man, Robert Catell, for appearing on WCW telecasts holding up various derogatory signs, including "PETER GOLDSCHMIDT LOSER 4 LIFE." Apparently, the two used to be friends on Long Island. Then, one day, Catell asked Goldschmidt to help him move. Goldschmidt supposedly said he was unable to because it was a workday, and the friendship came to a bitter end, leading Catell to travel around the nation and hold up disparaging signs at wrestling events. The number of lives that WCW ultimately affected is staggering.

The September 4 *Nitro* from Dallas was built around the *Nitro Swerve*™, which had been popularized a few weeks earlier. The swerve was that two bad guys would tease turning on each other, but in the end, they'd reveal that they'd planned some horrible deed all along. It got to the point where this swerve happened so often that the only way it would have been a real swerve was if the two bad guys really did turn on each other. This week's bad guys in question were Russo and Nash. They feigned turning on each other as participants in a triple-tier War Games match, but, of course, in the end Russo gave Nash the belt and allowed him to escape. Yes, Russo had possession of the belt right before the finish, so theoretically, he could have made himself the WCW World Heavyweight champion. Sadly, this foreshadowed events to come.

The September 11 *Nitro* emanated from deep in the heart of Ric Flair Country. After years of booking their hometown hero to look like an idiot, the company succeeded in killing the town once and for all, as despite the show being built around Ric's return and David's story line wedding to Stacy Kiebler, they drew a paltry crowd of 1,657. The brilliant story line idea was to have him arrested and taken off the show, to which fans responded by chanting "BULLSHIT!" for five straight minutes. There was another *Nitro Swerve*™, this time with Steiner and Nash. They teased fighting each other, but then turned on babyface ref Booker T and double-teamed him into oblivion. Nobody was sure why the stupid babyfaces never saw things like this coming after having witnessed it week after week after week. And of course, there was also the David–Stacy wedding that, in a swerve, never took place, as Stacy revealed that David wasn't the father of her unborn baby. By the grace of God, the company went out of business before fans had to hear her identify Russo as the dad, which was his original plan.

The mere thought of Russo booking himself in an angle that saw him having sex with the hottest girl in the company was annoying enough, but on top of that, Russo had now also somehow become the number-one contender to the WCW title. But even that could not compare to the events of the September 25 *Nitro*, which took place in Long Island. See if you can put two and two together before you finish reading about what happened. Vince Russo, creative goof and top contender to the World title. His hometown.

The main event saw Russo get his title shot against Booker in the cage. It should be noted that Russo was so popular in his hometown that when they announced on *Nitro* that he'd be getting a title shot here, approximately 200 additional tickets were sold that whole week. The rules of this match were that you could win by pinning your opponent, making him submit, or leaving the cage. A hundred million men ran in, including Goldberg. We'd note that it sort of kills the entire concept of a cage match when folks can just walk in and out at will, but WCW had already been doing this for years. Finally, Booker moved to escape, but just as he was about to set foot on the floor and retain his belt, Goldberg speared Russo so hard that Russo went through the side of the cage and crashed into the guardrail. The guardrail, of course, was outside, which meant—oh yes!—Vincent Russo was the WCW Heavyweight champion of the world.

As much as Russo wanted to play wrestler, being tossed around a ring was starting to take its toll on him. He had been getting involved in a lot of matches over the previous few months, and it should suffice to say that he was no athlete. He certainly didn't resemble a pro wrestler. Although wrestling is predetermined ("fake"), the fact of the matter is that an untrained layperson who gets involved sets himself up for serious injuries. The human body does not like the idea of falling flat on its back, and learning to do so takes time—sometimes several months. If you land with your weight too low, your head can snap back and bounce off the ring, which, contrary to popular belief, is made of steel and wood and in absolutely no way resembles a trampoline.

Russo had suffered various injuries during his bouts, including a number of concussions. There was a reason why he wore a helmet to the ring for his later matches, and it wasn't for comedic purposes. His brain was swollen, and with concussions, once you've suffered one, the likelihood of suffering another is immensely increased. Bret Hart knew this first-hand; his career ended for that very reason.

You can say whatever you wish about Vince Russo as a writer and booker for World Championship Wrestling, but in real life, he was a human being with a family, and going into the ring after having recently suffered multiple concussions was putting his health, and even his life, in jeopardy. It was sad to see him do so, especially in light of the Bret Hart and Darren Drosdov situations, both of which had occurred that very same year.

And what did he get for risking his livelihood? *Nitro* did a 2.87 to *Raw*'s 5.44. Believe it or not, a lot of people thought that *Nitro* was going to win that evening. The reason for this is that after seventeen years on the USA Network, the WWF moved to TNN. TNN at the time was The Nashville Network, and the belief was—seriously—that wrestling fans weren't going to be able to find *Raw* after it switched. Now keep in mind that it was still airing Monday nights at 9:00 P.M., so all fans would have to do was run through all the channels—at some point, if their cable service had TNN, they were going to find the show. This did not matter to many so-called wrestling experts. They were sure the WWF was done for. They were wrong.

It should be noted that on the show Russo won the World title, there was a Goldberg versus Scott Steiner cage match. This match took place with zero hype, and zero warning. Their previous match, which took place on PPV, was an awesome dramatic affair, so theoretically, WCW could have drawn some decent money on a subsequent PPV by locking them inside a cage. Instead, not only did they give it away for free on *Nitro*, they gave it away for free with no prior warning whatsoever. Long story short, they made no money on pay-per-view and drew a 2.17 quarter.

On the October 2 *Nitro* in San Francisco, WCW World Heavyweight champion Vince Russo announced that he was vacating the title, meaning that not only did he win the belt, but nobody ever would beat him for it. He had two other major announcements. First, he wasn't going to fire Goldberg for spearing him out of the cage last week. Russo's punishment was that Goldberg had to win 176 matches in a row to get a title shot, and if he lost even one, he'd be fired. Many of the fans who'd lived through the Sid win streak strongly suspected that this might not be on the level. Russo also announced a Jarrett and Booker versus Steiner and Sting tag match, with the two winners squaring off for the vacant belt in the main event.

Jarrett and Booker won the match, and the two squared off in yet another Russo brainfart: the world's first-ever San Francisco 49ers match. Basically, there were four boxes hanging from poles. Inside one of the boxes was the belt. Inside the other three were, well, not the belt. Whoever got the box with the belt in it would be the champion. If Frank A. Gotch didn't turn in his grave after watching the Nassau Coliseum show, he sure did after this. The first box opened contained a blow-up doll. The second contained a photo of Scott Hall, who hadn't been seen in as long as anyone could remember, but was still way more popular than 95 percent of the active roster. The third box contained a glove that you would use for, say, gardening, but it was identified as a coal miner's glove. The finish saw a midget named Beetlejuice from the Howard Stern show give Jarrett a low blow, allowing Booker to open the last box. Unfortunately, the belt fell out of the box before he was able to get it, so ring announcer Dave Penzer had to pick it up off the floor and hand it to Booker for the win. Of course, following the rules to the letter, this should have meant that Dave Penzer was the new WCW World Heavyweight champion, but thankfully Russo wasn't fast enough on his feet to change everything around at the last second.

//

And now, some useless trivia: the San Francisco 49er title change was the twentieth in less than one year for WCW (thirty-five weeks, to be exact). Compare that to the fact that between 1949 and 1980, that same title (well, the NWA title) changed hands twenty times.

\\

In early October, the first serious rumors about WCW being sold began to make the rounds. There had been plenty of speculation in the past that Time Warner might be interested in selling, and that Bischoff was doing whatever he could to get investors together to make an offer. It was even rumored that offers had been made, but both sides were far apart on numbers. In fact, in the summer of 1999, Mandalay Bay Sports and Entertainment, whom Bischoff had been working with, had registered the WCWextreme.com and WCWXtreme.com domain names. This, however, was the first time that any of the rumors mentioned an actual time and place: October 23 in Little Rock, Arkansas, the first *Nitro* back after the Australian tour. The story was that Bischoff and Mandalay were teaming up to make a purchase. As it turned out, the day came and went, and no sale was announced.

Rumors of the company's "impending sale" grew hotter as October wore on. In fact, things got so out of control that Brad Siegel told Terry Taylor to meet with the boys on October 8 to discuss it. Taylor basically said that four companies were interested in purchasing WCW: in addition to Bischoff's group, there were three others in Japan, France, and Germany. None of the latter three was specified, although months earlier, rumors had spread that one of Japan's major wrestling organizations (either New Japan, All Japan, or NOAH) was interested in buying, though it was never clear which. Taylor said there was no guarantee the company would be sold, but they were entertaining various offers.

Another name that popped up that week as a possible buyer was Vince McMahon. The instigator of this rumor was Antonio Inoki of New Japan, who had a history of making up outlandish tales. Whether he knew more than he let on or not, the fact was that McMahon was interested. Soon, *MultiChannel News* was reporting, through unnamed sources, that the WWF had the right to match any offer for the company as a result of settlement terms of their copyright infringement lawsuit. Both that lawsuit and WCW's countersuit had been quietly settled out of court in September. Since the details were sealed, nobody knew for sure whether or not this was true, but as the weeks wore on it was believed to have been a false story (WWF lawyers even publicly denied it). Regardless, McMahon had serious interest, and talks between the two sides continued for many weeks. By the end of 2000, however, it appeared that McMahon had decided to pass on the deal entirely.

In the midst of all these sales talks came what should have been a highly successful tour of Australia. Tickets had been going like gangbusters since mid-July, and this looked to be WCW's most successful house show run of the year. The reason, of course, was that Australia was starved for live pro wrestling and, unlike just about every building in America, hadn't yet been completely burned out by the WCW product. Over the years, many promotions learned that they could make great money overseas even when the U.S. market was depressed, either by running shows or by selling television tapes to local TV affiliates.

Almost immediately, however, things went wrong. Juventud Guerrera, apparently in a drug-induced fit, caused a huge scene at the Brisbane Mariott Hotel. The previous night, at a club, he'd smoked something given to him by an unknown person, and the authorities suspected it had been laced with PCP. He went to bed, and the following morning he went insane near the hotel restaurant where all the wrestlers were eating, tearing his clothes off while screaming that he was going to kill himself. Several wrestlers—nearly all of them much larger than Guerrera—tried to subdue him, to no avail. Cops showed up with pepper spray. Finally, he was tackled, handcuffed, and escorted from the building. Between fines and compensation to several officers he attacked, he was ordered to pay $1,850 U.S. He was also lucky enough to not have a conviction placed on his record, because as a Mexican citizen who traveled internationally, that would have seriously impacted his career. A WCW spokesman, speaking to a local newspaper, said that Juvie's behavior was, among other things, "unexpected," so apparently him taking all of his clothes off and going insane in a drug-induced rampage was not on the itinerary for that day.

JOHN LAWSON

Yet another luchador that Bischoff felt the need to unmask, Juventud Guerrera would eventually go insane in an Australian hotel.

WCW was so outraged by Juvie's behavior that they promptly fired Scott Hall, who, as you might recall, went crazy on an overseas tour back in February. As you also might recall, he thought he could never be fired because of the trademark-infringement lawsuit, and, as coincidence would have it, that lawsuit had been settled a month earlier. And yes, Juvie was canned too. WCW never bothered to tell him initially, though, and he wasn't aware of it until a bunch of friends called and told him they'd read about it on the Internet.

There wasn't much to the Australian shows in terms of content, but, as expected, they all did tremendously well business-wise. In fact, every show drew at least 9,000 paid, and even *Thunder* completely sold out. Of course, since this was WCW, they actually managed to lose money on the tour. Apparently, the company had signed a contract with the Australian promoters saying they'd buy back any seats unused at the shows. Unfortunately, this included seats that could not be sold due to the TV production equipment. Because they ran four shows taped for TV, the faux pas resulted in WCW losing $400,000 on a tour that should otherwise have been profitable.

And so back to America the company came, and, as usual, they brought their crappy shows with them. The October 5 *Nitro* was one of those horrible shows where everything that could possibly go wrong did. It was supposed to be pushed back a half-hour due to a NASCAR race. In the past, WCW had often forgotten to alert viewers that their programming was being moved to a different time or even to a different day, but this time, they made it very clear that the show was starting at 8:35 P.M. Unfortunately, when fans tuned in at 8:35 P.M., the show had already been on for a half-hour since the program hadn't been preempted after all. There were a bunch of hideous matches, including Wall versus Jim Duggan, a match so horrible it made one long for a Vince Russo WCW title defense. The Jung Dragons, three great Cruiserweight wrestlers, were all squashed at the same time by Scott Steiner, putting a damper on the whole idea to push the Cruiserweight division. Lex Luger, in an interview segment with Stevie Ray called "Suckas Gots to Know," asked if what he was about to say was just between the two of them. Apparently he was unaware that the program was being broadcast nationwide to several million people. Stevie was apparently unaware as well, since he responded that it was "just between you, me, and 5,000 viewers." Yes, 5,000 viewers. Tony Schiavone tried to make the save by claiming—really—that he meant 5,000 viewers in each house.

The following week, Russo cited brain damage—post-concussion syndrome, to be exact—as his reason for "temporarily" removing himself from the creative process. Even though he'd stayed in the U.S. and faxed all of his story line ideas to Australia for that series of shows, he suddenly announced that he would not be able to do his job anymore since his doctor had banned him from leaving the house until November 16. Some theorized that his fax machine must have been broken.

While it was unfortunate that Russo had a concussion, at least he got to keep his job. Bret Hart wasn't so lucky, as on October 20, he was released. The termination notice came literally days after he received another letter that said he'd been re-signed for two more years. It was a business decision, as he hadn't wrestled since January due to the head injuries that resulted in him suffering 10 percent brain damage, and he was theoretically the second-highest-paid wrestler in the company behind Hogan, pulling in roughly $25,000 a week while injured.

"At this point in time," Brad Siegel wrote in his termination letter, "we have been unable to utilize your wrestling services for over nine months and according to your doctor, you remain incapacitated. Based on your ongoing incapacity, WCW is exercising its right under paragraph 8 (e) to terminate your independent contractor agreement effective Friday, October 20, 2000. Your contributions to the wrestling business are highly regarded and we wish you only the best in the future."

With Russo gone, the interim booking team of Bill Banks and Ed Ferrera was told to keep his story lines intact until he made his return. Imagine being told such a thing. The problem with this was that none of the story lines could really advance, and it was obvious to viewers at home that nobody in the ring was giving anything even close to 100 percent. As a result, the holding pattern on TV did not lead to a holding pattern for the ratings, which continued to slide. The November 20 show did a 2.27 rating, the lowest ever in the history of the show running opposed in its normal timeslot.

What was sad was that the shows weren't even that horrible; they were certainly better than the programs Russo had written at his most insane. Unfortunately, by killing off all the belts, the Heavyweight title in particular, Russo had created an atmosphere in which everyone was fighting each other for really no good reason. Since the belts had been rendered worthless, there was nothing worth fighting for, and fans had no reason to get behind any of the wrestlers. And never was the company's future more evident than the day tickets went on sale for *Starrcade*. A few weeks earlier, the WWF had put tickets on sale for their biggest show of the year, *Wrestlemania X7*, to be held April 1, 2001, at the Houston AstroDome. On the first day they were available, 48,395 tickets were sold. In late November, tickets went on sale for WCW's biggest PPV of the year, the Grandaddy of Them All, *Starrcade*. On the first day they were available, 926 tickets were sold.

The main event for the *Starrcade* show was set to be Steiner versus a "major superstar" that Ric Flair was bringing in. Flair even went as far as to claim that this man was as big a superstar as Rock or Steve Austin. The man ended up being Sid Vicious, who was about as big a superstar as the Rock's jockstrap. The story line was that since he had been forced to give up his belt in April for no good reason (when Russo vacated all the belts), he deserved a chance to get it back. Yes, a rare logical story line. Unfortunately, there was no logic in the interview, as "Sid Vicious" accused Steiner of having a "fictitious name." More fun was in store in the story line, as Sid would later beat up a valet and steal all of his keys, then drive a bunch of cars into a circle so he could fight Steiner in the middle of it. Sadly, the footage of Sid attempting to match twenty keys to twenty different cars never aired on the program. As if things weren't ludicrous enough, yet another *Nitro* angle portrayed Sid as being so stupid he couldn't even find the arena! The entire evening, he kept calling in from his cell phone and saying he was lost. "Guys, can you hear me?" he asked in at least three different segments.

JOHN LAWSON

"See, there's only two things I care about, and I'm gonna see is the man who wins the title and the belt, and that man will be me!" Sid cuts yet another fantastically cryptic promo.

As much of a moron that Sid appeared to be, realistically, few in the entire company appeared to be any brighter. Case in point: no one seemed to know whether the December 11 *Nitro* was airing or not! Months back, a David Copperfield special had been scheduled to air that day, so Turner executives had bounced the idea of moving *Nitro* to Tuesday back and forth. On November 6, Craig Leathers, head of production for WCW, sent Terry

Taylor a letter informing him that it was going to be moved. Taylor supposedly never told anyone about it. So on December 7, the Friday before *Nitro*, everyone suddenly figured out that *Nitro* wasn't going to air on Monday, and they hadn't mentioned a thing about the time change on the previous *Nitro* or *Thunder* shows. As if that weren't enough of a production nightmare, *Thunder* had become so horribly produced and edited that it seemed as though they were attempting to build their audience by putting on the most absurd programs of all time. Following yet another Scott Hall arrest, head of WCW Legal, Diana Meyers, outright banned his name from all company telecasts, despite the fact that Kevin Nash didn't do a single interview without mentioning the words "Scott Hall". This led to another legendary segment on the December 6 *Thunder*, in which Nash and Dallas Page again talked about Hall. During the taping of the interview, there was a major lighting problem, and the overhead lamps were swinging back and forth as if they were in the middle of a windstorm. There was also a loud clanging noise, as if someone was pounding on a garbage can lid. This wasn't expected to be an issue, because the plan was to edit in footage of Hall to cover up these technical glitches. Unfortunately, when Meyers heard that Nash again mentioned Hall's name, she blew a gasket and refused to allow the footage or any verbal references to Hall to air. Instead of pulling the segment, they aired it on TV anyway, so fans nationwide saw Nash and Page eyeballing a wandering overhead lamp while several dozen words were bleeped, making it totally incomprehensible. *Thunder* had become the wrestling equivalent of the Ed Wood cult flick *Plan 9 from Outer Space*.

The week of December 18 saw everything go to hell again, as both participants in the *Starrcade* main event were stirring up problems behind the scene. First, Sid walked out, unhappy about being asked to lose to Steiner at *Starrcade*. He claimed he'd been promised the finish would be a double count-out, but then WCW double-crossed him and changed it to him getting pinned. He told people that he wasn't ultimately upset about the change, but rather about the fact that nobody was man enough to come up and tell him to his face, instead of just handing him a piece of paper with the new plan written on it. In the end, Sid agreed to lose, and plans to change it to a three-way so someone else could do the job were scrapped.

Then, the big fight. It started with Steiner cutting one of his now-famous unscripted promos, this time on Dallas Page. It was always funny to hear company officials get upset about things like this, because historically, it was entirely their fault. Steiner, for example, had never really been reprimanded for his behavior; if anything, he'd been rewarded, time after time after time. Earlier in the year, he buried Flair in an unscripted promo and was told by management that it was one of the best interviews of the year. Months later, he threatened Terry Taylor and was rewarded with a paid vacation over the weekend of July 4. So his antics continued, and instead of being fined or suspended, he found himself the WCW World Heavyweight champion. If management was upset with his behavior, they had nobody but themselves to blame. Even more depressing, the guys who actually worked hard, behaved themselves, and followed the rules were rewarded by being buried on television, and consequently, they gave up all hope.

Steiner's promo against Page included the following line: "Why don't you convince Diamond Dallas Page to get a sex change, so he has the balls to come out here and face me?" Page was stretching in the locker room when Steiner made his comments. Ironically, this was the same building where, earlier in the year, Steiner and Page's wife Kimberly had a verbal incident that resulted in her quitting the company for good. As soon as Steiner said Page had no balls, everyone in the locker room immediately turned and looked over at him, as if to see what he was going to do about it. According to one witness, "the air was totally sucked out of the room."

Page finished tying his boots and walked down the stairs near the curtain. As soon as Steiner walked backstage, Page reportedly said, "So, I don't have the balls to face you, huh?" They started swearing at each other, and a fight broke out. Steiner took Page down and started to pound on his face, with multiple witnesses saying he went straight for Page's eye. One source said that Steiner had been cutting his fingernails earlier in the day, and that if he hadn't, it would have been much uglier. The other wrestlers immediately jumped in to break it up, and it reportedly took them over a full minute to pry Steiner off of Page. Page was bleeding and had marks all over his face. He later told friends that Steiner wasn't just scary, he was a killer, and that he was glad he walked away from the fight alive. Page and Nash immediately grabbed their stuff and left the building, with some sources saying their last words were "We'll be back when there are new owners." Steiner then responded by cutting another promo, this time focusing on Kimberly and saying some very bad things about her.

Steiner's punishment? He continued to receive the biggest push of his professional career.

The final PPV of the year, *Starrcade*, took place on December 17 at the MCI Center in Washington, DC, before 3,465 paying fans. It was a decent show, featuring a great opener, a few decent undercard matches, and a shockingly good main event. Page and Nash—whose walkout lasted all of one week—beat Palumbo and Stasiak in a surprisingly good match to regain the tag titles, thanks mostly to Page's great job working as the baby-face in peril. Goldberg versus Luger in the semi-main was surprisingly good. And when Steiner beat Sid with the recliner in the main event, the match could only be classified as a miracle.

Sadly, by this point, good show or bad, it didn't matter. *Starrcade*, traditionally WCW's biggest show of the year, did a dismal 0.11.

With the year's end came the announcement of $62 million in losses. How did it happen? Hideous booking and one bad show after another caused pay-per-view buy rates and house show revenues to plunge. Advertising revenues plunged, due to *Nitro* being cut to two hours and to the elimination of *WCW Saturday Night*. Wrestlers, both on TV and in media interviews, buried the company for its incompetence, making fans feel stupid for having supported the product for so long. Countless millions were spent on stupid things: limos getting destroyed, helicopters, junkyard battle royals, contract money paid to guys who never appeared on television even once, commercials and newspaper ads plugging the wrong air dates for shows, and so on.

The company had become a money pit, the likes of which had never been seen before in wrestling.

And Time Warner was upset.

PART IV

The Death

"WCW is not a core business for Turner Broadcasting. We've decided professional wrestling in its current incarnation just isn't appropriate for the high-scale, upscale brand that we have built on TNT and TBS Superstation. We're no longer interested in carrying the product."

—Jim Weiss, Turner Spokesperson

CHAPTER 7

2001: The Ultimate Swerve

From the beginning to the end—even as Rome burned around them—those in charge of WCW felt that if they had nothing else, at least they'd always have television.

While Vince Russo had driven both buy rates and house show attendance into the toilet, many believed the *Nitro* and *Thunder* ratings were still OK. Sure, they weren't even in the same universe as the *Raw* ratings, but many cable shows did less than a 1.0, and most *Nitro* and *Thunder* shows were in the 2.0 range. The reality, though, is that *Thunder* was dipping below the TBS ratings average, and in the last few months, the show's rating was regularly surpassed by *Ripley's Believe It or Not*. Seeing no signs that the downward ratings were going to reverse anytime soon, TBS officials decided to axe *Thunder*.

Things were only slightly better for *Nitro*, the flagship show. Ratings were above the prime-time average for the station, but they were below average in terms of ad sales. Still, while things had declined since the height of WCW's popularity back in the late '90s, there was always the possibility that the company could rebound simply by hitting upon a hot story line or having a wrestler catch fire with the fans. While it didn't look like there was any chance of either of these things happening in the immediate future, it wasn't like they could *never* happen. After all, this was *World Championship Wrestling*. This was the organization that had reinvented the entire wrestling industry with the advent of *Nitro*. It was certainly conceivable that they could do it again at some point. WCW was, if nothing else, a company that survived. It survived times it should never have, like the lean early-'90s period when, on average, less than 1,000 fans came out to each house show. Things would turn around; they always did, and this time would be no different. All the company needed to become profitable again was to find just that right character, that right angle, and the fans would return.

WCW's ratings prior to the nWo invasion were flat, people argued, not unlike the numbers the company was doing during the collapse of 2000. Obviously, things turned out fine back then, so there was no reason to expect anything different now.

Except that there was. While the numbers in 1995 and 2000 may have appeared similar on the surface, there were major differences. The biggest was that, in 1995, the company had a $35 million to $40 million budget, compared to 2000's $185 million budget. More importantly, they'd never lost more than $6 million in any year, and all of a sudden, they'd lost $62 million in one. This sort of performance was not acceptable.

Ted Turner had been approached about shutting the company down several times in the early '90s. He'd always ixnayed the idea because he truly believed that wrestling was cyclical. Plus, because wrestling had been such an integral part of the Superstation that gave birth to his media empire, he had a soft spot for it in his heart. Pretty much everyone in the industry believed that as long as Uncle Ted was around, WCW would be safe.

But something happened in January 2000 that shattered this supposed certainty. Time Warner CEO Gerald Levin struck a $183 billion deal with America Online's Steve Case to merge the two companies into what they believed would be the ultimate media superpower. Turner ended up with 3 percent of the new company's stock and a mostly figurehead job as Vice Chairman. Suddenly, his days of spending millions at will on frivolities like professional wrestling were finished. In his place were boards of directors, financial analysts, and CEOs looking at the bottom line. These men were going to do something that no one ever had: make WCW fiscally responsible for its actions.

With the company losing money at an astronomical rate, it didn't take long for AOL–Time Warner to conclude that WCW was a hopeless proposition. Therefore, a shocking decision was made: the company was to be sold.

And, for the first time ever, there wasn't a damn thing Ted Turner could do about it.

At some point, Ted Turner probably regretted having sold Turner Broadcasting to Time Warner in the mid-'90s. And although he had voted in favor of the merger, he definitely regretted having agreed to the AOL deal. His woes included a huge stock crash that cost him between $7 and $8 billion. Wrestling fans should take solace in the fact that WCW, as horribly mismanaged as it was, could not hold a candle to the incompetence of AOL–Time Warner. Sure, WCW lost $62 million one year, but did they ever lose $54 billion in one *quarter*?

"I'd rather go back and be with one of my ex-wives than go through this again," Turner once said. "It's a fascinating story of how to do everything wrong. I think part of it was that it was just too complicated. If you ever have the chance to merge with AOL, stay away."

With the company for sale and with McMahon having pulled out in late 2000, the door was left open for one man, a person who dreamed of autonomous power and the chance to once again turn *Nitro* and *Thunder* into ratings gold: Eric Bischoff. Following his first demotion in September 1999, he spent some time hunting and fishing near his home in Colorado while still collecting large paychecks. Once Russo had thoroughly proven his incompetence, Bischoff was called about coming back.

In a 2003 interview on WWE's *Byte This* radio program, Bischoff tried to shift blame for the death of the company away from himself:

> The problem with WCW was that it really didn't fit within the Time Warner profile, meaning a lot of senior executives at the highest levels didn't want the company to be there and didn't support it. When I came back, that situation was a lot worse than when I left originally. So, I left again, and basically I was honest with Brad Siegel, who I was dealing with at the time. And I said 'Brad, the company is so screwed up, it's never going to work, I can't fix it, no one's going to fix it. Why don't you let me buy it?

Of course, one question remains obvious: if he claimed that nobody could fix it, including himself, why would he want to buy it? The answer is that he was lying. The truth is that the company didn't fit into the Time Warner profile because, thanks in good part to Bischoff, it collapsed and lost $62 million that year. If the company had still been making the kind of money it made in 1998, it would no doubt have fit the profile just fine. And his claim that his idea to buy it was a last-minute decision is false, because he'd been trying to convince Turner to sell since at least late '98. In fact, enough people were aware of this that when things really started to implode, some assumed that he was purposely trying to kill it in order to lower the price.

Bischoff continued:

> [Siegel] laughed at me, he thought I was nuts. And I left again, I went home again. And about two months later they called me back and said: 'If you're serious and you can raise the money, we'll talk to you.' So, I raised the money. And we had commitments for $63 million from some of the biggest blue chip investment bankers on Wall Street supporting us and some very, very smart people. And we spent about six to eight months going through a process called Due Diligence, where you do all the things you would need to do to buy a company, going through the books and making sure the documents are all in order and all the legal crap that goes along with it. We had a deal in place, a letter of intent had been signed, everything was going fine.

So fine, in fact, that on January 11, 2001, Bischoff and his investment group, Fusient Media Ventures, announced that they had purchased the company. When we say "announced," we mean that they told everyone: they told the press, they told everyone in the company, they told their friends, they told their families. A few noted the "coincidental" timing of the announcement, which came just hours before the AOL–Time Warner deal was finalized.

"Wrestling fans can rest assured that we will give the WCW the adrenaline shot it needs to once again become the most exciting brand of wrestling in the world," Bischoff stated in a press release.

Yet buried in all the hoopla and excitement was the tiny little part about how the sale wouldn't be finalized for forty-five days or so.

Everyone seemed to have the same question: how could Bischoff possibly turn the company around now, when he couldn't before? And more precisely, how could he do it now that he actually had to be fiscally responsible to his investors? The days of going to Turner himself were now long gone, so exactly how he planned to revert WCW back to its number-one position had everyone more than a little perplexed.

Not that it mattered to Bischoff himself. This was his chance to prove that he wasn't just a one-trick pony, that the success he'd created with the nWo was just the tip of his creative iceberg. He felt, even with a depleted roster in comparison to the glory days, that he still had the talent to get him there; he just needed time and good booking to push them over the top. He brought in Johnny Ace as his lead booker. Ace had been lauded for his creative match scripting, and he also knew the business inside and out, having worked for virtually every wrestling promotion on the globe. If anyone knew how to properly book a promotion, it would appear to be him.

Bischoff had grandiose plans: there was going to be a brief shutdown, perhaps as long as a month, and then a huge, fresh restart. He was going to push the Cruiserweights to the moon. He was going to set up a salary system similar to the WWF's, whereby guys would be paid "downside guarantees," then bonuses based on how successful house shows and pay-per-views were. He didn't want to fall into the "trap" of guaranteed contracts again. He said he was going to phase out the older guys and push the younger guys harder. He was going to open relations with Japanese companies, including Ultimo Dragon's Toryumon group, to introduce American fans to new, hot, high-flying stars. And, perhaps best of all, he vowed there would be no more Russo.

Basically, he said all the right things.

Wrestling fans, however, did not care about all the right things being said. They wanted to see action. With the major booking duties delegated to others, Bischoff began to look at the roster for anything he could trim. If he was going to own the company, that meant that he and his investors would now have to foot all the bills. No longer could he afford to pay his friends exorbitant salaries due solely to friendship. He was going to have to make the company work as a business, and realistically, the high pay rates demanded by the likes of Hulk Hogan, Kevin Nash, and Scott Hall didn't fit into his budget. So not only was the rise of such guys as Steiner and Booker T coming at the right time, but he had to make them the top stars even if they hadn't caught on yet—financially, he had little choice.

His first major plan was to do a company shutdown following the February 18 *Superbrawl* pay-per-view. The idea was to take several weeks off to build new sets, write new story lines, and get everything set up for a brand-new beginning on March 12. Time Warner, however, said no. Ratings had dropped to such a degree that WCW had to make good to advertisers. One month with no TV whatsoever would cost them some serious cash, and with the company already losing tons of money, that was out of the question. If you're wondering why Turner cared about a company they didn't own losing money, it was because the forty-five days were not yet up, and the sale wasn't completely finalized. Everyone figured it would happen within the next week or so.

Bischoff, therefore, came up with what he thought was an ingenious story line. He'd have Steiner, still the top heel and Heavyweight champion, take out all the remaining babyfaces one by one, leaving only Dallas Page. They'd headline the March 18 pay-per-view in Jacksonville, and then, the following night, the "new WCW owners" would be revealed and save the day by bringing all the babyfaces back at once. WCW would then scrap the April pay-per-view, so they'd have seven weeks to build up to their biggest show ever on May 6, when the entire company would be reborn.

In late February, Bischoff reconsidered his ingenious idea. The ratings were sinking fast, and he didn't think they'd be able to hold off until May before reintroducing the major stars.

Despite a few changes, programming still ranged from good to awful, depending on the week. *Thunder* was by far the worst, and every program seemed to be an effort to set the record for worst in history. Sid's promos became more and more nonsensical. "See, there's only two things I care about, and I'm gonna see is the man who wins the title and the belt, and that man will be me!" he once threatened. Or stated. Or asked. Or something. The story lines were absurd. One week, a masked mystery man bedecked in what appeared to be a bumblebee costume constructed by a five year old, attacked Rick Steiner. The next week, he unmasked, revealing himself to be—three guesses—Rick Steiner. On another show, Heavy D sold a neck injury by stating, "The doctors told me I can never wrestle again. The slightest thing and *snap*, my head could actually fall right off my shoulders. That's sad." Announcer Scott Hudson apparently took him seriously by replying with a straight face that yes, indeed, the fact that his head might spontaneously fall off his shoulders was sad. Perhaps saddest of all was that the main event of that show was DDP versus Jeff Jarrett, and as the ring filled with brawling men following the usual DQ finish, Tony Schiavone screamed, "THEY WON'T STOP UNTIL SOMEONE DIES!" Guys retired forever on a weekly basis, including Goldberg.

Tragically, Sid's career really did end forever when, in a mishap at the *Syn* PPV in January, he jumped off the middle rope and landed on one leg, shattering his tibia and fibula in one of the most gruesome injuries anyone had ever seen.

With no major changes taking place, viewers continued to tune out. In early March, *Nitro* and *Thunder* set brand-new ratings records. Unfortunately, they were record lows, 2.05 and 1.52 respectively. The investors decided now would be a good time to really investigate the books, and they were not pleased with what they discovered. In fact, to put it gently, they totally freaked out. Time Warner then freaked out because potential brand-new owners freaking out didn't sound very promising. The deal, which still had not been finalized, nearly fell through. Fusient's lead investor, Warburg Pincus, began to realize that this was a company that was in deep, deep debt, had tons of lawsuits on its hands, and a fan base departing in droves. In fact, the only real assets the company had included a name that had been horribly devalued by years of bad booking, several high-priced superstars who weren't cutting the mustard, and the fact that, once upon a time, it had a hot run. These were not generally considered valuable assets. Pincus, suddenly wondering why anyone in their right mind would invest in this company, hit the bricks. Once they pulled out, Fusient, which had been offering around $70 million, cut their offer almost in half. Their new plan was to offer $5.7 million down, then $2.15 million per year for twenty years. Yes, they believed they could keep WCW in business for twenty more years, or, more likely, that they could convince Time Warner that they could keep it alive for twenty more years while simultaneously looking for a new parent company to sell to.

And then it happened. A new adversary entered the fray, and it was an adversary that nobody in wrestling had ever even heard of. This man, however, would single-handedly change the entire course of pro-wrestling history. His name was Jamie Kellner, and he was the new Chairman and Chief Executive Officer of Turner Broadcasting Systems.

Kellner was not new to the television industry. He had, in fact, been the driving force behind the creation of both the FOX and the WB Networks, as well as FOX Kids. He was a strong advocate of television targeted towards the young female demographic, which led to the creation of shows such as

7th Heaven, Dawson's Creek, and *Gilmore Girls.* He also stirred up a hornet's nest when he stated, in a 2002 interview, that personal video recorders like TiVo, which allows viewers to skip commercials, were tantamount to stealing from the networks. If folks didn't watch the commercials that the networks aired, he reasoned, they therefore wouldn't buy any products, and if they didn't buy any products, advertisers would stop paying for future commercials. Strangely, Kellner did not go on a crusade against the remote control.

His wacky, industry-polarizing views and theories, however, were simply his way of looking at the bottom line. And that was a *huge* problem where WCW was concerned.

But that wasn't even the biggest problem. In addition to WCW's excessive financial losses, wrestling just wasn't the type of program Kellner wanted on his network. It was lowbrow, low rent. Even when ratings were sky high, selling ad time on the programming wasn't the easiest thing to do. Car manufacturers such as Lexus and Toyota would balk at spending precious ad revenues on folks that they imagined were driving around in fifteen-year-old pickup trucks. At the end of the day, the fact was that Jamie Kellner simply didn't like pro wrestling.

And so, in his very first week on the job, Kellner simply ruled that all wrestling programming was to be cancelled on TBS and TNT.

No more *Nitro,* no more *Thunder,* nothing.

This no doubt led Bischoff to this articulate conclusion: OH FUCK.

OH FUCK OH FUCK OH FUCK!!!

This was not good. To say Bischoff was banking on those timeslots would be like saying WCW lost a few bucks in 2000. How could this have happened? Wrestling had been on the Turner networks for twenty-nine years! It was a legacy, for God's sake! How could one man, some corporate suit at that, come in *on his first week* and put an end to a relationship that had lasted this long? This could not be happening.

It could NOT be happening.

None of the wrestlers believed it. After all, why would they? For six years, Bischoff and his cronies had booked story lines designed to fool not only the fans, but also the wrestlers and company employees. The company had often done this in years past, with the Ric Flair heart attack to fake fights in the back to Hogan walking out in the middle of matches. The theory behind doing this, it seemed, was that if they could fool their own employees, they'd really shock their audience.

Why, you might ask, would the company continually lie to its employees? Because in 1996, Bischoff and Brian Pillman briefly had everyone in the wrestling world talking about the fact that Pillman was out of his mind. The former "Flyin' Brian" morphed into the "Loose Cannon," a madman who could not be controlled and would say or do anything he wanted on television. He "went against the script." He had "real fights" with the bookers on live PPV. And what was the end result of this pioneering shoot angle? The wrestlers, upon discovering that they'd been lied to, stopped trusting management. Zero dollars were made by anyone other than Pillman, who got to plug his 900 phone line on *Nitro*. With everyone in a tizzy, Pillman convinced Eric to give him a real-life WCW release to make the angle "seem more legitimate." Upon receiving the very real release, Pillman immediately signed with the WWF.

So the wrestlers figured this whole "WCW sale" was just another swerve by Bischoff, an attempt to shock viewers into thinking they had lost WCW forever, only to bring it back again when it seemed things couldn't get any more bleak. The boys knew Bischoff's modus operandi, and also figured that Vince Russo, another swerve-happy booker, was likely in on it as well. It didn't help that on March 16, Brad Siegel sent everyone a memo that basically outright lied about what was going on:

> In early January, we told you about an agreement that we had reached to sell WCW and its related assets. At the time, we said that we would apprise you of any changes to the way WCW operates. Effective Tuesday, March 27, WCW programming will begin a period of hiatus. During this hiatus, WCW will review its programming plans and determine the course of future WCW-branded entertainment events. On Wednesday, March 28, please plan to attend an all-staff meeting at 10 A.M. at the Power Plant, at which time we will share with you further information regarding WCW plans. In the meantime, I hope that you will maintain the level of professionalism that distinguishes our organization, particularly as we prepare for the upcoming Panama City, FL, event.

And so Bischoff watched his dream fall apart right before his very eyes. The company he'd made was now being pulled away from him—just when he thought he had it in the palm of his hand. It was scramble time—no way was he letting his baby get away again, not this time, not when he was this close to having it all for himself. Bischoff raced from network to network in the hope of landing a television contract for the company. Even at the end, *Nitro* had drawn strong ratings in comparison to your average cable fare, so there had to be a network out there that would help foot the bill for the company.

SFX? No.

USA? Barry Diller, head of the network that hosted WWF programming for eighteen years, said of the WWF's tenure, "[An] audience of twelve- to nineteen-year-old pimply faced, mean-spirited males came, watched, and went on to whatever God-awful other pursuits." Um, that would be a no.

That left just one last possibility: FOX. Bischoff had been negotiating on and off with the network for over a year. One of his original plans was to create a spin-off group with their own TV show on FOX to build up to an eventual interpromotional feud, something he'd been wanting to do for years prior. As a last-ditch effort, Bischoff tried to reopen negotiations in late March, but unfortunately, to no avail. So on March 20, 2001, Fusient Media Ventures announced that they were pulling out.

"Once you took the television part out of the deal," Bischoff said years later, "it really wasn't worth anything. Without television, that company wasn't worth anything to us. So we walked away from it."

Even upon cancellation of the shows, with the end drawing ever nearer, many wrestlers refused to believe the truth. Siegel's memo didn't help. The fact that WCW never told them anything in the weeks leading up to the final program didn't help. The fact that on the final *Nitro*, instead of saying it was over, the announcers said it was simply the "season finale," didn't help. And, most of all, the fact that the company had been trying to work all of its employees since the mid-'90s didn't help. This makes little sense to those outside of wrestling, but a stunning number of performers within WCW, despite having read news stories about how their show was being canceled, thought this was just another big con, and that everything was going to turn out all right in the end.

It didn't.

And the only reason those wrestlers finally came to understand that they weren't being worked is because they stopped receiving paychecks.

It seemed a shame that WCW should end in such a manner. It had, at one time, a tremendous fan base, the largest the wrestling world had ever seen. Sadly, the egos of men such as Kevin Nash and Terry "Hulk Hogan"

Bollea crippled the company by forcing its spotlight to remain focused on them instead of other, younger stars. This caused many wrestlers, who could have helped WCW usher in a new era, to instead help usher in a new era in the WWF. When they left, so did much of WCW's fan base. Those wrestlers that stayed with the company until the bitter end had lost all their drawing power, and were eventually nothing more than another paycheck the company had to write when it could ill afford to do so.

Eric Bischoff was also largely responsible for the company's demise. Ironically, he was the mastermind behind the unlikely rise of the promotion, which, after years of mismanagement, was perhaps even more shocking than the fact that he tanked the company in the manner he did. The way Bischoff took the reigns of WCW and completely turned it around in 1996 is something that should be studied by every wrestling promoter. He was nothing short of brilliant. Sadly, those same promoters would learn even more by looking at what he did to quickly destroy the very same empire he had built. He had come up with one great idea, the nWo, which he presented over and over and over again, long past the point fans cared about it. He overspent on contracts, and when the ship began to sink, he panicked and overspent to a ridiculous degree on quick fixes like rock bands and celebrities who did nothing to help resolve WCW's primary dilemma—the fact that they were putting on horrendous TV shows, all of which were being presented with Bischoff's approval.

By the time Vince Russo came into the company, it was in pretty dire straits. Fans had been abused by WCW for years, which had presented bad show after bad show and failed to push new stars. When Russo came in, he had the opportunity to turn things around; the first week's rating showed that fans were still willing to give the company a look. Instead, he not only continued the trend of horrific television, he actually created programs that were far worse than those his predecessors had presented. This was due, in large part, to his desire to re-create an industry that had worked in more or less the same manner (two guys don't like each other, people pay to see them fight) for the past century. Despite claims that his "creative genius" was held back by Turner's Standards and Practices department, the fact of the matter is that he presented a product that the fan base at large completely rejected.

In the end, however, it wasn't Hogan, Nash, Bischoff, Russo, or any of the other usual suspects that killed the company. WCW's fate was sealed not by nonsensical story lines, horrendous TV, ridiculous overspending, guaranteed contracts, old guys holding down young guys, or anything else one would have expected. Make no mistake about it—all those things played a role in bringing a once-great empire to its knees.

But the final blow was a decision made in a boardroom by a TV executive who'd never attended a wrestling show in his life. He didn't see pro wrestling for what it really was: a business that could reinvent itself countless times over. He saw it as a TV program with a shelf life like any other. It was the *A-Team* or *Seinfeld* or *Married with Children,* a show that had done gangbuster numbers for a period but eventually ran its course.

When Jamie Kellner decided to pull the plug, WCW's guardian angel, Ted Turner, could do nothing about it.

And *that* was the death of WCW.

Those in charge of the company never predicted that things would turn out this way, and that was perhaps the biggest irony of all: for a company that took pride on fooling its fans and even its own employees, it was WCW itself that got the ultimate swerve.

"Being in WWE (formerly the WWF) sucked. I hated it. You had to kiss everybody's ass . . . you had to be on your political toes all the time. You would not believe the backstage politics. You were getting stabbed in the back constantly. I was so happy when I was told I was gone [fired]."

—Mike Awesome, former WCW and ECW performer on his WWE tenure

EPILOGUE

Spitting on the Grave

With the Fusient deal dead in the water, that left just one real potential buyer: Vince McMahon. The lack of timeslots meant nothing to McMahon, who had four hours of prime-time TV of his own in which to promote the brand name. And with the price coming down from the $500 million (yes, *five hundred million dollars*) Time Warner had rejected a year earlier to less than $3 million with no other buyers on the horizon, there was absolutely no reason not to pursue it. "This is a smart business decision and a good investment for us," cheered Linda McMahon in a press release following the purchase. "We're grabbing it because it is simply that kind of opportunity."

To buy out your largest competitor and create a monopoly for yourself for under $3 million? Yeah, that would be an opportunity you wouldn't pass up.

When it was officially confirmed that McMahon had finally, after twenty years, completed his goal and claimed sole ownership of major-league wrestling in the United States, many questions remained. How would he integrate the WCW brand? Would McMahon give WCW its own show? Could he bring WCW back to the prominence of its glory days?

And, perhaps most importantly to McMahon himself, how on Earth was he going to spend all the money he was about to make?

This was no ordinary wrestling story line. This was history in the making. For years, hardcore wrestling fans debated which company had the superior wrestlers. Who would win if Bill Goldberg wrestled Steve Austin or the Rock? What about WCW Champion Scott Steiner versus WWF Champion Triple H? Now, finally, McMahon would be able to promote the matchups fans had been salivating over for years and, in some cases, for over a decade. This was too good to be true.

And indeed it was.

Though most fans were delighted at the prospect of the inevitable WCW-WWF war, a few people were a bit skeptical, given Vince's track record. For example, in 1991, he'd secured the services of Ric Flair, who left WCW never having dropped the NWA World Heavyweight championship in the ring. Throughout the '80s, hardcore fans always talked about the ultimate dream match, WWF champion Hulk Hogan versus NWA champion Ric Flair. Flair's jump to the WWF opened the door for that, but instead, the WWF totally dropped the ball, not even mentioning the title by name and booking Flair as though he was some goof off the street with a fake belt calling himself the "real World's Heavyweight champion." The feud was a bust at the box office compared to what it should have been. Then in 2001, Chris Benoit jumped to WWF without having lost the WCW title in the ring. Again, the possibility existed for a dream interpromotional match, with the holder of the WCW crown facing off against the WWF champion. Instead of taking full advantage of what he'd gotten, Vince instead had WWF champion Triple H beat Benoit on his very first night in, ending all hopes of a serious money-drawing program.

Although McMahon's track record with interpromotional programs was, quite frankly, miserable, many felt that this was just too easy to screw up. WWF loyalists always had some way to justify what Vince had done previously: he *had* to beat Flair and Benoit, because even though he now had ownership of their contracts, the company they'd worked for still existed. Therefore, if they got early wins in a feud, it would show fans watching at home that the competition was in fact superior to the WWF wrestlers. This, however, was different. Vince *owned* WCW, he *owned* all the wrestlers, and WCW no longer existed except as a subsidiary of the WWF. There was therefore no logical excuse not to allow the "outsiders" to run wild on the WWF talent early to build towards big pay-per-view main events down the road.

So, believing that this was a foolproof angle, fans went crazy coming up with different fantasy booking ideas.

As any longtime wrestling fan is aware, the mainstream doesn't exactly look at followers of this sport in a positive manner. For years, books about wrestling weren't published because the belief was that wrestling fans could not read. Angles were booked to cater to the lowest common denominator, because even those inside wrestling believed the "marks" were just one step above Neanderthals. The main characters in *Ready to Rumble*, a mainstream movie about wrestlers that supposedly catered to wrestling fans, were portrayed as the dumbest human beings walking the planet. Advertisers shied away from buying time during wrestling shows because they believed wrestling fans were poorer and dumber than the average buyer. Obviously, this is all ridiculous, and while no scientific study has ever been done to measure the brain capacity of the average wrestling fan, chances are they're just as smart as the average fan of mainstream sports or entertainment.

Everyone who follows this sport, however, has certainly run into a fan or two who displays a shocking lack of anything even remotely resembling intelligence. This is not just a wrestling thing, though; people like this attend other sporting events, and we see them on the street on a daily basis. But the fan so stupid that you wonder how they can even exist in society without constant aid does exist in wrestling.

Now, with all that said, the most pathetic thing about the WWF's booking of the huge and epic WCW invasion was that not even the dumbest fan could have come up with a story line as bad as what Vince McMahon ultimately did.

One need look no further than the New Japan versus UWFi feud to see a truly successful invasion angle.

Japan's UWFi was formed in 1991 by Nobuhiko Takada. The company, which promoted "shoot-style" matches (fake wrestling bouts designed to look as real as possible), quickly took off, and at one point a few years later it was drawing over 15,000 fans to every single one of their monthly shows. By mid-1995, however, the UWFi was in horrible shape. With the company dying, New Japan, which was on a business roll and had profited from promotion versus promotion angles for decades, stepped in. Booker Riki Choshu understood that he had complete booking power over the outsiders and sought to exploit it. The company soon announced a joint show on October 9, 1995, with a main event of IWGP Champion Keiji Muto versus Takada. Tickets went like crazy. The first major battle between the two companies took place on September 23 at Yokohama Arena before 16,000 fans and a $1.3 million gate. In the best match of the night, UWFi's Tatsuo Nakano and Yoji Anjoh beat New Japan's Yuji Nagata and Choshu. Yes, not only did the guy in charge of the story lines put the bad guys over, but he put them over in a match he was in. Impossible to believe, but true. Even with some major botchery (Muto won the match and largely killed the feud), the huge and well-promoted dream match still drew a packed-past-capacity house of over 57,000 fans and a $6.1 million gate. Not only that, but they also sold $2 million worth of merchandise, so the total one-day take was over $8 million. At the time, no show in history had ever done that kind of money without pay-per-view, and even among those who did, the only two larger were *Wrestlemania III* and *Wrestlemania VII*.

McMahon had plenty to learn from when it came to putting story lines together. He'd made his own dumb mistakes with Flair and Benoit in the past. He'd seen successful invasion angles booked overseas in Japan, angles that drew sellout after sellout to the 55,000-seat Tokyo Dome. And closer to home, there was the infamous UWF interpromotional battle with Jim Crockett Promotions in 1987.

Well, to call it a battle would be to give Crockett and his company way too much credit. When they bought the promotion from Bill Watts, the idea was to keep the companies separate and build towards a huge Superbowl of Wrestling card at some point down the road. Unfortunately, ego got in the way long before anything like that could even start to build. Because the two sides had been feuding for so long, Crockett wasn't able to grasp the fact that purchasing the competition meant the war was over. Instead, he was still determined to show fans that JCP was the superior organization, and to do so, he sent many of his lower-card wrestlers over to UWF's TV and had them quickly win all the major titles. The UWF title was portrayed as a secondary title is portrayed in WWE today (say, the Intercontinental or U.S. belt), and the champion would wrestle early on in the card as a "warm-up" for Crockett's big stars, who worked all the main events. Not only did this absurd booking not lead to a boom period, but things got so bad for Crockett that he ended up going out of business about a year later.

Did Vince—who surely knew this story since his Head of Talent Relations, Jim Ross, lived through it—learn from this and book his invasion in a different manner? That is for you to decide. But first, the literal definition of the word "invasion":

NOUN: 1. The act of invading, especially the entrance of an armed force into a territory to conquer.

How about "invade"?

TRANSITIVE VERB: To enter by force in order to conquer or pillage.

Presumably, the dictionary at Titan Towers had a different definition:

TRANSITIVE VERB: To cause to be destroyed; failure to win.

The highly anticipated WCW Invasion turned out to be truly preposterous. It's hard to imagine a feud booked more poorly than what should have been the simplest, biggest moneymaker in the history of pro wrestling.

Before we get into that, though, we should note that the WWF did not have all the top WCW stars at their disposal. The WWF did absorb the contracts of twenty-four mid-carders, including Lance Storm, Chuck Palumbo, Sean O'Haire, Mark Jindrak, Mike Awesome, Elix Skipper, Shane Helms, Shannon Moore, Stacy Kiebler, Chavo Guerrero Jr., Mike Sanders, Hugh Morris, Shawn Stasiak, Kaz Hayashi, Jimmy Yang, and Billy Kidman. Men like Sting, Goldberg, and Hulk Hogan, however, were under long-term deals with Time Warner, and in order to break those deals, the WWF would have had to pay to cover the difference. The same was true of the very embodiment of WCW, Ric Flair: the company claimed they couldn't afford to bring him in as part of the invasion.

Apparently, the WWF couldn't afford to bring in the big-name stars, as it had been a very lean year for poor Vince McMahon. After all, his company was only able to gross a record-high $456 million. In fact, had it not been for his decision to start a renegade football league known as the XFL, McMahon's company would have generated a profit of $27.4 million that quarter and $84.9 million for the year. Despite the burden of the XFL, the WWF still had hundreds of millions on hand, thanks to the incredible numbers it had been producing in buy rates, ratings, merchandise, and house show attendance.

But this was not McMahon's only excuse. He also argued that if he bought out, say, Goldberg's contract for an estimated $6 million, it would upset the salary structure of the WWF and create grumblings in the locker room. What he and many of the grumbling wrestlers failed to realize was that every effort should have been made, no matter what the cost, to get the big stars and make the invasion a success. After all, if it was a success, *everyone*—from the top of the card to the bottom—was going to make a lot more money. And if the invasion was a bust because folks couldn't comprehend an "untested non-WWF performer" like Goldberg making so much money (and in reality, fans wanted Goldberg dream matches so badly at this point that he probably would have paid off his entire contract for the year with one PPV main event), well, everyone was going to end up with less spare change.

In the end, though, it didn't matter who McMahon brought in, because the WCW wrestlers weren't to be the focus of this invasion. No, the WCW Invasion was about the McMahons. That became clear on the final night of the Monday Night Wars, when Vince opened up the *Nitro* broadcast himself. Just in case someone out there didn't quite get the message, the final performer in a WCW ring on the final broadcast ever of *WCW Monday Nitro* was . . . Shane McMahon.

Yes, despite having Ric Flair, Booker T, Sting, and Scott Steiner available at the show, all of whom could have fired the first shot in the WCW Invasion and really put fans on the edges of their seats (and make no mistake about it, fans were prepared to open their wallets at the mere thought of interpromotional matchups), SHANE MCMAHON was the focal point. In the story line, Shane, and not Vince, had bought WCW, so Shane would lead the invasion.

The original plan was for WCW to have its own Saturday-night TV show and to run its own house show events and PPVs; basically it was to be its own company, with Shane McMahon as the story line president. Arenas were booked, and negotiations began with Viacom to secure a timeslot for the inevitable WCW television programs. All fine in theory, but Viacom, specifically The National Network (TNN) on which *Raw* aired, didn't want any more wrestling programs—they had enough. And they didn't want Vince to replace his highly rated WWF show with WCW, as they'd paid top dollar for the ratings that *Raw* drew, and they didn't want those numbers to be potentially sliced in half. So there were problems on the corporate end from the get-go.

This led Vince to change his mind in late May and opt instead for a "soft-launch." His new idea was to slowly introduce the WCW performers by having them attack WWF wrestlers on *Raw* and *Smackdown*, leading to a big interpromotional pay-per-view on July 22 in Cleveland. In what would eventually become the answer to an obscure trivia question, Lance Storm was the first guy to attack a WWF superstar. The next renegade was Hugh Morrus. Keep in mind that they didn't bother to attack top stars such as the Rock or Stone Cold Steve Austin, but went after mid-carders like Bradshaw and Goldust. The one time Team WCW did attack a huge WWF star, Kurt Angle, the fighting was done by—yes, you guessed it—Shane McMahon.

The first real shot in the war took place at the *King of the Ring* PPV on June 24 in East Rutherford, New Jersey, when Undertaker and the newly signed Dallas Page had an in-ring confrontation. Not a match, mind you, but a "confrontation." Page wanted to be a part of this historic angle so badly that he took a contract buyout at approximately 50 cents on the dollar, a decision he probably regretted years later. Upon entering the company, he was immediately placed in a story line in which he portrayed a perverted stalker who had a thing for the Undertaker's wife, Sara. Of course, those who'd followed WCW for years knew that Page's wife was the white-hot Kimberly, so it made little sense that he'd be making advances toward Taker's horse-faced old lady. Regardless, this led to their epic confrontation, which saw Taker beat up Page for approximately 5:39 minutes of the 5:40-minute encounter. Instead of being deadly adversaries, they were nothing but impotent goofs. This, combined with the fact that the WWF had been telling its fan base that WCW sucked for years (and, truth be told, WCW had told their own fans this for years too), led WWF fans to violently reject anything associated with WCW.

Therefore, what happened when Shane McMahon "secured" a WCW World title match for his men at the July 2 *Raw* from Tacoma, Washington, should have come as no shock. It would be the first time ever that a WCW-sanctioned match happened on a WWF show, and would feature two more newly signed wrestlers: WCW and U.S. champ Booker T (who beat Steiner on the final *Nitro*) taking on Marcus "Buff" Bagwell (who, ironically, McMahon had vowed to never hire on that very same final *Nitro*). Many questioned the decision to even allow Bagwell into the company, let alone put him in such a high-profile match. He was anything but a model employee in WCW prior to the buyout, often crying like a little baby when he was asked to job. His attitude only worsened when he was informed that he was getting the title shot; he became pompous and aloof, failing to show up for required workouts. In short, his hiring did little to appease the boys in either WWF or the new WCW.

The match itself, a disaster of Biblical proportions, didn't help much either. Despite announcer Arn Anderson's claim that this was "bigger than

Buff Bagwell was the man Vince McMahon felt should main-event the first ever WCW *Raw*. Why he felt this way—why anyone could feel this way after all the trouble Bagwell had caused in WCW—no one knows.

MIKE LANO

the moon landing," Bagwell and Booker tiptoed through a very mundane match, and proceeded to blow spot after spot. The crowd (those who hadn't filed out, that is) entertained themselves with competing chants of "BORING!" and "THIS MATCH SUCKS!" and "GOLDBERG!" In fact, the only time the crowd truly seemed to enjoy themselves was when Steve Austin and Kurt Angle, the WWF's two lead heels, came into the ring and beat the crap out of both men. In the midst of this—the biggest event since the moon landing, remember—the cameras cut backstage to Vince McMahon making out with WCW diva Torrie Wilson. This led to *Raw*'s finale, a scene in which Vince, wearing only his boxers, was caught by his wife Linda with his hand in the nookie jar.

Many labeled this the worst WWF show of all time.

It also put an end to the invasion as it was originally conceived. Prior to the show, McMahon's plans had become grandiose. On the *Raw* after the *Invasion* PPV, Vince and his wife Linda were going to do a divorce angle that would lead to the two of them splitting all their assets—assets that included the WWF itself. All of the wrestlers, WWF and WCW alike, would be drafted to one of two shows, *WWF Smackdown* on Thursday or *WCW Nitro* on Monday nights. Starting in October, the WCW crew was going to start running their own house show tours and PPV events.

Tacoma killed that idea. Vince took one look at the crowd reaction and decided there was no way WCW could survive as its own entity. With the invasion falling apart, McMahon knew something needed to be done to save the angle. And a savior of sorts appeared to have fallen into his lap.

In addition to WCW, a major independent promotion based out of Philadelphia by the name of Extreme Championship Wrestling had gone under. ECW was a rogue promotion under the management of Paul Heyman, who had come up with a novel concept for wrestling in the mid-1990s: tons of sex, lots of violence, and the complete abolishment of cartoonish characters and family-friendly story lines. Ironically enough, that was the same blueprint that McMahon had borrowed (some would say "stole") for his vaunted "Attitude." ECW had a rabid fan base—even to this day, when someone gets slammed through a table in wrestling, it is not uncommon for fans to chant "ECW! ECW!"

Realistically, though, the promotion was little more than a glorified regional outfit with great booking. The company rarely drew more than 1,000 paid to their events, and their weekly television show drew less than 20 percent of what McMahon's did. Despite the brilliant story lines and groundbreaking characters, Heyman simply didn't have the funds to compete with McMahon or Bischoff on a national level. This led both of the larger companies to raid his talent and his best ideas more or less at will. By the end of 2000, ECW was in shambles, and its workers' checks were bouncing on a weekly basis. The company collapsed, and McMahon, ever the opportunist, was there to pick up the pieces. He hired Heyman and a few of his better workers on the spot, and believed, since ECW was out of business, that he could use the name and logo as he saw fit. The White Plains, New York, bankruptcy court thought otherwise. The irony of this is that WWF itself blew a gasket in 1996 when WCW did something similar with Hall and Nash, though much less blatantly. McMahon, undeterred for the time being, continued to use the name and logo while attempting to work out a settlement.

Heyman was nothing short of brilliant following the death of ECW. Ever since he replaced Jerry Lawler as color commentator on *Raw*, he'd been dropping ECW references constantly. Not only that, but strange e-mails suddenly began to arrive at all the major wrestling websites, always mentioning the same thing:

Heyman was great, WCW sucked, and ECW should be resurrected with all of its former stars on WWF TV. In a "shocking coincidence," that's exactly what happened shortly thereafter. And because of it, the ruins of ECW were finally purchased by the WWF, effectively absolving Heyman of all responsibility.

Therefore, during the July 9 *Raw* in Atlanta, an ECW faction was formed when longtime ECW workers Rob Van Dam and Tommy Dreamer showed up out of the blue. All the men on the WWF roster who had ever competed for ECW joined them. Heyman himself entered the ring, giving a spirited promo about how much he hated McMahon for stealing his concepts and his talent. After teasing that the WCW and ECW factions were going to go to war with each other, they suddenly teamed up in a big swerve, with Heyman claiming that both sides were going to link up (forming the "Alliance") and kick the crap out of the WWF.

Despite running through eithteen months' worth of angles in about eithteen minutes on *Raw*, this was truly a landmark moment in wrestling. This is what the invasion should have been all along: the two promotions that Vince ran out of business teaming up to destroy McMahon and the men who had driven them into bankruptcy. All was right with the world again.

Until, of course, the final two minutes of the program, in which the viewers at home were introduced to the new owner of ECW: Stephanie McMahon.

Yes, now Vince's *daughter* was brought to the forefront of the invasion alongside her brother Shane. Again, the entire focus of the so-called "invasion" was shifted away from what fans had been dying to see for years, which was ECW or WCW versus the WWF. This not only alienated the hardcore ECW fans who might have bought into the story line, but also many longtime WWF fans who'd already been bored to tears by the McMahon family feudin' angle.

Behind the scenes, things were even worse: the on-screen tension between the WWF and WCW guys was boiling over into a real-life feud. The WCW group felt the WWF crew looked upon them as second-class citizens (and unwanted ones at that). They felt they had to walk on eggshells around the WWF guys. Many within the former Turner wrestling company knew that this was realistically their last chance in the business—if this version of WCW were to fail, they had nowhere else to go now that Vince owned the U.S. wrestling industry.

It was due to the hard work of the loyal WWF wrestlers that McMahon was able to do this. At least that's how the WWF'ers felt, and that's why they thought that the WCW boys should be kissing their asses. Look at them—here were the guys who'd driven an entire company down the drain. Why should they get any special treatment? And, perhaps more to the point, why should they get opportunities that would otherwise belong to the WWF's loyal workers?

And right there in the midst of all this tension was Vince McMahon, stirring the pot as best he could. Over the years, McMahon had often pushed his wrestlers' buttons behind the scenes, hoping that fueling the real-life flames might make for better television and in-ring product. He'd done this five years earlier with Bret Hart and Shawn Michaels, resulting in the infamous Montreal double-cross that prompted Bret to leave the company.

In an effort to antagonize both sides, McMahon handed out WCW shirts for the new guys to wear, just in case someone had forgotten which side they were on. The shirts became nothing short of giant bull's-eyes, and further enraged the WWF crew, who made sure to get in a few extra stiff shots whenever the camera called for a beatdown.

And beatdowns happened often. Far too often, in fact. The biggest money-drawing feuds of all time all had one thing in common: fans believed that either side could win. That was the key to wrestling: that feeling that the men pitted against each other in the squared circle were each capable of pulling off the victory. Think back to any sporting contest you've ever seen. The most intriguing matchups are those in which both sides appear to be on equal footing. Why would anyone want to watch a wrestling match, a predetermined one at that, in which one side was portrayed as never having a chance?

But such was the plight of WCW under the rule of Vince McMahon. Perhaps it was because Vince never really wanted to acknowledge that WCW was on equal ground with his own creation. He had, after all, refused to even acknowledge their existence on WWF television until the late 1990s, when *Nitro* was beating *Raw*'s ass in the ratings. They were the only wrestling company to successfully compete with him, and not only that, but for a while, they beat him at his own game. It was a humiliation that Vince's fragile ego seemed unable to endure. Therefore, it probably shouldn't have come as much of a shock that when he finally got the chance to pit the two companies "against" each other, he had the WWF side completely annihilate WCW.

It shouldn't have come as a shock, save for the fact that there was so damn much money to be made.

From almost the first moment that the two sides went to war on Vince's playground, WCW was made to look like a troop of pathetic losers. Page was killed dead pretty much immediately. From the moment the feud began until it ended three months later, he got in virtually no offensive moves. WWF fans hadn't seen squash matches the likes of this since the glory days of jobbers such as Mario Mancini and Barry Horowitz. Time and again, Page was humiliated in losses against the Taker, and the "feud," if you can even call it that, culminated in yet another loss—this time to Taker's wife.

Other WCW stars shared similar fates, except that the vast majority of them weren't featured anywhere near the main event. Most of the WCW crew were stuck battling men who always had been and would always be in the WWF mid-card. And the WWF guys liked it that way—God forbid these WCW slackers to come in and take their spots.

Of course, if anyone from the WWF stepped back and looked at the situation objectively, they would have realized that if this invasion were a success, more people would buy tickets to the events. More PPVs would be ordered. More merchandise would be sold. And, perhaps most importantly, WCW would become reestablished, meaning that there would be even more PPVs, arena events, and merchandise. In short, there'd be more cash for everyone involved.

How much cash? This was illustrated at the *Invasion* PPV, a show so successful that it was devastatingly sad; it was a very clear demonstration of just how much revenue the company blew. The event, from the Gund Arena in Cleveland, drew a sellout 15,535 paid for an $848,060 gate. But that's peanuts compared to the buy rate: a 1.6, which translates into a whopping 760,000 buys, or about a $10 million gross.

Yes, a *$10 million* gross, for just one show.

That would have more than paid off the contracts of the three biggest stars in WCW at the end, Ric Flair, Goldberg, and Scott Steiner. And God only knows how big the buy rate would have been if those men had actually been involved. You see, it was the very concept of WWF versus WCW that sold this show, but it wasn't an actual WWF versus WCW match. The main event ended up being the Dudleys and Rhyno and DDP and Booker T ("Team WCW") versus Steve Austin and Kurt Angle and Undertaker and

Kane and Chris Jericho. In other words, of those ten men, eight were WWF guys anyway (Rhyno and the Dudleys were in the WWF long before the invasion ever began), and it wasn't like Booker T and DDP were the biggest stars WCW had at the end. It's tough to fathom the kind of number they might have done for this show had Team WCW consisted of Flair and Goldberg and Steiner and Booker T and DDP.

It's even harder to fathom the kind of business they'd have done for at least a year afterwards had they brought all the big stars in on day one and promoted this the way it should have been promoted. The WCW stars, portrayed as equals, would have given the promotion enough dream matches to last at least a couple of years. Instead, the invasion was watered down by WWF guys pretending to be on the other team, as well as more McMahons than anyone ever wanted to see.

Ratings picked up a bit at this point, since a bunch of teenagers suddenly started to tune in, likely expecting something new and exciting. Unfortunately, this was the most interest fans would ever show for the angle, and things slowly began to drop off.

Thankfully, McMahon figured out the problem: the WCW and ECW guys didn't know how to work. Seriously, that's what he thought. Never mind the fact that WCW turned business around with Kevin Nash, who was worse as a worker than all the invasion guys put together. To rectify this issue, Vince simply had two of his top stars, Steve Austin and Kurt Angle, turn heel and join the Alliance. So now, not only was the spotlight of the Alliance on Shane and Steph, but on Austin and Angle as well. The WCW and ECW guys weren't relegated to second banana, but rather to about fifth-banana status. The plan did the exact opposite of what it was designed to do: within twelve weeks of the *Invasion* PPV, *Raw* viewership had dropped a staggering 30 percent.

Does the date September 8, 2001, ring a bell? No? That right there should indicate the kind of flop the angle had become by this point. On that day in Dallas, Steve Austin faced the Rock in the first-ever WWF champion versus WCW champion title unification match (it ended in a DQ). There was a day when this would have been one of the biggest stories in wrestling history. Within six months of purchasing WCW, however, the WWF's idiotic booking had turned it into a match virtually nobody remembers to this day.

A month and a half later, the WWF presented perhaps the most poorly booked *Raw* in history. Sure, there had been worse shows in the past, but never had a show been booked not to make money to this extent. First, Vince and Linda came out all smiling and happy, which made zero sense since, as you might recall, just prior to the invasion the story line was that they were about to get a divorce. They were about to kiss mid-ring when Shane and Steph came out and challenged them to a winner-take-all match at *Survivor Series*. The WWF considered this to be such a huge match that they never bothered to specify what "winner-take-all" meant and quickly dropped the subject (it meant WWF versus Alliance, with the losing group having to disappear forever). Then—and this is absolutely true—to give the Alliance team, which had no credibility, that one last big push towards the PPV, they had four title matches, and in all four, *the Alliance guys lost their belts to the WWF guys.*

It was like someone from WCW had started to book *Raw*.

And that brings us to the final showdown between the Alliance and the WWF at *Survivor Series 2001*, in which the loser of the match would be forced out of wrestling forever.

The first man introduced as part of Team Alliance? Duh—Shane McMahon. Next up was Austin, who had been the embodiment of the

WWF since McMahon introduced his "Attitude" concept in 1996. Then there was Angle, who had never competed anywhere but the WWF. Rounding out the team as afterthoughts were Booker T and Rob Van Dam, who were eliminated midway through the match so as not to take the focus away from anyone who, you know, hadn't worked for the WWF the majority of their career. And so, in the final match to determine the survival of WCW, the last two men in the ring were Austin and the Rock. The first person they showed after Rock pinned Austin was naturally the embodiment of ECW herself, Stephanie McMahon.

Ironically, who should appear the very next night on *Raw* but Ric Flair. Over the next year, the newly dubbed World Wrestling Entertainment, in increasingly futile attempts to reverse the downward ratings and buy rate spiral, would bring in not only Flair, but Hulk Hogan, Kevin Nash, Scott Hall, and Scott Steiner, many of the names they "couldn't afford" to bring in for the invasion.

And the two men who could potentially have meant the most, Bischoff and Goldberg? Both were eventually signed as well. Goldberg, whom fans had been dying to see in the WWF since the late '90s, was killed his first week in when he was put in a comedy sketch with Goldust that included the latter putting a shiny gold wig on the former's head. Never had a wig cost more people more money. Instead of being booked as the ultimate outsider, he was portrayed as—SURPRISE!—just another guy on the roster, and as a result, his first-ever PPV match with the Rock—which would have shattered all records years earlier—ended up doing along the lines of what every other PPV during that period did. And remember how, right after WCW folded, people said that if WWF signed Goldberg it would upset the salary structure and piss off the locker room? And how folks said that they were going to eventually sign him no matter what, so they may as well have done it for the invasion? Well, sure enough, when he was signed, a year too late, it was for an overinflated price that upset the salary structure and pissed off the locker room.

In a 2004 interview with Alex Marvez, Goldberg reflected on his WWE tenure: "I think the way they handled my character was moronic. Any businessman who has business first and foremost on his mind wouldn't have done what they did. But as much as they tried to demean the character, they couldn't do it. The fans know the true story. And everyone knows what should have happened from a story line and entertainment standpoint. I pretty much believe every member of WCW that came over, they had a grudge against us because we were kicking their ass when wrestling was at its pinnacle. Instead of using us to their advantage business-wise, I truly think they wanted to squash us and build us up and reinvent us as WWE entities and erase what we had done prior. When they wanted to expand the Goldberg character and make him understand people more and make people able to feel what I feel . . . people didn't want to see Goldberg have emotions or laugh. They wanted to see him rip people's heads off. That's what made me who I am. That's why I had a 176-match winning streak and Hulk Hogan and I put 40,000 asses in the seats in Atlanta. It wasn't because there was a wig on me and I was made into the laughingstock of fans. The situation was pure ignorance."

Bischoff's debut was even more absurd; instead of coming in and amassing a new horde of ex-WCW stars to try to get revenge on the company that put them out of business, his first move in his very first appearance on *Raw* was to give Vince McMahon a hug. You read that right; they HUGGED. Like the wig, never before had a hug cost so many people so much easy money. There was a time in WCW when Bischoff was known as "ATM Eric," and if ever there was a chance to do an angle in which he could live up to that reputation, this was it. Instead, he and McMahon might as well have taken millions and millions of dollars in cash and burned it all in a giant barrel on the ramp under the TitanTron, laughing maniacally at how they'd put one over on the rest of the world. The bottom line is that, no matter what anyone thought about the WWF having learned a lesson from the invasion debacle, they clearly hadn't learned a thing.

The ultimate irony is that WCW, the most incompetent wrestling organization there ever was, did an invasion right. They had three guys, Hogan, Nash, and Hall. Hogan at the time was a lame babyface who'd overstayed his welcome. Hall was a high mid-carder who'd main-evented a PPV or two in the WWF, but aside from his matches with Shawn Michaels, he'd never really lit the ring on fire. Nash was, without question, the worst-drawing WWF champion of all time. Yet these three men had helped to turn WCW business around because they were promoted as the biggest threats to the company that had ever existed, and they laid waste to WCW main-eventers left and right, month after month, until fans were dying to see them get what was coming to them. Of course, the fact that WCW never got their revenge was one of the reasons fans lost faith in them at the end. Still, Booker T and DDP were realistically at the same level of stardom in WCW as Hall and Nash were in the WWF when they left, and if you really want to know why the nWo worked and the invasion was a disaster, go back and look at how each pair of men was promoted upon switching sides.

In short, there was a ton of money to be made, but it was all flushed away due to petty ego. A feud that should have lasted years and years, one that had been built up in fans' minds as the ultimate battle in pro wrestling, collapsed after less than six months, and the end came in front of 10,142 fans paying a little over half a million dollars.

In 1984, Vince McMahon began a long quest to become the sole major-league wrestling promoter in the United States. Through a combination of cutthroat business practices, ingenious maneuvering, and flat-out good luck, he got himself to a point in the late-'80s where he was making more money than many ever dreamed was possible. He had shows on network TV, *Wrestlemania* and Hulkamania were household words, and the sky looked to be the limit. Although his company was rocked by a series of sex and drug scandals in the early '90s, he survived, and by 1995 he had only one major competitor: Ted Turner's WCW. ECW was there, and while its product was revolutionary and changed the business, financially they were always just hanging on. Bischoff created *WCW Monday Nitro* to oppose McMahon's flagship *Raw* show, and the battle was on.

The WWF lost $6 million in 1996, but by adopting many of ECW's formulas and putting everything behind the push of a WCW outcast named Steve Austin, things began to turn around. The war intensified, and by 1998, both companies were making tens of millions of dollars and broadcasting their programming to as many as 12 million viewers every Monday night. Forget Flair versus Steamboat, Funk versus Brisco, Hogan versus Andre, and even Austin versus McMahon: the biggest feud of all time was WWF versus WCW. By 2001, however, as a result of everything you've read about in this book, WCW suddenly found themselves $62 million in the hole. Still, *Nitro* was doing acceptable ratings, and between the four prime-time shows the two companies aired, almost 10 million people tuned in each week. Vince, the onetime wacky announcer in the cute red bow tie, was now an evil billionaire. He'd purchased WCW and finally, after all those years, all the battles, all the raids, the final great wrestling war was about to begin, and fans everywhere anticipated perhaps the most exciting programming of their lifetimes.

Little did they know that Vince McMahon would ultimately prove himself worthy of owning the WCW name.

1988-1996

McMahon, Vince. *Monday Night Wars* DVD, Sony Music Distribution, 2003.

1996

Hall, Scott. *WCW Monday Nitro*, 27 May 1996.

1997

Taylor, Terry. Prodigy Chat, 1997.

1998

Bischoff, Eric. Prodigy Chat, 1997.

Heenan, Bobby. Personal interview by R.D. Reynolds, Indiana.

1999

Hart, Bret. *Wrestling Observer Live*, 2000.

Kuczynski, Alex. "Cue the Music, Roll the Mayhem; Wrestling, Once Ad-libbed, is Now as Carefully Scripted as a Top-Rated Soap Opera." *New York Times*, 22 November 1999.

2000

Hart, Bret. Bret Hart's Weekly Column, *Calgary Sun*, 17 January 2001.

Heenan, Bobby. Personal interview by R.D. Reynolds, Indiana.

2001

Bischoff, Eric. Interview by Tommy Dreamer and Josh Mathews, *Byte This* radio show, 18 December 2003.

Olavsrud, Thor. "Turner Prefers 'Ex-Wives' to Reliving AOL Merger." *Internetnews.com*, 19 March 2003.

Weiss, Jim. Interview by Dave Meltzer. *Wrestling Observer*, 19 March 2001.

Epilogue

Awesome, Mike. *Voice of Wrestling* radio show, 2003.

Goldberg, Bill. Interview by Alex Marvez, 19 August 2004.

Like Death of WCW?

Then you'll love *Figure Four Weekly*, Bryan Alvarez's 12-page weekly insider wrestling newsletter covering every major promotion in the world today, including WWE, TNA, independent groups, promotions in Japan and Mexico, plus mixed-martial arts groups like UFC and PRIDE.

F4W is widely considered the most entertaining wrestling publication in the world today, and you can impress your friends with your knowledge of the backstage politics and future story lines of your favorite organizations.

Subscription to *Figure Four Weekly* in US rates are:

6 issues for $21	52 issues for $130
12 issues for $40	104 issues for $250
24 issues for $70	

International rates (in US funds) are:

6 issues for $25	52 issues for $160
12 issues for $48	104 issues for $300
24 issues for $85	

Checks or money orders in US funds can be sent to *Figure Four Weekly*, P.O. BOX 426, Woodinville, WA 98072. VISA or Mastercard holders, please call toll-free 1-800-960-3366, or write to figure4@ix.netcom.com.

For more information on the newsletter, click on the *Figure Four Weekly* link at www.wrestlingobserver.com. Don't miss out of the fun, order today!

And be sure to check out WrestleCrap at www.wrestlecrap.com for all the worst in pro wrestling!